THE PASSIVE VOICE

Ohio University Press
Athens, Ohio

An approach
to modern fiction.
Harold Kaplan

THE PASSIVE VOICE

TO ELIA AND GABRIEL ELIA

Contents

Foreword

It should be quickly apparent that this book is a selective study, both in its thematic concentration as well as for the novels it considers. The interest itself is ambitious, and it seemed best to me to proceed by example, to pursue my ideas qualitatively and do some justice to a few subjects in order to illustrate by hypothesis what could be done for the better understanding of many subjects.

Anyone who conceives a thematic principle of criticism is afflicted by misgivings on his own behalf as well as on behalf of his readers. He might be believed too well, or he might not be believed at all. Such alternatives oppose themselves in a conceptual world which presumes that literature can be or should be contained in a massed or multi-dimensional perspective. But we see what we can see, one pair of eyes at a time. We must write criticism with the intensity and absorption of the literary imagination itself, with its love for qualities and authentic forms. We must also leave the impression that the world is larger than the glass through which we look at it, close as that may bring us to what is so complicated and alive. Confronting life or literature, every categorical thought acknowledges its limits. And yet we are determined to read with the full intelligence, and we are convinced that we see the marvelous shadow of a coherent vision, not only within the work of one writer, but also among several, who thereby report on the collaboration of human experience. We remain critics, but we are always forewarned. Those who are devoted to the sophisticated real being of literature cannot be too jealous for mastery by their own intellectual powers. But I must hope that my words will have credence for others, and that this book can have some share in the collective intelligence which continues the long dialogue with classic writing.

In these chapters I have dealt with several related topics which grow from one source, the crisis of knowledge in modern intellectual history. The effects of solipsism and of moral passivity, the split consciousness which divides action and understanding, the perspectives of primitivist naturalism and stoic naturalism, the variations of the comic mood, and the example of tragedy, are all themes which associate themselves with the problem of knowing and the problem of acting, which the modern mind, in its greatly developed capacity for self-criticism, has released for treatment by the literary imagination. At the center of the literary issues involved here is the problem of action and its adequate motives, and to deal with this theme properly I have written a final chapter on *King Lear*, seemingly as distant as Mt. Everest from the novels of the twentieth century. But the height of its peak is brought suddenly close, and the view from it may give us an interval of climactic clarity for the issues entangled in modern fiction.

I wish to acknowledge the assistance given me by the Bennington College Faculty Facilities Fund. I also address my thanks to Stanley Edgar Hyman, Barbara Herrnstein Smith, and Rush Welter, my colleagues who gave me their responses and advice. Thomas Smith of the State University of New York at Albany, and Robert M. Adams of Cornell University also read the manuscript and were helpful with advice. Also my students at Bennington had their own share in the writing of this book and I thank them. Finally, grieved by his recent and untimely death, I wish to acknowledge the support of Cecil Hemley, the Director of the Ohio University Press: he was an editor and writer of great distinction, and a man whose mind and spirit were a continual honor and delight to his friends.

For the sensitive poet conscious of negations, nothing is more difficult than the affirmations of nobility, and yet there is nothing that he requires of himself more persistently, since in them and in this kind alone, are to be found those sanctions that are the reasons for his being, and for that occasional ecstasy, or ecstatic freedom of the mind, which is his special privilege.

It is a violence from within that protects us from a violence without. It is the imagination pressing back against the pressure of reality. It seems, in the last analysis, to have something to do with our self-preservation; and that, no doubt, is why the expression of it, the sound of its words, helps us to live our lives.

WALLACE STEVENS,
The Necessary Angel

"Unaccommodated man is no more but such a poor, bare, forked animal as thou art."

King Lear

THE PASSIVE VOICE

The solipsism
of modern fiction

I

We know major works of literature by their capacity to survive discussion and the continous stimulus they offer to the renewal of it. We return to those works which have spoken to us so strongly that they have become the existing cultural wisdom, and this is the significance of that endless dialogue of criticism in which we are all gathered. In propounding the judgments found in the major writers of our time, we know that these judgments have penetrated our minds as well as reflected them, shaped our actions as well as expressed the shape of them. Assuming this, the critic is himself led to the role of the expositor of wisdom, much like the exegetists of the Bible or any other holy or magnified text.

We think of the task of commentary then in terms of a scriptural text or basic myth in order to illustrate the demands made on our understanding. The sacred story portrays life in order to energize the living of it, bringing motives to their highest peak by reciting the drama of salvation. This gives us the largest outline of possibilities for the narrative literary imagination, but within it we see better the orientation of judgment for works that are less heroic in scale. The religious imagination has a primitive frankness and unity; it recreates experience in the same impulse which would give an ideal order to life. The aim is insight, the product of a maximum curiosity, but one that is the servant of a maximum need. The sacred text increases knowledge to its possible range, but only to apply it to the problem of action in life.

The problem of action is the key to my approach to the writers I treat here, and as my title implies, I find that the ruling spirit of modern fiction is unfriendly to action because it has found no way of putting action first as the beneficiary of insight. Rather, in the great transcendence of anthropocentric issues which modern knowledge expresses, the pursuit of knowledge necessarily becomes autonomous. Does knowledge serve experience, or does experience serve knowledge? That would seem a fruitless question unless we think of it as directed toward the temperamental priorities within the search for knowledge. When the human interest, in teleological and metaphysical considerations, was outdistanced by the human intelligence, the momentum of the latter was obliged to find its own force, its own justification. If the slogan of modern intellectual and spiritual life became truth for the truth's sake, it was because the majesty and power of that enterprise so far outran the possibilities of human action, or the possibility of finally satisfying any value except the intellectual value itself. We are then in the case where we know or can imagine more than we can do, more than can concretely concern us, more than our tangible futures as subordinate physiological organisms can possibly encompass. At the same time, in the ultimate destructive paradox, we know so much that we are suspicious of what we know, and are forced to condition thought with so much criticism that it has become clear that a large part of our thinking is essentially after-thought, or thought about thought. It is enough to take a look at the activity among contemporary academic philosophers to see this extreme effect. This might be called the end of the road in that progress of Western thought toward its autotelic existence, where it finds its largest function in defining its own limitations. Whether it is observed that we know too much or know too little, the main effect is that the intelligence which could support action, or the motive-values of action, is undermined by its own sophistication.

The key to the development can be understood generally and simply in the death of the anthropomorphic spirit, which might be called the most important intellectual event of the last two centuries, unless we say rather that it was busy dying for that time and longer. It is with this understanding that I propose to introduce my discussion of modern fiction. If it could be openly acknowledged that "God was dead" at the time when Nietzsche made that announcement, it was to be expected that the news would have penetrated fiction and made its effect felt. That goes without saying, but a deeper implication of nineteenth-century naturalism was that man, as the hero of the dialogue with both God and nature, had lost his dramatic role in the universe, and this information was bound to have a more radical effect on fiction than its parent premise.

Perhaps what happens most vividly to most of us as we grow into intellectual maturity in our culture is a memory of passing from an anthropomorphic consciousness, expressed openly in children's literature, to a skepticism directed particularly against homocentric and egocentric illusions. We grow to respect the skeptical mode as the strongest trait of an enlightened modern consciousness. The austerity as well as the counter nostalgias of that sophisticated consciousness can be seen expressed in the work of George Santayana, a philosopher as inquisitorial as he was sensitive to the appeal of a complete and harmonious metaphysics. Santayana describes the "animal arrogance" and "moral fanaticism" of the anthropomorphic spirit, "that early unregenerate claim (by men) to be enveloped in a protecting world designed for their benefit and vindification." [1] Its simplest proposition was this: "That the world is made for man and that even God is just such a God as man would have wished him to be, the existent ideal of human nature and the foregone solution to all human problems." [2] This aspect of specific religious anthropomorphism began to lose its dominance in the west as early as the seventeenth century. There were other teleologies to replace it, as the colorful philosophic history of the eighteenth and nineteenth centuries would indicate. As Santayana put it, the tendency of human thinking "to hypostatize home values into a cosmic system" will do its work. Nevertheless, the principle of criticism reached a climax with Kant, and the enterprise of framing a metaphysics at all fell under increasing suspicion and restraint. The later nineteenth century presented to many minds what seemed like a final triumph of science over metaphysics, and positivism had established its reign with disturbing implications for people whose vocation (in writing novels, for instance) was making assertions about reality. It appeared that the valid instrument of knowledge had transcended the human sensibility itself. Any simple introduction to scientific method proposed disbelief in the power of the individual consciousness, the ordinary, unspecialized consciousness that is, to make important statements about the truth. The mind which was not disciplined by the laboratory and not part of the collective truth instrument of science, was considered a consciousness under suspicion, subjective, ridden by emotion and prejudicial interest, and limited even in the basic power of perception.

The intellectual suspicion of the human intellect is the great theme which pervades modern fiction as much as it challenges

1 *Platonism and the Spiritual Life*, Harper Torchbooks, p. 249.
2 "Modernism and Christianity," *Winds of Doctrine*, Harper, p. 45.

philosophy. What is at stake for both is not a set of substantive ideas so much as the dramatic problem of knowledge. In literature this is to state the condition of an alienation from reality, a sense of broken communication with both that which exists and that which matters. It is literature in the first place which is most deeply committed to the anthropomorphic sensibility, really the *full* sensibility, in which a perception seeks harmony with the life sentience and the life thought of the perceiver. The abstracted, skeleton sensibility of modern science implies a violence to feeling at its root, where it is the animal instinct to place a value on truth before truth itself is known. The mind creating the widest consensus of modern belief, the mind which is scientific and not religious or literary, clearly asserts that nature is neutral, that the human interest, modestly conceived, is imposed upon nature and not received from it, and that the absolute human interest, no matter in what dream of perfection or immortality, has no correspondence in nature at all. The world is viewed as *exterior*, and the protagonist suffers a painful series of cross-purpose actions aimed at placing himself in relationship. The repeated themes of writing become the search for an identity against the threat of dispersion, and the search for a sense of reality that could meet the most drastic tests of authenticity.

When we think of the early history of realism and naturalism we find that their characteristic mode is to outline the human capacity for self-deception. A moral revulsion from falsehood seems to provide the energy for most of the manifestations of naturalism, particularly in its impatience to enter the fields of experience which conventional faiths or conventional complacency concealed. We can say actually that the novel as such began its long history in the climate of skepticism, taking its mission as the prose criticism of the mythopoeic imagination. As Lionel Trilling observed, the presiding spirit of the novel goes back to Cervantes, himself produced by the century of the birth of modern science.[3] But the dramatic principle of prose narrative could not remain simply the confrontation of illusion with reality, when the changes in knowledge maintained such speed and complexity that the literary imagination found its ground for the distinction between illusion and reality more and more difficult to hold. The style of the imagination seemed itself to be the style of illusion, and this pointed the way to the ultimate threat of intellectual beleaguerment and solipsism.

We might say that modern fiction has this fear of solipsism in its heart; it labors under the implied accusation to the extent that its styles and techniques of narration can be understood largely as a set of defensive maneuvers against the charge. The most extreme of such maneuvers was to invite subjectivity openly and frankly, a form of knowledge which would be authentic in proportion to its degree of faithfulness to actual subjectivity. This was to say that though the full sensibility was incapable of knowing the world as it is, it was at least capable of rendering a full report of itself. Its instinct was expressive rather than recording, transforming facts into values and associating events with responses. The problem for modern literature was how to maintain the human sensibility alive in its full range, how to make it speak and have its voice heard with respect. This could be done by allowing it to speak only for itself. It could keep the freedom of self-expression, so long as the locus was clear. That locus was in sentience itself, hovering always on the border of irrelevant solipsism both in relation to the world as it is and in relation to the rival sentience of other listening minds.*

3 *The Liberal Imagination*, Viking, p. 208.

* Santayana describes the philosophic parallel, and no doubt the direct intellectual influence on impressionistic writing, in the work of Bergson. Here the problem of knowledge which particularly afflicts literature has been solved triumphantly, for now "the world and the knowledge of it are identical." Santayana continues, "With this we seemed to have reached the extreme of self-concentration and self-expansion, the perfect identity and involution of everything in oneself. And such indeed is the inevitable goal of the malicious theory of knowledge, to which this school is com-

There was, however, another alternative. We see the general problem in its clearest outline when we observe the direct literary response to philosophic naturalism expressed in the factual documentary, or objectivism, of the naturalistic novel. In that medium the writer assumed as much of the costume and apparatus of the scientist as possible. He became the camera who saw what was there, and reflected it without immediate judgment, though he might frame his evidence in a theory of social and biological behavior, as any scientist would be interested in doing. The main point was that he assumed, or attempted to assume, a psychic neutrality for himself, nor did he care to penetrate very far into the psychic experience of his characters. As we read Dreiser, Dos Passos, and Farrell, to think of American fiction, where the method had perhaps its widest practice, we are impressed by the fumbling irrelevance in the subjective consciousness of their characters. They are portrayed in terms of rather simplistic laws of psychological and social behavior, while their own consciousness is groping, penetrated by only brief glimpses of light. The field of vision is at the extreme of externality, so preoccupied by the super-personal design of social and biological process that the agents within it seem mindless.

We say then that the characteristic extremes in modern fiction have moved between the two sharply opposed perspectives of objective naturalism and subjective impressionism.* What

mitted, remote as that goal may be from the boyish naturalism and innocent intent of many of its pupils. If all knowledge is of experience and experience cannot be knowledge of anything else, knowledge proper is evidently impossible. There can be only feeling; and the least self-transcendence, even in memory, must be an illusion. You may have the most complex images you will; but nothing pictured there can exist outside, not even past or alien experience, if you picture it. Solipsism has always been the evident implication of idealism; but the idealists when confronted with this consequence, which is dialectically inconvenient, have never been troubled at heart by it, for at heart they accept it." ("The Intellectual Temper of the Age," *Winds of Doctrine*, Harper, p. 13.)

* I say extremes because, of course, it is misleading to infer that it is possible to divide modern fiction into the two categories. The conventionally defined naturalistic novel occupies a narrow segment of the history of

they have in common is a fear of the solipsistic impasse and a compulsive drive to establish the sense of reality. The modern doctrine of the perspective nature of truth has forced its self-consciousness into every postulate of the creative imagination. It accounts for the extremes on both sides and the inadequacies which match each other as if the parts of a whole vision were divided into neat halves. Naturalistic fiction, imitating the neutral reportage of science, tends to drown the subject in the context, because the context or scene is the medium for credibility. The opposite excess of the subjective method is of course to maroon the subject in a private consciousness, and question reality itself by the isolation of the subjective life.*

The effect upon character and action is instructive. The largest effect I note is a sustained passivity in character, whether keynoted by passive sentience or by determinist or automatistic action. Modern knowledge itself features passivity; this is to say that the modern knowledge of character takes its credibility

---

fiction. So would such specialized subjectivist fiction as that of Virginia Woolf and Dorothy Richardson. But the examples illustrate the range in technical perspectives, the ends of a scale that can be applied to other fiction where in fact these perspectives are often mixed and alternated. Joyce, for instance, established a triumphant capacity to reach both ends of the scale. The implication remains, however, that there are sharply divided perspectives for knowing, to be inside or outside, to be subject or object.

* It might be observed that Freud reversed this threat entirely by demonstrating that subjective analysis was itself the way to the effective world of process and reality. However, the Freudian theory could not do more for subjectivist writing than it had already done for itself. It in fact might do much less; it could be argued that Freud has undermined the last refuge of the autonomous literary imagination. The authority of Freud only made it clearer that the mind gave a view of experience from the inside, a limited view, as it dramatically appeared, by the stress on the aberrations of consciousness. Freudianism therefore stressed what the physical sciences had already emphasized, that the ordinary consciousness was a liar, and furthermore, by developing a set of principles to describe the operations of the mind and sub-mind, it restricted the real freedom of the artist more than ever. What the sensibility speaks for, dominated by a Freudian understanding, is no longer even the unique reality of its own experience but rather the abstract code of behavior of a species. This is the objective viewpoint taking over strongly, entirely, in the actual province of the subjective consciousness.

from science and is oriented toward analysis rather than action. Its effective curiosity is psychological rather than moral, if we think of the latter as a value and action dominated conception of character. Analysis has its power before or after the point of action; in that sense its knowledge is inert until it is taken up within the moment of action. To function *within* the scene of action and to provide a dramatic experience, the values of dramatic choice must transcend the nature of data, for as data they have no "withinness" in the scene. Passivity is the effect when value judgments lose their active nature as values and become psychological or historical information. It is also the effect when, at its highest reach, the human intelligence is self-regarding and detached from action, like the intelligence of Stephen Dedalus or Proust's Marcel; when brought to action, the intelligence descends to a lesser order, like the minds of Emma Bovary and Leopold Bloom, though Stephen and Marcel themselves exhibit the same descent. It is their power in retrospection and analysis which makes them exceed themselves, not their powers in action.

Characteristically the human agent of action becomes the object of his own contemplation, whatever the approach from bifurcated perspectives. It might be considered that the naturalistic novel puts action first, whatever else it does; things happen, events in movement are continuous. However, action in the essential dramatic sense summons a full role for consciousness, or else it has the effect of mere movement. Action can be distinguished from movement only when choice, responsibility, or causation is clearly featured, and the further these are placed from the protagonist himself on the scene of action, the less he has to offer as a dramatic agent. Dramatization has always been a troubling problem for typical naturalistic fiction; it has wished to say that history is the protagonist, or the race, or it has seemed forced to say that there is no protagonist but rather a focus for converging forces and events. The naturalistic vision may be pessimistic and necessitarian, or it may follow the more or less optimistic evolutionary creeds, as in Marxism for example. But whatever the quality of faith, the view of individual action leads to a sense of victimization and passivity. Even in novels of revolutionary social action, the small suffering and the small contribution of each individual within the large context diminishes the sense of action as such, except as the massive inching or eruption of the stream of history. The effort to give relief to this might come in the climax of collective action, the revolution or the strike, surely designed to offer a cathartic release from passivity. I think usually these effects resemble the naturalistic novel of violence, which features the same sort of explosive breaking out from a chain of causation or compulsion. This is the outburst of a repressed force that may indeed be in search of a personality, like Joe Christmas in Faulkner's *Light in August*, but has at that point only its disintegrated fragments to exhibit.

II

The solipsistic modern consciousness can trace what might be called its temperamental history to the exuberant dialogue with nature which gave revolutionary confidence to romanticism. The inspired romantic was a newly revived anthropocentric prophet, listening to revelations within himself and from nature which made an intelligible harmony in his experience. This release of the sensibility to freedom and autonomous authority is surely the distinctive trait we have in our minds when we consider the term romanticism most usefully. Romantic art was frank in conceiving nature as an extension of the person, or the dream of the world as an extension of the dreamer. This avoids the entangling anthropomorphic assertions of a supernatural metaphysics and the results are perhaps unpleasant to a traditional moralist or religionist, but the business of being made at home in the universe has been accomplished. The truth of course was, as Irving Babbitt pointed out long ago, that the strongest philosophic base of romanticism was its own naturalism, though it might be called, as he did, an emotional or sentimental naturalism. As such it was calculated to challenge the cold, anti-anthropomorphic naturalism of science, whose implications could not be mistaken in the early period of its dominance.

In the context of thought which surrounded romanticism at the outset and which followed it for later generations, the great theme of a personal communication with nature sounded desperate in its intensity, an effort, as some would put it, to substitute for God. All of the nineteenth century, it seems to us now, was intent on listening to nature and announcing its messages. The blankest answer of all is the one heard by the "underground man" of Dostoevsky, pre-eminent among the solipsistic heroes of fiction, when he declares to himself that nature had nothing to do with his wishes, nothing at all in fact to say to *him*, and upon that basic frustration builds his life of impotent self-destruction. We remember also the answer felt by Melville's Bartleby, as he faces his own blank wall, and responds thereafter to all invitations to act or speak with his one sentence of passive misery, "I would prefer not to." This large contrast, the basic spiritual exchange of yea and nay, as one might hear it between Tolstoy and Dostoevsky, or Emerson and Melville, is in the background of our considerations here. Romantic or redemptive naturalism can not be left out of sight in any consideration of the traditions which affect modern fiction. It acts in its own right or it acts in ironic mixtures, to contrast with the bleaker forms of naturalism, ranging from biological or social determinism to outright metaphysical nihilism. The poignance of this interchange of standpoints is what sometimes shapes the characteristic effects of American writers, whose tradition of sentimental naturalism is strong, as in the fiction of Hemingway and Faulkner. What we have in a good deal of modern fiction is a heightening of ambivalence in the consideration of nature, confronting the doctrine of sympathy with the rival doctrines of mechanism and alienation.

In other words we must see that there are contradictory intellectual traditions fostering the modern novel, deeply naturalistic though they are in the broad sense, if we think of naturalism as a life philosophy which bases its view of the human order on what is found in the natural order. These traditions divide first in the reading of affirmative or negative response in nature and second in their tendency to subjectify or objectify nature. Romanticism preached a subjective power, expressed in freedom, founded on sympathy, which organized the large harmonies of experience. Objective naturalism stressed the external order of necessity, and understood human behavior largely in terms of self-wounding anthropomorphic illusions (the largest perhaps was the sense of freedom) which break down in conflict with the natural order. When literary naturalism as such, in its narrow definition, arose, it did so in protest against romantic subjectivity. Even more basically it arose against the conventional anthropomorphism of social moralities and mythologies, which spread a screen over natural truth and seemed mass self-deceptions. For this aspect we keep in mind particularly the work of Flaubert who, as Zola himself said, is the true father of the modern novel.

However, we must distinguish sharply between the naturalism associated with Zola and the real work of Flaubert. The distinction has major importance for the understanding of twentieth century fiction, which the influence of Flaubert dominates. The key to the distinction is precisely in the issue of a redemptive doctrine of nature, the issue which separates the modern consciousness from the affirmative forms of naturalism, whether romantic or scientistic, which the nineteenth century cultivated. The so-called experimental novel of Zola accepted scientific knowledge as the instrument of understanding, and implicitly or directly, as the instrument of redemptive human goals. The avenue to reality was open, provided one obeyed the rules and seemed to follow the methods of the official bodies of knowledge, self-confident for their achievement in the physical and biological sciences and now reaching out for a science of society and history.

The consequences for the novel were clear. It meant that those writers with a searching intelligence would deal with causation where its force arose, or destiny where its significant meaning could be understood. Man could only be understood in terms of the large processes which formed him. Since significant dramatic change no longer centered in the individual life, the naturalist who would retain a teleological hope for human destiny had to transfer his major interest to society and history.* It was inevitable that so many naturalists beginning with Zola were social revolutionaries and reformists, if we cite the cases of Dreiser, Norris, and London in the American first generation of naturalists. The brutality of naturalistic documentation enforced a shock, but it was a shock with a moral protest implicit in it. This prophetic and moral strain searched for the means of historical redemption. It needed only the exact example of Marx to provide that. His ingenious and covert moral imagination reversed the gloomy perspectives of nineteenth century economics, and transformed what presumed to be a scientific report of history into an outline of history's process of self-redemption.

It was a plausible irony that neo-scientism, as it was absorbed by the social naturalists, should pursue the same ultimate goals

---

* It was understandable that the nineteenth century should have been the era of the philosophies of history and social ideologies. The struggle to escape the solipsistic threat supported them to the degree of making them fetishes. The point is that social ideologies are shared truths of shared experiences, and when subjected to post-Kantian criticism, the essential element which survives skepticism is the fact that they are shared. As Santayana put it, speaking of nationalism, "Of this distinction (nationality) our contemporaries tend to make an idol, perhaps because it is the only distinction they feel they have left." ("The Intellectual Temper of the Age," *Winds of Doctrine*, Harper, p. 7.)

as romantic naturalism, working from difficult premises through the process of hypostatizing "home values into a cosmic system." No longer idealist but materialist, no longer subjective but objective and seeming to accept the authority of science, nevertheless the common need expressed was to find human values supported in nature and the large design of history. We know them both, these two strains of naturalism, in the nostalgic aura of the nineteenth century, the age of hopeful ideologies.

These two dominant traditions in the nineteenth century dialogue with nature, were, it might seem, last appeals for the survival of the anthropomorphic principle. Because they were redemptive and because they found the force for redemption in natural causes, it seems to me fair to say they were particularly high-spirited forms of anthropomorphism, even though their characteristic literary expression was accompanied by an undercurrent of irony, or manifestations of pathos and brutality. If we look, however, for the distinctive moods of the most important fiction of the twentieth century, we find them neither in the vision of Rousseau nor of Marx. We see now that the philosophic spokesmen are more and more obviously Nietzsche and Kierkegaard. More directly, the literary ancestors who must draw our attention are, I believe, Dostoevsky and Flaubert, and perhaps, in a restricted range of influence but progressively more visible, Melville. However, Dostoevsky and Melville conceived a great stage of metaphysical drama which in the temperament of the twentieth century could only be occupied with diffidence and reserve, as in the indirect parables of Kafka, for instance. With concentration on Flaubert the essential note is struck. The temper of Flaubert is hard and ordealistic in an acutely modern sense, and it seems to me that he signals the shattering of the anthropomorphic consciousness. He indeed taught Zola and all naturalists much, but what distinguished him was that he could not release the unique personal being as the important subject for his fiction, nor could he soften the dilemma of personal being in the incommunicative universe. In *Madame*

Bovary he dramatized an opposition between the consciousness and the force which ringed it, and that drama was so harshly written that no naturalistic pieties like those of the romantics or the neo-scientific humanitarians could break the tension. In its light we see the effective qualities of such writers as Joyce, Conrad, Faulkner and Camus.

What I would call stoic naturalism, deriving from Flaubert, is without redemptive hopes or claims; it is the pure form of naturalism we might say, because it is uncompromisingly free of any wish to exchange one form of anthropomorphism for another, or to define nature in terms that are congenial to man. Those writers who dominate our contemporary consciousness found their material precisely at the point where imaginative human freedom met conflict with an unresponsive nature. Here the sensibility cannot master the world, nor does the world translate necessity into its own supererogatory design.

Perhaps this theme expresses itself more clearly in the work of Hemingway and the work of Camus, than in greater writers who complicate the issue with their richer sensibilities. Hemingway's initial romanticism cannot be mistaken; it is not a cold dissection of Bovaryism which we find in Hemingway; rather it is Bovaryism itself and the pathos of its destiny. Hemingway's characters seek fulfillment in the expected ways, in love, in nature, in the aroused vitalism of the hunt or the fight, but they do so with death already in their hearts. They suffer the ordealistic consciousness that experience is at the margin of an inhospitable truth, despite the reversions to typical sentimental naturalism in much of his writing. Camus' stronger philosophic interest takes the theme to its intellectual fulfillment. In the classic manner deriving from Flaubert, action is described as movement outward from the circle of subjectivity, surrounded by a barricade, so to speak, of individual and collective deceptions. The denouement is the purge of hard experience, and if the ordealistic protagonist breaks through the circle of untruth, it is to find himself alone, powerless in the exact sense of a frag-

mentary life consciousness in the physical swarm of nature.
The typical resolutions of what I have called stoic naturalism force the acknowledgment of pain, but pain is a great heightening of consciousness, if it gives nothing else. The compensation of the ordeal of experience is to capture the sense of reality. Camus describes this as the single reward of his broken hero in The Myth of Sisyphus: he offers the triumph of consciousness, which is simply truth knowing, truth telling, and this implies by its own necessary courage, the courage to exist. Perhaps this is the residue in its purest form of what has traditionally been meant by catharsis, the offering of stated meanings behind the foreground of destruction, death and silence. There are no more austere or paradoxical rewards in this vein than those which stoic naturalism offers, the bitter victories of the lucid mind, the integrity of consciousness acknowledged at the last point where all voices disappear into incoherence.*

In further paradox, what survives is an implicit moral passion. The representative modern novels I deal with in this series of essays tend to find their justification in the lucidity of consciousness which becomes a virtue, implicitly, the virtue of honesty. That is frequently the only virtue which supports the moral regime under which characters are presented and valued, if we accept the contingent values of intelligence and courage which are the requirements of the heroic consciousness. Under that moral regime the villain of the piece is illusion in all its forms, whether conventional anthropomorphic belief or individual self-deception. Thereby the redemptive act in the moral

* A substitute term for stoic naturalism might be existential naturalism, but existentialism has too many implications to be useful here. In any case, the fiction of Sartre, like that of Camus, in its self-conscious intentions has deeply clarified the issues latent in an era of writing which precedes rather than follows his example. It is instructive to remember Sartre's whole-hearted acceptance of modern American fiction. "To the writers of my generation the publication of The 42nd Parallel, Light in August, A Farewell to Arms, effected a revolution similar to the one produced fifteen years earlier in Europe by the Ulysses of Joyce." (Quoted in Henri Peyre, "American Literature Through French Eyes," The Virginia Quarterly Review, Vol. 23, p. 438.)

drama is disillusionment, the quality of revelation which more than any other describes the modern temper.*

We thus pursue virtues which are the virtues of the heroic consciousness. In literature at least intelligence is the god we serve, but a particularly passive and unpragmatic intelligence. Others may find use for the enormously magnified instruments of knowledge, but their chief effect for literature has been to inhibit the representation of the full cycles of action, and to define the ability of the intelligence to master life in inverse proportion to its ability to perceive it.

In the most blunt demonstration of modern metaphysical impotence, Camus describes the role of sensate awareness in this way:

> For the absurd man it is not a matter of explaining and solving, but of experiencing and describing. Everything begins with a lucid indifference.
>
> Describing—that is the last ambition of an absurd thought. Science likewise, having reached the end of its paradoxes, ceases to propound and stops to contemplate and sketch the ever virgin landscapes of phenomena. . . . Explanation is useless, but the sensation remains, and with it, the constant attractions of a universe inexhaustible in quantity. The place of the work of art can be understood at this point.[4]

This has the resilient toughness of Camus' own temperament but it is also pathetic; it is a climax of pathos for the retreating sensibility of modern man. Who remembers at this point the anarchical self-confidence expressed by Nietzsche as he confronted the same dilemma?

* Disillusionment is the act of piety, the negative gesture of truth, which the relentless self-criticism of modern thought inflicts upon itself. All other values find themselves transvalued by the effect of truth or purity of perception, as the forms of naturalistic ugliness became more readily the substance of art than naturalistic beauty, or as the purity of line and color replaced the pretensions of representation and meaning.

4 The Myth of Sisyphus, Alfred A. Knopf, p. 99.

The falseness of a given judgment does not constitute an ob-
jection against it, so far as we are concerned. It is perhaps in
this respect that our new language sounds strangest. The real
question is how far a judgment furthers and maintains life, pre-
serves a given type, possibly cultivates and trains a given type.
We are, in fact, fundamentally inclined to maintain that the
falsest judgments (to which belong the synthetic a priori judgments) are the most indispensable to us, that man cannot live
without accepting the logical fictions as valid, without measur-
ing reality against the purely invented world of the absolute,
the immutable, without constantly falsifying the world by means
of numeration. That getting along without false judgments
would amount to getting along without life, negating life. To
admit untruth as a necessary condition of life: this implies, to
be sure, a perilous resistance against customary value-feelings.
A philosophy that risks it nonetheless, if it did nothing else,
would by this alone have taken its stand beyond good and evil.[5]

We emphasize that what Nietzsche thus introduced is the
solipsistic hero of modern fiction, though the figure was to be
extended in a broad range of success and failure. The Nietzschean ideal was the power-increasing personality who acted
in independence of both "truth" and traditional values. I do not
think that modern literature has ever lost the heady exhilaration
of freedom in this respect, the recognition that the person in his
own will was ultimately the only authority for his life. However,
the insight maintained a constant and dispiriting ambivalence.
Nietzschean egocentricity had its stimulus from the solipsistic
principle; to extend the circle of one's own being was to fill an
empty space, to go beyond good and evil was to stress that good
and evil, "truth" and "value" were non-existent. The Nietzschean
superman was perhaps an hysterical appeal from the void.

The theme of much of twentieth century fiction seems to support this by inverting the Nietzschean prototype. Active within
one degree or another of the isolated imagination or the isolated
will, the protagonists in this vein tend to be Nietzschean failures

5 *Beyond Good and Evil*, Henry Regnery Company, Chicago, p. 4.

who dramatize the reduction of the power impulse to futility, anarchy, stultification, and self-destruction. Gide's Lafcadio, Faulkner's Sutpen, Conrad's Lord Jim, Fitzgerald's Gatsby, Joyce's Stephen Dedalus are examples which come to mind.

The example of Joyce reminds us again that action after all is the subordinate interest in much of modern fiction. We recall Stephen Dedalus in his earlier phase, presented in A Portrait of the Artist as a Young Man. Deeply related as he is there to the Nietzschean hero, he openly transfers his search for dominance from action to consciousness. It is in fact implicit in Joyce's work that "action," conveyed by the instrument of the naturalistic insight, is properly the material for the mock-heroic, for comedy. In this he extends the ironic naturalism of Flaubert to an appropriate conclusion. The estimable hero of Joyce's work, one who truly conquers a world, is the consciousness which accompanies and regards Leopold Bloom on his journey. The figure of the nose-picking futilitarian Stephen Dedalus is there to represent its material agent, descended into the flesh, so to speak. Superbly ironic and self-mocking, nevertheless, that exemplary consciousness leads to a great sociological as well as fictional mode of our times: the artist, or the sensibility itself, conceived as hero. Here, the description of Santayana was borne out, experience became itself the only possible object of experience, and the solipsistic threat became art's great asset, a precondition for understanding the sensibility of the twentieth century.

Madame Bovary: the seriousness of comedy

Emma Bovary is the protagonist in a great example of modern fiction, building itself upon the dramatic isolation of an individual consciousness in a world which resists both her will and understanding. Emma is surrounded by a cold light, she is seen objectively, almost clinically, a fragment of life spinning on its separate path. The reader knows Emma, but as he might know a sick, mad, or otherwise self-absorbed person who cannot return communication. He knows as a scientist knows, not in a dialogue, but as in the observation of an unanswering thing. This drama, typically naturalistic, splits the point of view so that to be the actor in life is one thing, and to know life, quite another thing, is to be the spectator of it. Emma's consciousness cannot deal equally with that of the reader. This is the key of the work and its effects. In that sense it is a modern novel, one of the most remorseless in method and brilliant of modern novels. No one went further than Flaubert, except perhaps

Joyce, in administering an epistemology that we understand so deeply. This defines knowledge as solipsistic and private when it is knowledge in action. Emma is alive in her own context, but her life is a distant flicker so long as the point of view is truly given up to a neutral omniscience.

A literary empiricism or positivism is in the position of the laboratory. It remains outside the object of experiment, and pursuing its own interest, widely outside the fatal personal interests of the agents in the drama. In that sense there is no dialogue, as I put it, between character and reader. Flaubert concentrates on the stage, as if the only hold we have on truth is the immediate scene, and every secondary report is a subjective distortion. When the report comes we are interested in it *because of its subjective distortion*. A context of coldest, precise objectivity is prepared for Emma's illusions. As protagonist, locked in her private world, she is mocked by the contrast, and the straining of desire is shown against the indifference of facts. This makes a drama of cross-purposes, working itself out brutally, pathetically, toward the final silencing of the consciousness and will. The terms must be brutal and pathetic because the antagonists are not evenly matched. Emma is defeated by the premises of the conflict; her antagonist is not so much inexplicable as non-communicating. It is not a personality, it does not respond, and as an antagonist it merely exists in her perception of the array of time, matter, circumstance set against her. It is, abstractly, a blind principle of resistance.

The objectivity of fate is recorded in the objectivity of the narrator. Like a spectator god he refuses to intervene, and he will not allow the dramatic loneliness of the protagonist to be comforted. He asserts nothing to give her life a share in a world of significant meaning, nor will he allow her illusions to wrest something from extinction at the end.

In any drama a character is set seriously at odds with his life's offering, or his destiny, as we may wish to put it, and classically the resolution of conflict calls for the intervention of a unifying insight. In general what we expect is that the resolution be teleological, in some sense, and although gods may not descend to give judgment and interpret the action, yet the elements of conflict have brought the antagonists into terms of communication. I think we might say that an instinct in all story-telling moves toward dramatic resolutions which depend in some form on the faith that men have in their ability to control or understand destiny.

The difficulty and special method of modern fiction has much to do with the difficulty of achieving teleological resolution in this aspect. The *values* of modern fiction, in the complex of esthetic and ethical effects, tend to be located in an impasse insofar as the instinctive search for a teleological metaphysics is concerned. That search must in fact be blunted and the curiosity of the reader directed not so much to substantive discoveries as to the nature of the struggle itself. That is what I mean by saying that although the protagonist of Flaubert's novel *intends* to bring fulfillment to her interests or make her fate intelligible in *their* terms, the reader expects nothing of the sort. The protagonist and the reader (or the author, which is to say the same thing) do not move on the same level of interest, and it is this characteristic of the esthetics of objectivity which concerns me most in this essay.

We ask ourselves what the values are in an esthetics which sees the human struggle impassively, with an implicit skepticism for the correspondence between subjective values and external reality. There is of course the value of a lucid report, the clarity and wholeness with which the life experience has been rendered. This has indeed been the chief ostensible claim for Flaubert's pure practice of naturalistic method. But is verisimilitude the major value in his art? That is not likely, nor can we be restricted to terms that aim for purely formal value, like clarity, completeness, coherence, etc. It was perhaps a symptom of the difficulty of defining the correspondence of interest between the subject and its audience which made a stress on formal esthetic values so much the rule in Flaubert's own thinking about his work.

We need to go beyond these terms if we wish to understand the values inherent in his great work as well as in the long tradition of fiction which it dominates. We need first to recognize a quality of pathos in *Madame Bovary* which seems proportionate to the cold violence of the writing, the kind of pathos which appears as the reduced vestige of tragic sympathy, and is the effect of suffering which is not understood and of a conflict between drastically unequal forces. The vein of pathos in naturalistic writing appears despite the coldness of surface; it can at times be quite sentimental or at the service of a moral polemic. The quality of pathos in Flaubert's writing is, however, restrained and absorbed into the spirit of irony. A neutral omniscience is after all most often the point of view of comedy, and will tend to provide some of the satisfactions of comedy. The effect of Flaubert's great ironic method is complex, and it might be described as applying the accuracy and coldness of juxtapositions familiar in comedy to matter treated seriously, in fact with the passion for ordealistic experience we find in tragedy. Erich Auerbach, discussing Flaubert and placing his work somewhere between the poles of comedy and tragedy, calls it the mode of "objective seriousness." Considering the term he goes on to say, "This sounds strange as a designation of the style of a literary work. Objective seriousness, which seeks to penetrate to the depths of the passions and entanglements of a human life, but without itself becoming moved, or at least without betraying that it is moved—this is an attitude which one expects from a priest, a teacher, or a psychologist rather than from an artist. But priest, teacher, and psychologist wish to accomplish something direct and practical—which is far from Flaubert's mind." [1] Auerbach goes on to conclude, however, that there was a didactic purpose concealed in Flaubert's artistic

1 *Mimesis*, Doubleday Anchor, p. 433.

aims, the simple hatred for nineteenth century bourgeois culture. This is no doubt largely true and objective naturalism
comes readily to the service of a didactic message or a polemic.
It seems to me, however, that Flaubert's neutrality deserves
greater credit. His later disciple, Joyce, in his portrait of the
archetypal artist, described how emotions are transcended in the
Olympian spirit of irony, based on a lucidly detached omniscience which purges anger, fear, and desire. The irony we speak
of may be a value for the artist, if not perhaps for the teacher
or psychologist, in that it satisfies the appetite for power in the
intelligence; it arises particularly from the discrepancy between
the wide consciousness of the observer and the restricted consciousness of the subject. The note of sadism it suggests is
typical enough for a deep trait of the modern intelligence. It
is precisely because the spirit of irony thus described is *not* at the
service of a didactic message, or the expression of a misanthropy
like Swift's, which gives it its special quality: not really to laugh,
not really to weep, nor to cry out in anger or hatred, but to be
released from a commitment to action and belief and to transcend all human limitations simply by acknowledging them.

In Flaubert's work then we find the expression of realism at
its philosophic extreme, the effort to report things as they are
with a scrupulously neutral teleological point of view. The most
austere realism can successfully avoid the effect of satire or of
polemic, but it cannot avoid the implications of irony and
pathos. These will arise in dramatic presentation in proportion,
in fact, to the distance or neutrality of the point of view. The
removal of the author from value judgments has the effect of
stressing and isolating the values of his protagonists, now seen
clearly in dramatic collision with things as they are. The contrast is with things as they *might be*, in this case imagined in
the subjective or solipsistic world of Emma Bovary. The center
for ironic treatment is not the world as found so much as the
human consciousness itself, moved by idealization and desire,
destined for self-deception and failure. The reality which sur-

rounds consciousness has a kind of neutral undebated existence which in fact tends to be as awe-inspiring as the traditional metaphysical power of God. It has dignity at the expense, we might say, of the principle of subjectivity. Nature is not a benevolent god in typical modern naturalism, but it is a god nonetheless, to whose omnipotence has been added the impressive attribute of indifference or incommunicability insofar as the human interest is concerned. There is a school of naturalism, in Zola and Dreiser for instance, more typical of the nineteenth than the twentieth century, which suggests that the God of nature is comprehensible at least, and when its *diktat* is known men can achieve some fulfillment in their living. That combination of scientific method and humanitarian purpose was long ago expressed by the Goncourt brothers (as Erich Auerbach points out) in their preface to *Germinie Lacerteux:* "Today when the Novel is broadening and growing, when it is beginning to be the great, serious, impassioned, living form of literary study and social investigation . . . ; today when the Novel has imposed upon itself the studies and duties of science, it can demand the freedoms and immunities of science. And if it seek Art and Truth, if it disclose troubles which it were well the happy people of Paris should not forget . . . ; human suffering, present and alive, which teaches charity; if the Novel have that religion to which the past century gave its broad and vast name: Humanity; —that consciousness suffices it; its right lies there." [2] But this is not the quality of Flaubert's naturalism, neither polemic, nor moral exposure, nor affirmation.

Emma Bovary, like any protagonist, is an agent of the sensuous, ethical and esthetic human imagination. When the content of that imagination becomes the object of neutral study rather than either assent or denial, then the normative function itself becomes depreciated and is patronized by the intelligence. The dialogue traditionally conducted between the reader and

2 Translated by Erich Auerbach, *Mimesis*, p. 437.

the protagonist of the narrative is broken. It is the way, as I have said, in which Emma's motivated consciousness is isolated from productive correspondence with her environment, and isolated in addition from a consensus of values; it is this isolation from world, audience, and author which strikes the characteristic quality of the novel, and I believe, the dominant tradition of naturalistic writing which grows from it. It is necessary at this point to offer some illustrations of the effects I have generally described.

* * *

Emma has begun to be bored in her marriage, and here is an example of her early dreaming:

> Didn't love, like Indian plants, require rich soils, special temperatures? Sighs in the moonlight, long embraces, hands bathed in lover's tears—all the fevers of the flesh and the languors of love—were inseparable from the balconies of great idle-houred castles, from a silk-curtained, thick-carpeted, be-flowered boudoir with its bed on a dais, from the sparkle of precious stones and the swank of liveries.

> The hired boy at the relay post across the road, who came in every morning to rubdown the mare, walked through the hall in his heavy wooden shoes; his smock was in holes, his feet were innocent of stockings.*

There is the immediate counterpoint. The hired boy in his heavy wooden shoes echoes outside Emma's dreams, illustrating the characteristic tension in Flaubert's writing. The brilliantly concise objective scene records itself.

> Charles jogged back and forth across the countryside under snow and rain. He ate omelettes at farmhouse tables, thrust his arm into damp beds, had his face spattered with jets of warm blood at bleedings; he listened to death rattles, examined the contents of basins, handled a lot of soiled underclothing.

* Quotations are from the translation of *Madame Bovary* by Francis Steegmuller, The Modern Library, New York.

Those tingling sensations define a reality. Its coldness presses against Emma's luxurious imagination, where the intense vagueness of desire moves in ratio with the resistless tendency toward solipsism. Her images . . .

> lived on a higher plane than other people, somewhere sublime between heaven and earth, up among the storm clouds. As for the rest of the world, it was in some indeterminate place beyond the pale; it could scarcely be said to exist. Indeed the closer to her things were, the further away from them her thoughts turned.

The force of the romantic imagination is passion searching for its objects. In that sense, as Denis de Rougemont stressed in his study of the theme, romantic passion grows from resistance, its basis is frustration from which it moves out to the limitless, the unrealizable where all terms are its own.[3] Experience is self-generated; wave after wave of private impulse moves outward to meet resistance, which serves only to send the flight higher or make a total collapse. There is no coming to terms because there is no communication of terms. The climaxes of the romantic experience are passive, in the sense that desire is separated from action and confined to itself. The most extreme of personal demands alternate with the passive retreat. The dynamics of Keats' "Ode to a Nightingale," for instance, might illustrate the subjective flight and fall. Desire finds its essence in imagined experience, the image taking perfection into itself. The climax moves into the fall, reality intervenes, and the fall into reality forces helplessness. The final position is inert, the will has lost its objects, the consciousness is lost between dream and reality. The poem plausibly ends, "Do I wake or sleep?"

The "fictional" basis of Emma's consciousness attaches her naturally to invented and transcendental worlds, romantic novels, the theatre, the church. Emma at the theatre is Emma in life,

3 *Love in the Western World,* Harcourt, Brace.

thoroughly absorbed in artificial forms. She identifies herself simply with the woman on the stage, though "no one had ever loved her with such a love." The experience is interrupted by the arrival of Leon, and Emma moves without a break, forgetting the opera completely, into her love affair with him as if to illustrate the continuity of her fantasies.

The church is more impressively the source for subjective experience, and the best themes for Emma's internal climaxes are religious. The images are absolute but they remain sensual, they are Emma's.

> . . . she gently succumbed to the mystical languor induced by the perfumes of the altar, the coolness of the holy water fonts, the gleaming of the candles. . . . The metaphors constantly used in sermons—'betrothed,' 'spouse,' 'heavenly lover,' 'mystical marriage'—excited her in a thrilling new way.

In these ironic metaphors Flaubert seems to put religion at the apex of the expressive human fallacy. In his story, "Un Coeur Simple" the consummation of Félicité's locked-in emotional consciousness is a vision of the Holy Ghost in the form of her stuffed and moth-eaten parrot, the latter intruding into her fantasy directly as the sign of the mundane and opaque reality of her existence.

After the illness provoked by her frustrations, Emma goes through something very like a religious experience which seems to spiritualize her excess of desire, but inexorably Flaubert turns it back. The lovers meet at the church itself, which to Leon "was like a gigantic boudoir suffused with her image," and again without much transition, religion reduces itself to a private sensuous fantasy. Leaving the church, in the same confused trance as it were, Emma passes into the arms of her lover and the process of her self-seduction is completed.

Here idealization is seen as close as it can be to its physical sources. The realism is reductive and man is viewed as a dreaming animal, his dreams a symptom of his biology. It is not ir-

relevant that Charles is a physician. He is part of the reality
trap for Emma, and he brings its naturalistic aspect to the foreground. The image of Charles examining the contents of basins
and listening to death rattles is a forecast of the end. Meanwhile
as Emma surrenders to her first lover, Rodolphe, his hyper-
bolic seduction speech is counterpointed by the political speaker
at the country fair, with his praise of scientific agriculture, with
the awards for the best breeding and the best manures.

Flaubert's intentions are clear in the lingering over the physical details of Emma's death. The blind beggar comes to Emma
as the messenger of fate, and he exhibits fate with his shredded
flesh and open wounds. His voice is the last sound in Emma's
ears. Whatever principle of meaning it has, nature answers ir-
relevantly to the question of the consciousness. This is expressed
in the "scientific" discussion among the medical men, while they
eat a good lunch at Homais' house and Emma lies dying.

> First we had a sensation of siccity in the pharynx, then in-
> tolerable pain in the epigastrium, superpurgation, coma.

This is the hammering emotionless tone of fact, idiotic in its
factualness. The scientific report speaks a language unintelligible
to the subjective life at its extreme; pain, grief, fear, these are
terms that have lost utterly their ground of reference. Their
source, their only knower, has herself become extinct.

The ironies of irrelevance are climaxed in the final argument
between the priest and Homais as they sit with the dead body.
At cross-purposes, unintelligible to each other, the dead body
is their audience, and religion and liberal science make their
claims in the heaviest resisting silence. Enforcing the point,
they both finally fall asleep.

> They sat opposite one another, stomachs out, faces swollen,
> both of them scowling—united, after so much dissension, in
> the same human weakness; and they stirred no more than the
> corpse that was like another sleeper beside them.

Although Christianity might have spoken to Emma's last flicker of consciousness, it has been betrayed by the object she has become, it now speaks in a world she no longer inhabits. Science, as expressed by the vulgar pharmacist to be sure, has some crude validity in describing the object she was and has become, but as a language, never has it been less in communication with the sentient spirit which made use of language.

The truth the novel has to tell is that Emma, the sentient, subjective being, is alone, and very few have pursued this insight with as much clarity and courageous finality as Flaubert. Emma chooses her death when the people in her life, one might say, have all become bill collectors, when they refuse her what she wants, when they ask for payment. Her desires require what is not freely given. She loves but Lheureux pays the bills and he says, "Do you expect me to pay your bills indefinitely?" A material arrangement has to be made, a physical power won before the will can be satisfied. An impersonal and abstract machine, in society as well as nature, has power over life, and it cannot answer Emma's language of desire.

In this way the novel ends with the progressive beleaguerment of the protagonist. She is overwhelmed by externality, both social and natural. There is a climactic series of refusals ending in total failure to impose her will. Leon, Lheureux, the notary, Rodolphe, these with the absence and silence of Charles, force Emma to the wall. She has purified the issue of being at odds. This is the acute psychological position and the one which suggests suicide.

Flaubert follows the stages of disintegration to the end, for he knows that it is the ruin of the great theatre of meaning itself, the theatre of the consciousness. He enacts in his writing the incoherence and disorientation of her mind; her subjectivity has closed in completely.

> Madness began to take hold of her; she was frightened, but managed to control herself—without, however, emerging from

her confusion, for the cause of her horrible state—the question of money—had faded from her mind. It was only her love that was making her suffer, and she felt her soul leave her at the thought—just as a wounded man, as he lies dying, feels his life flowing out with his blood through the gaping hole.

Night was falling; crows flew overhead. It suddenly seemed to her that fiery particles were bursting in the air, like bullets exploding as they fell, and spinning and spinning and finally melting in the snow among the tree branches. In the center of each of them appeared Rodolphe's face. They multiplied; they came together; they penetrated her; everything vanished.

Flaubert stresses at that moment the refusal of love, the greatest subjective claim itself. Like the wavering of a single light in the dark, the poignant principle of life is that its meaning is self-generated, the light has its source within itself.

* * *

Flaubert's ironic view of subjective beleaguerment gives special pregnancy to every view of the protagonist in the fiction of our century, which owes more to him than to any other nineteenth century master. Understanding his approach to Emma, we must deal with his work with an eye on the traits of earlier romanticism. In characteristic effect, the romantic hero is the subjective protagonist facing a hostile reality. However, in the earliest tradition he is the significant martyr of his experience, and if he is alienated, it is largely by his own effort at transcendence. His prototype is Prometheus or Manfred. In his isolation and suffering he glorifies the subjective principle and even within failure he justifies his sentiment or his will. In the end the romantic hero manifests an ineffable greatness of sensibility; that is his victorious principle when, like Tristan, he faces the ruins of a life action or meets his death. As de Rougemont suggested, that victory *requires* his frustration, or to put it another way, victory on the level of consciousness required defeat on the level of action.

In large terms the growth of realism in the nineteenth century is understood as the humbling of the romantic posture. Flaubert's novel regards the protagonist not as the hero of his own impulse or imagination, but as the victim, in the sense that the great block of external reality has all the power on its side and pushes the hero to diminutive size. Flaubert, in his novel, by a sharp exaggeration of the principles of romantic irony, creates a mode of literature very familiar to us, with immediate examples that come to mind in the work of Joyce, Kafka, and Beckett. We might call this a special form of dry comedy which stresses the cross-purposes between feeling agent and unfeeling object, a sense of the absurd which conveys intelligible motive into an unintelligible and unresponsive field of action. The effect in *Madame Bovary* is that of the spirit of comedy without humor, and of the perspective of tragedy reduced to the grotesque. The theme is most serious, it universalizes itself; it has the sobriety, in fact, of metaphysical comedy. In the ordinary view, I think, comedy is representative enough but not universal or absolute. That is, it exhibits a feebleness and a capacity for error we all recognize but in such special circumstances or caricatured semblance that we single out what is laughable without including in our patronage all of humanity and the human experience in its *essential* quality. The pure effect of comedy requires an implicit comparison with norms which are serious and are conceived as possible.* The metaphysical comedy is impure, that is to say, it is changed by the threat of nihilism which makes laughable comparisons pointless. The universal comedy of humanity is appreciated best by gods or Martians, and it is written as both Joyce and Flaubert imply, in imitation of that stance.

It may be that Flaubert's novel is a miracle of literature in its achievement of deeply luminous perception without the qualification of feeling. Emma's death is accompanied by a curiously interrupted response, an abstractness of vision in which the basis of any emotion dissipates itself, because the objective

---

* Even Swift wrote from that standpoint, though perhaps he had to invent the Houyhnhnms to achieve the comparison.

distance between the character and the reader is proportionate to her own solipsistic dilemma. When the consciousness of the subject and her reality in the world are to this extent separated, we have an incomplete dramatic experience, ambiguous, intellectual, but without that emotional release which depends upon at least a temporary fusion of motive and action or insight and reality.

It is the coldness of an intellectual hazard, of a thing seen with curiosity and strain that the reader feels pressing upon him as he reads Flaubert's novel. He is looking at Emma as through lenses which see too much to let her touch him directly, or else he has her own eyes to see through whereby he loses the sense of any reality but her own. A curious numbness invades him and though he may sense very sharply Emma's suffering, the experience seems to refuse any emotional or intellectual fulfillment.

In Flaubert the ambiguity resembles the dilemma of the "underground man" in Dostoevsky's story, a work equally expressive of major effects in modern fiction. In that story there is a cycle of canceling out for each insight, each confession, because the grounds for belief have been sapped. The threat of a zero in interest and a zero in value arises in every standpoint, and even truthtelling becomes a mask which stripped away will expose nothing, a vacuum. What Dostoevsky's story illustrates is the anxiety of telling the truth when there is nothing but a subjective ground of reference for truth. The man confesses his life, but he knows and says he will have no audience, and further he does not believe himself after each assertion and cannot in his desperate alternations see anything but a revolving series of masks for his real being. His ultimate desperation is that he wants authenticity, a basis, beyond being true, or good, or loved, things which he has left far behind. He dangles, a man without a basis, and though he keeps the energy of his mind, and functions intensely in his emotions, his feelings and words have been hopelessly compromised; they are finally pointless and he dangles in empty spaces.

This sense of an ultimate pointlessness read between the lines illustrates that aspect of a normative or teleological impasse we postulate for Flaubert's novel. It has, as I said, something like the detachment of comedy and the passionate seriousness of tragedy. But the ambiguity of thought and feeling makes a sharp contrast with what we associate with traditional tragedy. Thus one remembers Othello speaking just before his death:

> *I have done the state some service, and they know it;*
> *No more of that:—I pray you, in your letters,*
> *When you shall these unlucky deeds relate,*
> *Speak of me as I am; nothing extenuate,*
> *Nor set down aught in malice; then must you speak*
> *Of one, that lov'd not wisely, but too well;*
> *Of one, not easily jealous, but, being wrought,*
> *Perplexed in the extreme; of one, whose hand,*
> *Like the base Judean, threw a pearl away,*
> *Richer than all his tribe; of one, whose subdued eyes,*
> *Albeit unused to the melting mood,*
> *Drop tears as fast as the Arabian trees*
> *Their medicinal gums: Set you down this:*
> *And say, besides,—That in Aleppo once,*
> *Where a malignant and turban'd Turk*
> *Beat a Venetian, and traduced the state,*
> *I took by the throat the circumcised dog,*
> *And smote him—thus.*

This is Othello united with his own experience. It would be trivial to say that he has corrected his error, but in a large sense he is in a transcendent relation with the truth. His speech is the absorption of a situation which sums up his life, and it is in fact his meaningful consciousness which now has dominance over his survival. His life is about to end but significant knowledge and feeling are firmer than they have ever been.

Similarly, enacting the tragic principle, Lear moves from incoherence to sanity,

> Pray, do not mock me:
> I am a very foolish fond old man,
> Fourscore, and upwards; and, to deal plainly,
> I fear, I am not in my perfect mind.
> Methinks, I should know you, and know this man;
> Yet I am doubtful: for I am mainly ignorant
> What place this is; and all the skill I have
> Remembers not these garments; nor I know not
> Where I did lodge last night: Do not laugh at me:
> For, as I am a man, I think this lady
> To be my child Cordelia.

Lear receives a communication from his real condition and from Cordelia which cannot be deflected by further events. Emma Bovary on the other hand descends to a true mental chaos which is the consequence of isolation and is not to be reversed. Emma is alone at her death, and cannot receive a person or a truth in any communication. Flaubert puts up the intellectual barriers and keeps them there—by establishing Homais and the priest at her bedside. No insight and therefore no identification with her can cross these barriers. They are there to maintain distance and propose irony for the resolved point of view.

There is a reservation to be made to this and perhaps Flaubert does not intend Emma's isolation to be absolute. Charles exists and he is at her bedside too. "And in his eyes she read a love such as she had never known." This sounds as if Flaubert had for a moment lost the courage of his convictions, and I think really that this is a stroke unworthy of him, little as it is related to anything which precedes or follows. If Charles is the agent for sympathy it is abortive and cannot get through. He joins the priest and the pharmacist at the deathbed, he comes to say good-by and this is the moment for a possible leap across barriers. But possessed by his great ignorance, with less knowledge than anyone of Emma's secret life and consciousness, he is not a recompense for the priest and the agnostic pharmacist. He is simply dumb emotion reduced to its own private gesture, and finally as in curiosity he lifts the veil over Emma's face, all that comes from him is a scream of horror. There is an allegory speaking here, as if the protagonist of feeling, divided from intelligence and belief, (the priest and the pharmacist are now sleeping) were capable only of blind revulsion.

Now at this climax grief itself illustrates the solipsistic principle. Charles refuses the evidence of Emma's unfaithfulness almost to the end. Opposed as he was in his external being to Emma's consciousness, he now himself becomes possessed by an idealized person with no correspondence in reality. He is more complete in his befuddlement than Emma, in love with a non-responding object, the dead woman who never loved him.

> The strange thing was that Bovary, even though he thought of Emma continually, was forgetting her; and he felt desperate realizing that her image was fading from his memory, struggle as he might to keep it alive. Each night, however, he dreamed of her. It was always the same dream: he approached her, but just as he was about to embrace her she fell into decay in his arms.

When the truth of Emma's life is finally forced on him, confusion is only succeeded by silence. After his first rage he has nothing to say, not even to Rodolphe, in his resignation. This evaporation of any basis of judgment, or the possibility of truth at all, reminds us of Dostoevsky's story. Meaning itself disintegrates in the shock, the characteristic note again is passivity:
"No one is to blame. It was decreed by fate."
Just before he dies the next day, there is this:

> . . . a vaporous flood of love-memories swelled in his sorrowing heart, and he was overcome by emotion, like an adolescent.

In these respects the conclusion of Charles' life parallels Emma's. He is not the respondent of knowledge and grief, but is taken on the same path of isolation from facts, toward passivity in the final confrontation of them, and to death in the condition of a subjective fix, mild and pathetic as it is. The comedy of cross purposes comes to an end with pathos heightened, as if to say that this kind of confused grief is the proper monument to Emma's life. That pathos, which is a special or limited form of sympathy, patronizing, though to be sure it patronizes universally, is the necessary response to a suffering which has withdrawn to a vanishing point in the subjective consciousness.

Whatever other spiritual relief the novel provides comes in the austere effect of empirical insight. However, as I've said, if truth, whatever its value elsewhere, did not have a poignance in the human consciousness it would have no literary value. Therefore this truth is inseparable from irony—the irony of appreciated differences and perspectives. The spirit of irony is in analysis the jubilant exercise of intellectual power. The power to criticize life is tested, while the power to assert values, which the full spirit of irony surrenders, is replaced by as strong an appeal in the power to devalue valuations. The spirit of irony expressed in Flaubert's masterpiece is not limited and vulgar— it does not jeer or express contempt. Rather it is superb in detachment and by its detachment it measures its own success. It does the almost inconceivable thing, it transcends in the perceiving consciousness the limitations of the active consciousness. To describe a failure can give the illusion of power. To trace the errors of the human consciousness requires a perch above error as well as above involvement. The heady special catharsis suggested by Flaubert's work is that recompense in awareness which transcends both desire and action. A moralist might say that nothing has enfeebled the modern human race so much as this critical patronage which the intelligence gives to action and belief and which is deeply implicit in what I have called the esthetics of objectivity.

It may be possible to say that this is an esthetics which is the natural product of an era of science. In what we may for convenience call anthropomorphic esthetics, which is at its extreme point a religious esthetics, life is viewed comprehensively, but the viewer is a part of the picture, action is given purpose, the knowledge given belief. In this respect the knower and the known are one and they move together toward a common principle of action. The goal of religion and the literature based on the religious impulse is an act of faith which unites the several levels of experience, a universe of meaning, the hero, and the audience receiving ritualistic testimony. It unites two levels of occurrence, the events of the play or story and the universal consequences in which they have a part. Above all, however, it unites the consciousness of the reader with that of the protagonist in the communication of a common experience and a commonly valued destiny. A religious or teleological literature conceived in this way is the extreme contrast with what I have defined in Flaubert's school of fiction. This in its primary example is an ambiguous tragi-comedy, where action and knowledge are disjointed, where the motives of the active consciousness take prat-falls in reality, and a luminous spectator mind observes them, acknowledges an impasse, and makes its own skeptical clarity its recompense. If there is an educated sensibility produced by this literature, it seems to me that its moral quality is one where man patronizes man, and the ultimate consequences of this standpoint have yet to be measured in our civilization.

Stoom:
the universal comedy
of James Joyce

I | THE SPOILED PRIEST

In "Ivy Day in the Committee Room" a mysterious character appears who is described as possibly a defrocked priest or else an unemployed actor. This might be presented as Joyce's own sly signature. The priestly imagination claims a performance on the stage of the infinite, and it claims the sacramental power of fusing spirit and matter, or putting it closer to our interests, the power to reconcile illusion and reality. However, Joyce, the radical modern ironist, who, I think we can say, built his career as an artist on the basis of destroyed religious thought, offers his metaphysical premise in the implication that the priest is really a man of the theatre, the performance a mime, the performer a seedy actor.

Broken, transformed, dying and dead priests make their appearance in several of the *Dubliners* stories. As Harry Levin said with great effect, the chalice which broke in the hands of the ruined priest of "The Sisters" was the symbol of a broken communion and a theme throughout Joyce's work. The priest is paralyzed, a suggestive principle for the impotent high intelligence and imagination, removed from their vocation. Was it the ruling figure in Joyce's imagination, that mad and paralyzed priest, laughing alone in the confessional, with the abortive communion on his conscience? It is in the back room where a priest had died that the boy in "Araby," fathering child of Joyce's artist protagonist, finds his precious books which plant the pure but secularized seeds of romance in his mind.

When we contemplate the successful communion we understand the ambition of the artist; it is specifically the urge to transcend limits. Joyce makes that clear to us in *The Portrait of the Artist as a Young Man*, which in declaring the ambition of the artist and the terms of his vocation, becomes the necessary introduction to his great work, *Ulysses*. Everything he wrote before that, smaller masterpieces though they may be, were exercises and lessons for himself and the reader to prepare them for the task of *Ulysses*. Joyce's theme is the world, but in the total effort to conceive it, like a god creating a world, he first has to account for the creation of himself.

In Stephen Dedalus' young imagination the priest is the human figure who has come closest to sharing the omniscience and omnipotence of God. He has the power to act with his knowledge, and in his great action, the mass, which is crucial and cathartic, he makes his knowledge penetrate life and change it. The mass is a new act of creation, repeated endlessly in the ritual, whereby the imagination viewed as spiritual meaning inhabits and redeems passive matter. The wine which becomes blood concretely makes the fusion of terms whereby expressive meaning, held to its highest concept as God, has absorbed the object, the everlasting externality which the priest contemplates as he holds up the chalice. His ritual resolves the problem of life and declares it a unity and a success; the God of meaning arrives at his call with teleological purpose. The priest who cannot breach the external in that ancient miracle has failed, and Joyce's artist conceives himself at that point of failure.

The priestly ritual has a mimetic principle based on dramatic belief; it intensely wishes to achieve its purpose and does so. However, the source from which Stephen, the frustrated priest, the yet unborn artist, must draw his work is dramatic disbelief, a radical understanding of the limitations on both his knowledge and his power. The intensity of purpose exists but without hope for success. Nevertheless the call still remains, the vocation must be fulfilled.

We say then that the theme of Joyce's early work was the struggle of the priest-artist for his old vocation. The story of Stephen Dedalus is the record of a consciousness yearning to exceed itself, and finding out the limitations of both knowledge and action. The childhood, boyhood and youth of Stephen is one of progressive alienation and paranoia, starting out with the first shocks of sensation, the plunge into the cold muddy water, the consequent fever of the troubled body in its experience. He suffers experience which is difficulty until he rebels, at which point the boy becomes a personality, distinguished by his alienation from the oppressive world. The shock of the muddy pool, the swish of Father Dolan's soutane, the cut of Heron's cane, all demand submission and retreat. The answer is no, and that monosyllable becomes Stephen's prepared response to all impositions upon his personal power, freedom and knowledge.

His rebellion gives him a personal consciousness, but the basis of his rebellion is a truly exorbitant demand for a universal consciousness. All the challenges to interference, the struggle for personal liberty, only lead the way to the real issue which is his own total victory over the world, a transfiguration of knowledge and power. Stephen follows the classic routes of love, literature, and religion. He writes the poems of the unreal or exorbitant imagination. "Elements which he deemed common and insignificant dropped out." His poems make their own world and invite the subjective trance. He waits for love: "A tender premonition touched him of the tryst he had then looked forward to, and in spite of the horrible reality which lay between his hope of then and now, of the holy encounter he had then imagined at which weakness and timidity and inexperience were to fall from him." These last words have stress; love is a domination of experience in Stephen's mind. However, the "horrible reality" grows and he proceeds at this point to his first sex experience in "the squalid quarter of the brothels."

The consciousness that strives for dominion discovers its limitations in action. As a child Stephen begins to understand the limitations upon knowing as such when he thinks of God. Only God can know everything and think about everything everywhere. God understood French, for instance. The restrictions are placed when Stephen writes his name on the flyleaf of his geography book, followed by "Class of Elements, Clongowes Wood College, Ireland, Europe, The World, The Universe." This is a diagram we must remember as we read Joyce's work and try to understand the theoretical discipline of his art.

Stephen, in the passage of his youth, is the ironic butt of the effort to know everything. In Joyce's unmerciful hands, the absolute imagination, the religious imagination, for instance, as expressed in the prolonged episodes of Stephen's religious struggle, turns back upon itself, hears its own voice and becomes nonsense. Stephen, as he tells Cranly later, has to understand the prospect of spending eternity with the Dean of Studies. In the long retreat sermon, the voice of the impassioned priest argues itself down with its own hyperbole, its own faltering imagination. Superbly mock-heroic, the retreat sermon presents anthropomorphic fallibility given its head. Heaven and hell are furnished with the inept details of the priest's invention, though the bathos is very subtly placed and his rhetoric has traditional resonance. At a climax we hear the ring of the priest's great cash register in heaven, adding up sins and the redemptive account of man. And Stephen must ask himself, drunk with possible salvation, what shall he do in this scheme with his devout mother's sneeze? Reality keeps breaking in, as when he hears the swish of Father Dolan's soutane at the crucial moment of choice for the priesthood.

We might say that all of Joyce's moody and brilliant genius focuses at this point. His work might be most simply described as a series of elaborate, highly ingenious strategies for treating the theme of romantic irony. The parable remains that of Dedalus and Icarus, with the latter falling from a flight too close to the sun, and the former surviving to record it. That legend of a fatal flight establishes the dilemma of the most ambitious consciousness in the world. The crafter Daedalus is "a symbol of the artist forging anew in his workshop out of the sluggish matter of the earth a new soaring imperishable being." In Joyce's fulfillment of the parable, all particular instances of flight are doomed either to find themselves wingless in the outer circle of nonsense, the inexpressible inane, or to find themselves falling back to the sluggish earth.

In any case, the first need is that of flight from the commonplace, oppressive earth. We follow the curve of flight in Stephen's permanent sense of betrayal, his paranoia of suffering. His young life is largely spent challenging sluggish ties, as he makes and elaborates an unqualified series of rejections. As he flies past the nets of religion, language and nationality, as he rejects the possibility of love, the actual love of his mother, the offered friendship of Cranly, he is searching for what—beyond the ineffable freedom of flight?

The dilemma is strict. To fall back to the humiliation of commonplace being was one danger, but to continue flight was another. If he were saved in the religious sense, as Stephen says, "He could not see why it was in any way necessary that he should continue to live." To continue flight was a solipsism made sublime; it reached the placeless, timeless inane. This is evident when human knowledge attempts its most ambitious task, as in the retreat sermon. At the keenest moment of Stephen's urge to believe, when the teleological answer might be expected to appear, we confront suddenly that strange circular sentence which stridently echoes the sermon's last words: "We knew perfectly well of course that although it was bound to come to the light he would find considerable difficulty in endeavouring to try to induce himself to endeavour to ascertain the spiritual plenipotentiary and so we knew of course perfectly well—" That sentence will never complete itself; it provides the surest clue for interpreting the self-parody and self-defeat of the ambitous human understanding. The voice is heard far off, at the ceiling of Stephen's mind, transcribing ultimate nonsense.

The ancient logos of religion has been mocked; what form of knowledge can redeem the activity of consciousness? This is Stephen's demand and the answer has been predestined. The father, the great artificer Daedalus, returned from his flight to construct a giant maze for Minos. Stephen's experience has made him fall, but his artist's conscience can renew his flight. The artist recognizes his mission and his triumph when he chooses neither "the pale service of the altar," nor "the dull gross voice of the world of duties and despair." He is the dialectician who presides over both, the intermediary between the ideal and the real, the sacred and profane. This is the dedication which Stephen announces, "To live, to err, to fall, to triumph, to recreate life out of life." The alive and tangible consciousness expresses both a flight and a fall. It salves the injury of experience with its own awareness, and it interrupts the flight into the inane with the touch of a disabusing reality.

In The Portrait Joyce illustrates the theme at several points. Stephen, feeling the romantic agony when his girl E. C. does not meet him after his performance in the school play (the agony great in proportion to the tenuous fantasy of its cause), walks the streets and passes a stable. "That is horsepiss and rotted straw. It will calm my heart." What it calms is not so much suffering as the threat of unreality and solipsism. We remember the fancy vague babble of Stephen's poems, where "elements he deemed common and insignificant dropped out." To measure the development of Stephen's principle of art we must compare such poems (very much like those Joyce published in *Chamber Music*) with the substantial dross of the commonplace he here invites, and which Joyce made so much of in his fiction.

In the end we find that the greater enemy of the creative imagination is not the sluggish earth, but those intelligent personalities in life who make their flight to an idea, or an emotional value. In a series of encounters with Davin, McCann, and Cranly, one with his emotional claims, another with his abstract doctrine or program for living, Stephen expresses his typical resistance and silence. It is only with Lynch that he becomes voluble, and it is Lynch, the vulgarian and buffoon, who becomes the proper audience for the esthetic creed which is Stephen's only faith. He must talk to the man who writes on the backside of Venus in order properly to discuss beauty, because this man has a fundamental share in Stephen's vision of beauty. Lynch ate cowdung as a child, and as Stephen says, "we are all animals, I also am an animal." At the climax of his peroration on esthetics a dray carrying clanging iron comes along and interrupts him conclusively.

Thus the consciousness and matter speak directly to each other. Lynch is necessary to full awareness in art, though the way in which he is converted to value *in action* is not clear, for Lynch must remain Lynch, the eater of cowdung, an agent in endless dichotomies and unreasoned conflict, the object of baffled disgruntlement. The others cannot deal with Lynch, but Stephen can, and it has been the object of his education to learn how. Lynch, the ultimate rawness of material fact, cannot yield to a normative or teleological approach, but he must yield to an esthetic mastery of experience. Stephen says "I can't love God but perhaps I can unite my will with his." God, if he loved the world and could be loved himself, would be involved with material nature and move himself in it. But the God Stephen invites is the God of omniscient consciousness purely, removed from kinetic involvement, "raised above desire and loathing."

The theory of art with which Joyce ends *The Portrait* is essentially for Stephen a metaphysics and a program for living. He has responded to the vivid epiphanies of life and determined his vocation from them. At the crucial moment of his choice against the priesthood he has seen the naked bodies of the boys swimming, their splashes and shouts overcoming his thoughts, and in a later revelation, he has seen the young girl wading in the stream, her skirts lifted to her hips. But we notice that he does not join the boys in their swim, though they call him insistently, "Bous Stephanoumenos! Bous Stephaneforos!" Nor does he stop more than a moment with his vision of the girl, though from her, ". . . he strode . . . crying to greet the advent of life that had cried to him." If his creed is in any sense an affirmation of life it must be understood in consistency with his cold final rejections of religion, politics, friendship, family, and love. There might be less sense of contradiction if we expected that Stephen's life-seeking was a typical romantic revolt, rejecting conventional sterilities for the sake of "life" in a naturalistic, neo-primivistic aspect. That is a turn that Stephen's biography might have taken, but it doesn't. The possibility becomes grotesque if we think of Stephen as a character created by D. H. Lawrence. The life Stephen Dedalus has chosen has a special nature and definition, it is the life of the artist. It does not mean the rejection of one limited or unsatisfactory sphere of action for another, or the action of complex social relationships for the action of the instinctive body. Quite the contrary, the naturalistic vision had revolted while it inspired him. "It was a pain to see them and a sword-like pain to see the signs of adolescence that made repellent their pitiable nakedness."

Stephen's refusal to become a priest has as its complement a refusal to be immersed in the body and routine of lay life. These were drastic alternatives, and it reveals Stephen's representative philosophic dilemma to see that the choice of one meant the moving away from the other. *The Portrait* stands as a keystone in modern intellectual biography in thus describing a divorce between spirit and matter, or the irreconcilability of nature and mind. As I have said, the gross earth of Lynch would not offer itself to a moral or metaphysical communication, but it does become amenable to the esthetic understanding. The vocation of the artist we see finally and clearly as the triumphant alternative to the defeated vocation of the priest. The old priestly ambition, making a complete commitment of consciousness to action, would make a teleological understanding penetrate nature and bring it to the resolution which was salvation or grace. The vocation of the artist escapes the failure which awaits this commitment, by refusing all commitments entirely, natural or supernatural in their sphere, for the sake of the free omniscient consciousness which *acts* only in the creation of itself in the images of what it knows. In his rejection of religion, politics and friendship Stephen is declaring that action as such is failure, and that the conflicts of the ideal and the real are unresolvable. Consciousness transcends action, that is the theme of Stephen's final discovery, but it must first remove itself from the limitations of action. Art removes kinesis, "the object of art is to be raised above desire and loathing." Stephen even as a boy could not hold his emotions long. "He was divested of anger by some power." The fantastic pride which remains tells him that the only power which means anything is the power to know, "to know everything," and this cultivation of consciousness leads, as it does with Stephen, to the divesting of personality.

The creative principle is passive and spectatorial; knowledge carried to its limits confesses its limits. Knowing the repeated failures of action, the priest artist withdraws from action. He takes his mission at the expense of his life, imitating the asceticism of the priest, but going further toward a more extreme asceticism. His art *requires* his life, in the sense that his work survives on the principle of an omniscience which is neutral. In this view he holds the communicants, who are his protagonists, and the epiphanic or meaningful reality of their lives in permanent arrest, striving to reach other and failing. That failure is their creator's knowledge and that knowledge is his success.

We are aware in all of Joyce's writing, beginning with his early work in *Dubliners*, of the effect of static drama, or a cyclical movement which refuses resolution to a fixed point. If we have a temporal dramatic curiosity rather than what we might call a scenic curiosity, we are sure to be disappointed as we read him. It is in this sense that Joyce's fictional world presents a metaphysics without teleology, as if to say that all conventionally dramatic literature is anachronistic and inconsistent with our actual understanding of the world. This understanding is one of consistent cross-purposes and inconclusive meaning in the small actions of life as well as its larger involvements. Nevertheless the appetite for omniscience prompts the fiction, as it always has, and if it cannot offer teleological reasoning it compensates itself with its own lucidity, imitating modern science, which progresses in its empirical awareness as it gives up its power to explain. A kind of catharsis acts in the lucidity of consciousness to substitute for broken impulse and abortive action. The fragmentary human agent in Joyce's fiction, pathetic or comic in his stressed limitations, has the contrast of relief only in the rising general consciousness which absorbs him. We see the movement explicitly in "The Dead" where a final awareness, no longer Gabriel's, rises above the living and the dead, the commonplace realities and heroic images which have opposed themselves in Gabriel's life. This consciousness is closer to the dead than the living perhaps, but it sees them together, the snow falling on all. The story rises above personal involvement to omniscience, seeing and understanding everything. In this way also we understand the conclusion of *The Portrait*. The series of subjective, biographically inconclusive experiences in the book, presented essentially as mental monologues, end finally in silence. Stephen's mental stream has become a series of increasingly fragmentary passages in his notebook, a writer's notebook. Detachment is complete, the communication and dialogue with others as well as the emotional rhetoric in his own mind, are finished. Presumably he no longer has personal experience at all, but has become the recording instrument of the life he has known and will recreate. We remember the early temptation toward the omniscience and omnipotence of the priesthood. "No king or emperor on this earth has the power of the priest of God!" Driven in the same direction but without the aid of supernatural power and knowledge, this modern artist, the voice of the conscience of his race, pays a strange and severe penalty. The price is his own passive neutrality; to become the knower of all that is knowable he must give up his own identity.

II | STOOM AND BLEPHEN

In *The Portrait of the Artist as a Young Man* Stephen begins as the beleaguered subjective hero enduring the pain of experience. He ends as the artist, that is to say, a pure consciousness, aware of experience but detached from it. When Stephen reappears as a character in *Ulysses*, however, he has become the object of an omniscience rather than the possessor of it.

Returning Stephen to life, Joyce found it necessary to return him to alienation, or discrete existence. He is not free in his detachment, but rather embittered and frozen in exile, not rejecting the world so much as being rejected by it. He knows an Ireland from his tower of exile, and that tower too is one from which he is being dispossessed by Buck Mulligan. The latter raises his shaving bowl to the sky in a new image of the mocked communion, and Stephen, the defrocked priest, as Buck defines him, contemplates that chalice. The circle of loss is complete as he remembers the bowl of sputum at his mother's deathbed.

Around Stephen the stream of life flows but he does not contain it. We feel in the episodes that involve him that his overt relationships have been reduced to a minimum; even when he is speaking to others he seems to be speaking to or answering himself. As the Proteus episode emphasizes, he is his own companion and for him the real theatre of experience is his own mind. Nevertheless he is helplessly subject to externality as in a siege.

Consciousness is at an impasse in Stephen; he is a man of fear and inaction. The threat is outside; he fears the sea and drowning, he fears Buck Mulligan. Chiefly he fears death and history. The theme of physical corruption never leaves his mind and when he thinks of God he calls him Hangman. Or God is a cry in the street, the dogsbody which floats at the shore, a sound in the flux, the immanence of matter. When he thinks of his mother and her deathbed request, it is as if mother love itself would imprison him in the corrupted flesh. Nature is an enemy and we understand what sort when we remember that Stephen is the spoiled priest without a faith, a man of intellectual reason who finds no reason in life. History is an enemy, it is a nightmare, he says, and "What if that nightmare gave you a backkick?" It does, adding to the kicking confusion of matter; they are his suffering and his comedy.

The artist hero of *The Portrait* has become in *Ulysses* one of the subjects of the most extended ironic perspective in all literature. He is the arrogant starveling, homeless, unhappy, inaccessible, passive in all mistreatment, easily offended and easily defeated. He is Stephen as Buck Mulligan sees him, picking his nose while speaking brief and brilliant epigrams. The aura of his immediate being is shabby and unpleasant. We are depressed knowing him in his impotence, particularly after the cold strength of his concluding posture in *The Portrait*. Perhaps this is what it means to see with the dual vision, for in *The Portrait* we knew Stephen as the master of his own intelligence, observing rather than observed, but in *Ulysses*, as I've said, he has himself become the object of omniscience.

The comedy pursues him in the expansive mock-heroic language of esoteric philosophy. Such favorite motifs as "metempsychosis," "omphalos," and "parallax," which reappear throughout *Ulysses*, in Bloom's mind as well as Stephen's, are the terms of the buffoon intellect, self-mystifying and self-mocking. In the double-face of comedy, however, they are terms to give structure to the novel itself from Joyce's own intellectual imagination. Thus metempsychosis is a theme word to be used as a basis for analogies, the recurrence of universals. The transmigration of souls isn't a serious theme, but the transmigration of experience is. So *omphalos* denotes the search for the common cord of reality, even though it is a mock search. Stephen is a comedian but he is also suffering against the extreme limitation of the "ineluctable modality of the visible." Here he announces his theme, wrestling as a consciousness against the flux of real experience. The confusion he knows is also the confusion against which *Ulysses* struggles in the effort to stabilize essence in flux, to control the change of forms in their endless changing. Stephen, like his creator, would like to know the immanence of things as well as his own identity in the protean stream.

Stephen is the agent then of the great intellectual comedy in *Ulysses*, in contrast to the physical and social comedy which features Bloom. When he speaks fully to the world, which he does for the only time in the Library scene, holding forth to his enemies, Eglinton, A.E., and Buck Mulligan, we must read carefully for the implications. They are rich because he is speaking in identification with Shakespeare, the ultimate hero of the intellectual imagination. From the start he extends his theme of banishment, usurpation and betrayal. The dispossessed Hamlet and Esau, the Shakespeare who has suffered from his usurping adulterous brothers, these have lost their birthrights. Is this not the allegory of the intelligent human spirit, alienated from the reality in which it lives? Shakespeare is the great "bawd and cuckold" who has acted and been acted upon in the reverses of nature. We compare this exclamation of Stephen with his other, "bawd and butcher," the "*dio boia*," or Hangman God he finds in nature. All of Shakespeare's art he finds proceeding from seduction and betrayal by women, thus pointing to the significance of Molly's liaison with Boylan on the universal Bloomsday. Stephen says that Shakespeare's tragedies were from his life, that he has suffered by his murdering cuckolding brothers and he has been banished in exile.

Cuckoldry is the protean principle; it relates to change in nature, and its resistance to the claim for stable immanence in the human consciousness. Nevertheless Shakespeare, the great tragic cuckold, wrested unity from life with his divine imagination and so Stephen worships him. Shakespeare is the father of his own grandfather as well as his own unborn grandson. That is to say he is the father of all his race and of all possibility, as the imagination in its supreme exercise can be the father of reality. "He is the ghost and the prince. He is all in all." Paternity may be a legal fiction, Stephen says, in the playful as well as tormented dialectic of the discussion. Fatherhood is a mystical estate, a symbolic estate, like the relationship between man and God. The relationship between the creator and his subject is like that of the gifted consciousness and reality. They are separated but brought together by the symbolic act of fatherhood, the act of art. "He found in the world without as actual what was in his world within as possible." In the act of art the consciousness equalizes itself with reality and becomes its voice. Shakespeare is the voice heard in the heart of his son Hamlet, and Hamlet, his created reality, is the voice heard in the heart of Shakespeare.

All this sounds to us as we first hear it with its comic mystifications and paradoxes like the parody of unrestrained literary exegesis. The scene and its characters are colored this way, with the vague irrelevances and interruptions of the discourse, the pedantically weighed contributions of the listeners, who clearly do not understand Stephen. We remember the dialogue with Lynch in *The Portrait* and understand again that conceptualization in Joyce appears buried in profane comedy. "Do you believe in your own theory?" Eglinton finally asks and Stephen says no. We remember also the meaningless circular sentence in *The Portrait* which is a comment on the elaborate metaphysics offered by the retreat sermon. The intellect exercises itself in futility, accompanied by its own negations. Stephen interrupts his discourse by saying, as if answering Eglinton, that motherhood and mother love may be the only "true" things in life. He is expressing his tormented conscience in a double sense here; apart from his rejection of her claim on him, he must mean that motherhood is a non-symbolic truth, speaking directly in nature, which contrasts with his own shadowy, inconclusive abstractions.

The dialectic in the library is more than comic; it is a serious demonstration of conceptual failure. We see more clearly that Stephen's exile is an exile of the mind. The penalty of that omniscient detachment he fought so hard to obtain in *The Portrait* is a reductive solipsism. He wanders among ideas as helplessly as he does among the suspicious fantasies of his human relationships. *Ulysses* does not spring from Stephen's mind, but we might say that it was written not only to draw his mind but to meet its dilemma. Stephen exists and holds the stage in the first three episodes of the novel, but he exists precariously. We know him on the verge of disappearing from a relevant or overt role in life, partly by the isolation offered by his own mastering subjectivity—so strong in effect that it would offer to replace the world in his imagination or art—and partly by the imposed exile expressed by his relations with Buck Mulligan, Mr. Deasy, etc. He must be bound to the novel, that is, the world of real experience, in the first place by his suffering in exile, and again by his suffering of conscience, agenbite of inwit, which in the larger sense involves his guilt toward immanent reality, figured in his own guilt toward his mother. But essentially he is bound to the novel by Bloom, his comic lost father, who surely represents what can be "found in the world without as actual." We remember that during Stephen's discourse, the patient silhouette of Bloom appears and hovers nearby in the library.

Bloom himself of course is an existent reality threatened not only by his own usurper, Blazes Boylan, but in the nature of things, by the large space and time in which he must be discovered. Much more expressively and continuously than Stephen he is a multiple man of fragments. His day is a day of transformations and reincarnations. All his identities are admitted by the first enlargement in his initial identity as Odysseus. Fantasy and reality make their interchanges, and vividly as we know him as Molly's mild, all-suffering husband, he is also Gerty MacDowell's dark romantic stranger, and even the Messiah and Savior Bloom in flight from persecution in the pub. His fate is to be known "in the world without as actual," as well as in "his world within as possible."

To live is to question identity, and the question that lifts uppermost in Bloom's consciousness, as well as in the novel, is simply, who is Bloom, where is he? Both Bloom and Stephen illustrate how the subjective consciousness lives in the world when we compare them to their opposite numbers, Malachi Mulligan and Blazes Boylan. These two are by intention denied a subjective dimension; as agents of the external they are the usurpers, whereas Bloom and Stephen are the usurped and dispossessed. Boylan and Mulligan are loud and ebullient, the sex boasters, the potent ones, therefore masters and at one with experience. They are not characters at all so much as the conceived rivalry of the external world, which the subjective man compares with his own lack of strength and his unsatisfied desires.

The division between internal consciousness and external being is thus dramatized, but its sharpness is an illusion of the point of view. The eye and the intelligence frame objects in static forms, as Blazes Boylan has a special fixed identity in Bloom's own knowledge of him. Bloom and Stephen are not so enclosed because they are consciousness itself, in a protean stream of "ineluctable modality." Objects are limited but the true subject is not, and moves toward a universality of being, astronomically enlarged beyond the immediate frame of a space-time event. Thus a deeply recorded personal consciousness in Joyce's work tends to disintegrate its form in becoming the voice of experience itself. All particular consciousness is fragmentary and all character incomplete in the great sphere of consciousness and being, the world-soul, which is the true protagonist of Joyce's novel. So Bloom and Stephen bob like corks in eternal separation and striving, as the whole stream moves on in search for its totality.

This principle makes the epiphanies of experience the more important, and Bloom essentially is the hero of immanent being in the novel. Truly a mock-savior after all, he wrests from the incoherence of experience a memorable existence. If we use Stephen's own scholastic terms, Bloom is the champion of *quidditas*, the whatness or thingness of reality, an element perhaps more admirable or necessary than either *consonantia* or *integritas*. Stephen's esthetic theory is a kind of elaborate epistemology, after all, a last though aggressive defense against the solipsism toward which all the things he does *not* believe have brought him. The *quidditas* of the thing is pure, the saving element, and Bloom, despite the restless activity of his mind, is always its guide and partner. From this point of view, a secondary hero of the novel, supporting Bloom, is the soap in his pocket.* Shifting from one pocket to another, regularly making itself felt, it is the detail which anchors confusion. Most per-

---

* The soap voices itself in the Circe episode:
  "We're a capital couple are Bloom and I;
  He brightens the earth, I polish the sky."

tinently it is a kind of therapy for the ubiquitous mental illusions which reflect experience. When the soap appears in newspaper headlines during the Aeolus episode, comedy is only one part of its effect. Trivia, because it is familiar trivia, has this transcendence in Joyce's created world; it is the luminous direct appearance of the thingness of life.

We understand this again when in the same episode we see Patrick Dignam's name appear spelled backward in newsprint. Recently dead, he is trivia now too, and his identity has been reduced to its incarnation in the printing machine. The men in the newspaper office have been discussing the grand allegories of life, biblical myth, the heroic legends of Irish politics. These have appeared in the headlines too, their pretentiousness mocked by their companions, the soap and "mangiD kcirtaP." The big words of men, blown up by the wind, create the solipsistic panic; consciousness seems to lose its foothold in history itself. But the tiny unchallenged reality of the soap asserts itself emphatically. We are returned to a familiar world and sanity clings to it. The dead man Dignam has been rescued to concreteness in the newsprint, a modest but significant resurrection.

We pose the dramatic issue of *Ulysses* generally as the problem of a meeting between Stephen and Bloom. We recall the theme of Daedalus' flight and we observe that Bloom, the protagonist of earth, is as necessary as earth to Stephen, the protagonist of flight. That cry in the street, that nightmare which will give one a back-kick, as Stephen fears it, is the phenomenological reality which Bloom carries with him as his own essence. Perhaps his function in the novel is to teach Stephen not to fear it.

There is no need to describe in detail Bloom's average sensuality, his average worldliness, his much greater than average curiosity. It is the latter which is his significant trait, and announces his indestructible allegiance to the concreteness of the world. It is not a poet's alertness to experience (a faculty which did not teach Stephen anything) but of course the opposite. The poet one might say is in haste to transform the world of fact to a world of ideas or symbols, striving to gain a superior essence which is intelligible and redeems the material world. Such a sensibility is arbitrary and rebellious in dealing with matter and time, wishing to transform the one and transcend the latter. Bloom has no such pretensions; in his first recognition concreteness appears without prejudice we might say. His vision of reality is in the utilitarian daylight of the simple businessman or the fact-grubbing consciousness of the amateur scientist. It is the practical interest which anchors Bloom; his time continuity is simple, as if to say, how shall we live today, how shall concreteness be used so as to survive tomorrow? It is emphatically, however, a time continuity, whereas the spoiled ambitions, the fallen metaphysics of Stephen lead him to the moment when he crashes the lamp in Bella Cohen's brothel, and "Time's livid final flame leaps and, in the following darkness, ruin of all space, shattered glass and toppling masonry."

The motif for Bloom is the speed of a gravitational fall, 32 feet per sec per sec. His speculations are endlessly vulgar because utility is constantly entering into them; he makes use of every observed detail to construct a world which functions. What is to be remarked in his mind is not his wisdom but his ingenuity, not of course his intelligence at all, but his spirit of survival. In this aspect he is Ulysses to perfection.

Bloom is essentially a man of the world, trying to stay in it, while Stephen is radically alienated and ready to destroy the concrete world in a symbolic gesture. The narrative material which comes from Stephen is a narrowing stream and he is receptive to very little new experience. Bloom, however, is expansively open to experience; he records his own basic sensations and he is responsively curious about those of others. He tries to know Polly Dedalus' hunger, Mina Purefoy's child labor, how it would feel to be the blind stripling, or the victims of the boat disaster. He belongs to a democracy of the flesh, and the basis of his power of sympathy is the dominance of the physical in him.

The reader is the more grateful for Bloom's existence, in revulsion from Stephen's excesses of spirit. He is not the superior Olympian imagination in this novel that he was in *The Portrait*. He has been exhausted and put into an intellectual and spiritual impasse, as we see at the end of the day, when he is finally put into communication with Bloom, following his outbreak at Bella Cohen's brothel. Even when Bloom is physically exhausted, however, his curiosity and his motives remain ready. It is he who speaks and questions in the Eumaeus and Ithaca episodes, while Stephen for the most part has subsided in an indifferent silence. In the essential dichotomy, the plain will to live in Bloom has come into relationship with Stephen's will to die.

It was inevitable that Stephen and Bloom should finally meet in the Circe or brothel episode; they meet in the den of animality at the deepest root of their common nature. The characters and lives of Stephen and Bloom are so far apart, that of necessity the meeting must take place where they are both stripped of surface being and have gone to the depths of the animal subconscious. Over this scene the whore symbol presides. It is a nightmare chaos in nature or subnature, the soil itself from which the visible life springs. The Circean magic is that of instinct and the unconscious, and the Black Mass which is a feature of the episode is a communion with the dark.

The climax of this naturalistic Dance of Death is the appearance of Stephen's dead mother. What Stephen cries out is "bawd and butcher," and he is addressing the god of nature himself. The "Corpsechewer" has appeared and Stephen's day-long despair now has focus. All he can do now is to strike the lamp in a destructive apotheosis, destroying all time in "its livid final flame." The real body of death is there to see and the great final fear. The abdicated priest has had the renewed witness of his failure.

Bloom is waiting, the comic savior, man of compassion and survival. It is rather clear what is happening. Kelleher, the undertaker, arrives in a car with his hearse driver. He would pick Stephen up and give him his form of transportation, but Bloom offers to take charge of him. The comic breath of his affirmative spirit comes to us in his remark, "A girl . . . Best thing could happen him."

Bloom has not come into this scene intact or unthreatened. He too has shared the nightmare, reduced to his own swinedom in the episode. Circe's wand is the wand of reductive nature, and Bloom too has been stripped of his supporting faiths which are a parody of conventional human wisdom. These philosophies and moralities become the comic agents of Bloom's nightmare, expressed as appeals, expostulations, fertile inventions, and excuses against the abusive reality of Bella. Under her whip, Bloom the man is a humiliated animal.

However, Odysseus with his sword and magic potion can conquer Circe. The magic drink to protect Odysseus was *Moly* from a dark root, and Bloom carries his shriveled potato in his pocket. The flower from *Moly* was chance, luck, and Bloom's potato is the root of the mundane. It represents his own naturalistic essence and it comes now as a counterpoise to the nightmare of nature, a chaos of unconditioned forces and threats. Bloom's body we have had always with us and know it so well that Bella's whip and her abuses cannot estrange us from it. He has eaten the inner organs of beasts, we have seen him in the toilet; we have seen him feed the cat, feed himself, and throughout the day run through the catalog of possible physical manifestations. Bloom, the conditioned animal, has expanded in restless speculation and memory from digestive, eliminatory and erotic stimuli.

Finally Bloom's mind has questioned death with as much absorption as Stephen, if we remember the funeral or Hades episode. He sees the grey rat in the cemetery and memorably calls it the "grey alive." He imagines flesh decaying, "hearts like broken pumps," he says. In his analogies and considerations we understand what a resurrecting spirit he is. The corpse is ordinary meat to the rat, he says. Cheese is the corpse of milk. This utilitarian spirit is nature's own, a kind of sanity if we listen clearly to it. He imagines the gramophone in the grave, the voices of the dead speaking from the parlor instrument. Thus Bloom domesticates life and death, and metaphysical problems are led comically back to the irrepressibly homely but reassuring human spirit.

As *Ulysses* extends itself, we increasingly expect that the communication between Stephen and Bloom is necessary to focus its structure and make its created world comprehensible. The passage of the day has been directed toward a meeting between them, and it brings them to the amalgam of the Circe episode, where for a moment they become one in a mystic sign of unity, the sign of Stoom, or Blephen. Stoom then is the hero of the novel. However, we would mistake the spirit of the work if we expected in this some sort of fusion and resolution of disparities.

In the slow turgid narrative which follows their meeting in the brothel, Stephen, the introspective exile who has brandished his ashplant at the god of time and matter, is now the companion of Bloom, the creature of time and matter. Bloom dreams of a higher consciousness, desires his son. He asks Stephen for enlightenment and culture. Stephen, though he does not ask for it, is certainly in need of some restoration to primary life. Together they sum up all the stressed dichotomies of *Ulysses*, science and art, spirit and matter, poetry and common sense, Irish and Jew, father and son. They are polarities which seem irreconcilable except for the most meaningful pair, as well as the most ironic, the father and the son.

Irony presides over this meeting of major dualities, since for all we can see, the communication between Stephen and Bloom is a failure. In the cabstand they are both still dazed by the phantasmagoria and debauch of Circe. Stephen is silent or monosyllabic, while Bloom, befuddled as he is, talks endlessly as though searching for the topic to evoke response. The discussion remains one-sided and at continuous cross-purposes. The fatigue and futility spread over the whole world of discourse, while the discourse itself, prompted by Bloom's restless curiosity, at the same time makes itself open to all the big questions of the human intelligence.

The dry comedy which follows dramatizes the defeat of the conceptual mind. The vulgar, half-educated intellectuality of Bloom invades science, philosophy, morality and religion. The style of the episode is that of a formal and at the same time stylishly colloquial essay, heavily over-written and full of intellectual clichés, but basically it is in Bloom's own voice, appropriate to his confusion and innocence. Stephen's silence or mumbled responses are his own expression of intellectual futility. We notice that when Stephen does show curiosity, it is on the subject of sweeping the floor of cafés in the morning.

As this episode moves into the next, the discourse continues, but the style becomes even heavier and more pretentious. It is not Bloom speaking any longer, so much as a disembodied intellectual curiosity. The standpoint is that of neo-scientific scholarship, stressing its neutrality and abstraction. This detachment, sacred as it is as a principle of research, is the surest note of comic futility in the investigation. The machine of analysis continues operating, the facts go on being collected, even though the subject has imperceptibly changed from major to minor; the result is a hash of inconsequence and irrelevance, delivered with the majestic intonations of logical method engulfing its mountains of evidence. The episode, apart from anything else, is a superb parody of the style of science, transfixed here as the example of human intellectual pretension.

The failure of communication between Stephen and Bloom in this episode actually asserts the general failure of communicable understanding. The dialogue at cross-purposes is heard in empty inter-stellar space. Nature stretches astronomically beyond Bloom's questions, the obtuse and turgid answers, and that sense of space reveals the cosmic irony toward which all the events of the day were leading. We feel the resignation of this magnitude, the purity of its indifference, and we understand again that omniscience straining toward its furthest limits, finds ultimately the border of the inane. Bloomsday is now passing into its natural future: "The void of incertitude, the lethargy of matter, the apathy of the stars." The intimate being of Bloom, with us throughout the day, is now recorded this way as he lies next to his wife: "At rest relatively to themselves and to each other. In motion being each and both carried westward, forward and rearward respectively, by the proper perpetual motion of the earth through everchanging tracks of neverchanging space." The two bodies of Bloom and Molly are marked in their relationship to the turning axis of the earth, but the final question in the catechesis of the episode is inevitably, "Where?"

Stephen and Bloom have met in the mind's defeat, in "the void of incertitude," and yet we say that exiled Telemachus in some sense had found his father. How do we understand this from the point of view of that alienated genius of the imagination who once demanded all or nothing at all? We have no word from him. Stephen refuses Bloom's offer of hospitality for the night as well as any relevant response to all his rambling and incoherent efforts at conversation. The last act of Stephen and Bloom together, before Stephen goes off into the night of Dublin and Bloom goes to bed, is a sociable urination in the yard in front of Bloom's house. Again we might say this is their only level of communication, the reductio of nature.

If Stephen disappoints us, Bloom does attempt to claim Stephen and all the emotion and the gratification of a search is on his side. Both Molly and Bloom think of Stephen personally, as son, as lover and as their teacher. The fumbling instinctive hungers of the flesh are there, but also the inchoate need for the lost metaphysician priest. But Joyce is ruthless in frustrating their hopes. They will not improve and refine their

lives with Stephen's help nor will he save them. They have
wanted to be instructed but their fate will be merely to be
understood.

We could if we wish interpret Stephen's rejection of Bloom's
fatherhood and Bloom's home as one last gesture of his irre-
deemable alienation from life. Yet if we remember Stephen in
the concluding scenes of *The Portrait*, and particularly his one-
sided dialogue with Lynch, we might feel something else in his
supremely noncommittal relationship with Bloom in the last
episodes of *Ulysses*. The message he may be receiving from
Bloom is simply the intense request to be embodied in his art.
Is this perhaps the hint in his answer to Bloom's request for
teaching, "maybe, but probably not?" What Bloom has wanted
from Stephen, comically, inarticulately, is a traditional redemption in knowledge. But the intelligence redeems nothing and the
"probably not" haunts all its efforts at teaching. The lucid consciousness can only recreate Bloom; he can be made known, and
this affirms him. Actually Bloom has already saved himself;
Stephen can do nothing for him. The artist only records what
he has achieved himself, his existence. He can have that monument and no other salvation. As for the saving to be done, it
is he who has reassurance to give to the intelligence and not the
reverse, as we have just seen.

This we can feel is Joyce's concluding theme. The problem
of the relationship between the artist and his subject is the
problem of relationship between the human intelligence and the
world without a directing intelligence. When Stephen and
Bloom first confront us, they seem to be oppositions that require each other. One is thought or the sensibility radically
alienated from its circumstantial being, and the other is existence comically fumbling for consciousness. When they meet
finally they find they cannot cross a bridge to each other. We
may say that what is implied by this is that there can be no
teaching from the spirit to material being, and apparently that
there can be no home for the spirit in the world's active and

mundane body. The ritual communion has been conclusively broken.

However, there is a Stoom or Blephen in the final outcome. Before Stephen wanders off into the night he has been the silent companion of Bloom; we think, has he been half-asleep, has he been listening, or rather has he for a period *become* Bloom? There is one godlike attribute left to spirit or intelligence, that of omniscience, not incarnating itself in reality but allowing reality to be incarnate in it. "I cannot love God but perhaps I can join my will to his." There is a *passive* relationship possible between the mind and reality, it can absorb it, it can reflect it, and the highest result is the work of art. In this sense *Ulysses* has been an extensive rewriting of *The Portrait of the Artist as a Young Man*, but beyond that the great achievement of its esthetic theory.

Telemachus finds his father in the man of flesh and Odysseus finds his son in the artist who recreates him. The two terms are art and nature but they have no unity except by reflection. The reflection is a flicker on the stream of time and matter; Stephen disappears and Bloom prepares for sleep next to Molly, sleeps and is absorbed again in endless inconclusive being.

If we remember the question "where?" which ends the Ithaca episode we find something to modify its uncertainty in Molly Bloom's monologue. It waits like a coda and resolution for the long activity of the day. The return home has been made to her bed. The Bloom-mind has searched outer space and ended in astronomical inanity. The mock-scientist has babbled, the artist-priest has been silenced, but Bloom the man is tired and has gone to bed.

He is at home with Molly where he began his day of wandering. Molly is the sign of self-sufficient reality which conducts no search; she is primary being which answers for itself. It is clear in the syntax of the episode that Molly's mind does not form thoughts, she doesn't contemplate herself in abstraction;

she is simply sensate consciousness and it is not traceable apart from her biological rhythm. Her only word of judgment or understanding is simply yes, represented in the coda, and with this she literally has the last word in *Ulysses*.

She affirms, but she is faithless, for a long series of men have entered her bed or her bedroom consciousness. We remember the words "bawd and butcher," "bawd and cuckold" in Stephen's torment. Nevertheless she remains Penelope and this is not mere comic paradox. Her word for her infidelities is simply "It's only nature." This is all sufficing; she still waits for Bloom.

In contrast to Molly, Bloom as we have said is a personality who exists by his division from total being. As such he can know faithlessness. His specialized male consciousness experiences life as a conflict, essentially the conflict of the part with the whole. Molly, however, is complete; her literary monument is a lyrical statement of her fused being, a poem really and not a dramatic narrative. Lying in bed she becomes massive and occupies all space.

This is as far as art's consciousness can go—it has fused with the immanence of being. The great themes of the work have been fatherlessness (and sonlessness), homelessness, and faithlessness. They have been the comic but important motifs, and in the end they meet only their permanent irresolution, but the comedy has its own affirmations. Stephen has a father, he is Bloom. Therefore he will still face fatherlessness despite his discovery. Stephen has nowhere to sleep, he has lost his tower, but he has found his home in Bloom. Nevertheless he goes off alone, but this merely means that Bloom's home is the whole world in fact. In the same sense Molly is faithless, will always be faithless, and Bloom's discomfort from this is endless. Yet she is his wife and Penelope, waiting for him. The last episode gives the final turn. Following one of the object and word motifs of the day (Stephen's key to the tower, etc) Bloom has forgotten the key to his house. Nevertheless he crawls into the window and is irresistibly home at last. And of course he has been at home all day, not in the active play of his mind, which we call conscious or discrete existence, but at home in his immanent being.

III | THE MANY VOICES OF REALITY

We must make some preliminary definitions to view *Ulysses* clearly for what it is, a superb synthesis of the modern intelligence. Fundamental in its method first of all is the positivistic knowledge of science, which requires the displacement of subjective and objective dimensions of knowing reality. The discipline of science has created devices which we might call self-transcending; that is, the subjective limitations on knowing have been transcended by an abstract language and a methodology which makes truth the product of a collective depersonalized mind. All this is simple demonstration that the universe as it exists is beyond the reach of the sensibility of the single man and is only distantly approached by the collective sensibility of science, which in large part is not human at all but the recording of instruments.

Furthermore, a science of history teaches that history is always larger than the grasp or the power of the agents acting in it, whether they be individuals or cultures, and that in fact, if history is a memory, it is a babble of many memories speaking at once and in frequent contradiction. The modern concept of time asserts that time has no closures at either end, that it has no dramatic structure as provided by a traditional anthropocentric metaphysics. In sum then the sophisticated modern intelligence constantly challenges and would exceed its own limitations. Its effect is to give us a strong awareness of subjective experience as something apart from objective being. Under this regime there are two perspectives of events, two realities and always two. One is the objective basis of being insofar as it can be distantly ascertained. The other is the existent reality of human consciousness, doomed forever to be out of phase or synchronization with the first.

In Joyce these two fields of events manifest themselves in the narrative. The narrative as a whole transcends the points of reference which are personal and subjective. No one writes *Ulysses;* it is rather the collected awareness of a neutral and distant sensibility. This artist sensibility is not unlike that of a master scientist who at the center of some collective project receives the reports of his scattered assistants and amasses the truth from them all.

The neutrality of that large perspective stresses the limited interests and limited knowledge of the subjects enclosed within it. Everyone is subordinate, everyone is powerlessly subjective, and therefore ultimately passive in the greater scheme of existence. Within that field, experience actually takes place in the form of subjective drama, an immediate reality expressed by the consciousness of living people. The breach between two truths, two realities is constant, and the reader, sharing the neutral omniscience of the creator, knows the constant effect of pathos or of comedy, depending on the turn taken by events.

What drama we can perceive in *Ulysses* is always an inner drama which becomes anti-climactic as soon as it is related to its outer frame of reference. The outer form is only pictorial, it is a map or chart of experience held in arrest. The sense of arrest is so stong, the dominance of pictorial circumstance as well as of the infinite time stream so pervasive, that in the traditional sense, character and action do not exist in *Ulysses.* Character would require some quality of strength or awareness which would bring a protagonist closer to an even match with his life circumstances. Action would require a sizable crisis where the agent in some sense can act upon his circumstances. In Joyce, however, the match is too uneven. Events are not really actions so much as effects recorded on the sensible screen of the consciousness, or they are tiny demonstrations from the protagonist which fade into the immense process of time and experience which contain them. We are never far from seeing Bloom as we do at the end of *Ulysses*, lying in bed with Molly, the two of them swinging at some point astronomically located among the stars. A character in Joyce is the creature of his context, sensate but relatively helpless, as he would be in the scientific point of view, which is interested in particulars only as they relate to a general field of events.

The consciousness which would transcend its limitations, must be generalized and impersonal like the map of the world itself, a large consciousness which is the sum of all experiences and so neutralizes itself. To achieve awareness is to become static, held in arrest oneself and detached from the personal drama of existence. This is the choice made by Stephen at the end of *The Portrait*, but it required the sacrifice of all his subjective commitments and all that distinguished him as a personality. It would seem as we read Joyce's work that there is only one other possibility for an uncompromised state of being. That is to be vitalistically at the center of process, unthinking and unified in being like Molly Bloom, who is reality itself.

In Stephen Dedalus as he reappears in *Ulysses* we have a brilliant illustration of what happens to an intelligence when it becomes committed to personal existence again. Stephen's experience, observed within the subjective perspective, becomes psychological, and consists chiefly of troubled fantasies and paranoiac moods. His dramatic problems cannot fill the stage, whether it be his conflict with Buck Mulligan or with his mother's ghost. His problems cannot be externalized convincingly, and in fact our viewpoint is not dramatic at all but clinical. This is because every one of his problems has the realistic exaggerations of Stephen's own point of view, his suspicions, resentments, clouds of anger and grief, presented in aimless impingement upon an indifferent stream of events.

The effect then on Stephen in *Ulysses* is to make him something like an emotional adolescent again, where his thinking and feeling are in excess of the objective correlatives of his experience. Stephen feels too much and doesn't know enough to support his suffering dramatically. Viewed from the external context, on the other hand, his reaction is too small to represent suffering. Seen within his own perspective, his experience is exaggeratedly large and non-representative. Even if he were not already so disposed the effect of the narration would be to emphasize his futility and impotence of spirit.* Under these conditions the sensibility is solipsistic and unreal to the extent that it is actually highly developed.

The problem of a dual point of view is the major task which Joyce set himself in the writing of *Ulysses*. No other modern writer has had the appetite for omniscience expressed by this work, and no modern writer has had the same degree of skepticism which defined the limits of the personal consciousness. In what sense could a novel achieve the language of omniscience without departing from the limits of this realism, or to put it another way, how could Joyce maintain a viewpoint much larger than any of his characters, without either becoming a character in the novel himself or losing versimilitude in some abstract or neutral jargon? In Joyce's concept of authorship all the languages of authorship were personal languages, steeped in a subjectivity which contradicted omniscience. At the same time the only objective language would be a kind of mathematics, or else some thing like the tortured universal language of *Finnegans Wake*, composed of the two dimensions of universal myth (and history) and the subterranean consciousness of the dream.

Without going quite so far, *Ulysses* is nevertheless a more convincing effort to achieve a universal consciousness. Joyce's solution to the problem of language was to give himself up to languages, all languages and subjectivities, so that in their amassing weight and variety the effect of a great totality of language would be achieved. Language is the voice of a con-

---

* Perhaps we can say he had been made so disposed by the affliction of this ambivalence in self-knowledge.

sciousness but the sum of languages might be the voice of all consciousness, equivalent then to the voice of real being insofar as it could be expressed. This is solipsism triumphing over itself. The subjective point of view is given total license, nothing interferes with its speech, and as Camus said in praise of consciousness, what the mind has lost in its ability to make unchallengeable assertions about reality, it has gained in the variety and inclusiveness of phenomena. Thus Joyce made his dominant subject the consciousness as agent in the world, interrupted in its stream at important intervals by such effects as the clanging of iron drawn by trucks in the street, or the automatic expressions of Bloom's body, which render convincingly the nature of consciousness itself.

The consciousness then is the last resort of the omniscient artist, the fortress into which he retreats, so to speak, against the onslaughts of an unrelieved epistemological skepticism. But there he surprisingly finds offered the gifts of intelligible form, indispensable to him even when obscurity and confusion are the features of his subject matter. The rule of association in the mind is antecedent to reason, and has a power of unity stronger than it. No historian or objective analyst can so plausibly adjust and concentrate the human record as Leopold Bloom. His innocence is his best authority. The exciting effect in Joyce's writing is that so much can be reflected in the mirror of a man. We know a world in Stephen Dedalus conceived by the premise that only Stephen as a consciousness is what we can truly know. But in him we know his Ireland, his family, politics, religion, and literature, his street, city and earth. It is *his* earth and thereby we have gained a coherent and complete world where we least expected to find it. The fact that we have also Bloom's world, and that of Father Conmee, Gerty MacDowell, and Molly Bloom, makes us the more convinced that it is indeed the world we have gained.

The subjective monologue is the medium of Joyce's work and it confesses its subjectivity at every point. But in doing so it breaks out of itself. It does not speak to the world as though to gain its assent, but rather it is overheard as by an omniscient ear. It is purely as an ear that omniscience survives, because the moment the author stops listening and speaks for himself the illusion of omniscience is broken, the limitations of his own subjective person admit themselves. Thus at the moment when Stephen understood his vocation he disappears. His words concentrate and become fragmentary, their style neutralizes, a personality evaporates, there is a declaration of a mission and Stephen vanishes. Where has he gone? He has sacrificed himself, as he must, to become the voice of other experiences. He will become the neutral medium for other voices, that is, other consciousnesses. His writing becomes a series of speeches or languages which are overheard.

In Joyce style is psychology, it defines the limits of a mind, the self-centering of experience. This has been true in *The Portrait* even before it is carried to its further extremes in *Ulysses* and *Finnegans Wake*. We remember the long retreat sermon and the narrative accompanying it which parodies the church doctrine through the medium of the priest's unctuous rhetoric, the theology made grotesque in the clichés and general ineptitude of his imagination. When Stephen is in love or writes poetry, the narrative style becomes purple and languishing. It isn't that language imitates experience, but rather that it *is* experience. This we are taught very early in *The Portrait* as Stephen interviews the words "belt" and "suck" and develops a kind of phenomenological existence for them. Joyce is clear on this, experience is the word itself, not objects nor actions, for the word is the fusing state where reality becomes consciousness.

Languages are voices, words are what we catch in the stream of experience, and we hear them in Joyce as though surrounded by a great silence. It is to this neutral space that Joyce's artist withdraws, paring his fingernails, watching and listening, above all listening, because it is in listening that he gains his knowledge, that is to say, his art. With him we have become obsessed by words, and the principle which makes language, consciousness, and reality fuse into one essence helps to understand Joyce's experiments with language. Stephen contemplates the ineluctable modality of the audible as well as the visible in the Proteus episode and he tells us in this literary testament that words are the signatures of things, their forms, and that a form of words is a form of forms. In that sense all of *Ulysses* is pastiche, a series of styles like parodies which render their subjects. Onomatopoeia becomes the first law of this literary creed. We remember Stephen in Proteus experiencing a line of verse he has just written. "His lips lipped and mouthed fleshless lips of air; mouth to her womb. Oomb, allwombing tomb. His mouth molded issuing breath, unspeeched: ooeeehah: roar of cataractic planets, globed, blazing, roaring, wayawayawayaway-awayaway." At the same time he notes the spatial silence in which his words appear. "Me sits there with his augur's rod of ash, in borrowed sandals, by day beside a livid sea, unbeheld, in violet night walking beneath a reign of uncouth stars. Throw this ended shadow from me, manshape, ineluctable, call it back. Endless would it be mine, form of my form? Who watches me here? Who ever anywhere will read these written words? Signs on a white field. Somewhere to someone in your flutiest voice."

Surrounded by this questioning silence, styles of the voice become the substance not the medium of the novel. It is a familiar principle that a style should voice a definite personal consciousness like those of Bloom and Stephen. But in Joyce a style is also the voice of general experience, that of an institution, a society, a history. We see this clearly for the first time in the Aeolus episode at the newspaper office, where the voice is not that of Bloom's inner experience, nor is it authorial (there is no authorial style in Joyce) but rather that of the scene itself. The mingled voices of journalism, history, law, pedagogy, and literature write this episode.

The voice of the bill collector who narrates the Cyclops episode is that of the man in the street, in his paranoiac phase.

He is the mass man hostile to separate individuals and minorities as well as to authority. All the stale voices which have echoed in that pub and an endless series of pubs, have joined in his consciousness and make him with his average ignorance and malevolence a public voice, a more certain reality than he could be as an individual. In the same sense the style of Father Conmee dominates the Wandering Rocks episode, which is otherwise the most objective scene in *Ulysses*. Father Conmee naturally thinks of himself in the third person, for he is not a man but an institution. Such a man, we could say, sleeps in his clerical costume; he is all one with himself and his public identity.

A public style is a parody which expresses an average consciousness, like the cheap rhetoric of shopgirls' magazines which narrates the Nausicaä episode. The public style is mock-heroic as when we hear Gerty MacDowell's self-flattering inventions and the genteel euphemisms which mask her eroticism. In the same way the mean motives of the Cyclops narrator are breathed in the grandiose accents of folk epic. These degenerated literary languages, voicing great echoes, emphasize the bathos of the commonplace. The bathos is always in the subjective limitation, the mark of the anthropocentric fallacy. The average man or the public man, as Joyce finds him, lives in a narcissistic daydream. The tones of popular journalism, popular romance, myth, and patriotic legend join with the subjective voice to express the over-weening self-interest which colors the forms of human expression. The most ambitious, the science and philosophy of the savants, are due to have their own mock-heroic parody in the Ithaca episode. We appreciate the fullest dimension of this inclusive satire in the tour de force of the Oxen of the Sun or maternity hospital episode where Joyce reviews the styles of literary history. After hearing the multiple voices of Dublin we hear the multiple voices of the historic consciousness speaking in their organic growth. This is the clearest example of Joyce's verbal expressionism. The narrative presides over the birth of the child Purefoy and leads itself through the natural cycle.

Language begins in the inarticulate chaos which precedes life and moves into the climax of the literary consciousness (which is almost the paradigm of an adequate consciousness) and ends finally in the drunken jargon and disintegrated speech of the medical students as they rush from the hospital to the brothel.*

As it develops then, *Ulysses* aims to become an omniscient and universal identity, speaking in all its voices. These express themselves first by being liberated from their author, and eventually by being liberated from their own separate sources, so that we have finally an amalgam of voices, first and third persons, scenes and institutions, history and literature and the dog barking in the street, all mingling to make a super consciousness which is that of experience itself.

Thus liberated Joyce goes so far as to mingle the separate subjective experiences of his characters, as in the Sirens episode. There we realize definitely that events are taking place neither in Bloom's personal consciousness nor in a three-dimensional reality, but rather in total sensate being. So the punctuation of the love song in the restaurant is Boylan's jingle as he approaches his rendezvous with Molly. Molly's arm is seen tossing a coin to the blind beggar, while Bloom eats his meal, belches, and adds his note to the fugal experience.

Music we know is the structural key to the episode. In itself we might say it is the art form which preeminently does most to depersonalize consciousness and abstract subjective experience. Personal emotion pours itself out into the collective art form, and its sharp characteristic is its social communicability. With such effects as "charmed him Gould Lidwell won Pat Blooms heart," identities have fused; enchanted, relaxed, released from themselves, the characters have floated into music, the collective day dream. Love accompanied by its betrayal becomes the universal theme, "All is lost now, when I first saw

---

* Perhaps Joyce commits himself to a judgment of history when we hear the accents of the American gospel preacher as the last articulate language before chaos.

the form endearing." In the conversation in the restaurant music itself is defined as numbers in a mathematics. Then it is called emotion, love; love is defined as sex, and the appetite for food mingles with music and love. Finally as if to perfect the universality of the musical consciousness, the image of Dignam appears with the cemetery rat, the voice of death. Together in the counterpoint we hear Boylan's knock at the door, the scrape of the rat in the cemetery, the tap of the blind stripling.

At this point we are prepared to see the fulfillment of a musical consciousness in *Finnegans Wake*, where subjective and objective worlds have completely fused and the private dream is indistinguishable from the collective, racial dream. There at the peak of his effort, if not his achievement, the meaning of all Joyce's experiments can be understood in his obsessive effort to resolve the antinomies of consciousness and reality, the individual and the race, the moment and history. The problem for Joyce was nothing less than how to enclose the whole world of meaning. Logical syntax, a space and time syntax, gave principles of unity but these were definite barriers to immediacy as well as universality of being. The analogy with music substituted a different kind of unity and comprehensiveness, based on recurrence and psychological relationships, rather than causal or spatial relationships. Most important it needed no teleological theme to make itself intelligible; the past and the future were not separate entities, and any passage on the stream of time, Bloomsday for instance, enclosed the whole.

The music principle is really the form, as I have said, of a super-consciousness, depersonalized as well as immediate, which crosses the breach of terms ordinarily existing between the particular and the general, the subject and the object. The barriers which the mind sets up as it begins to think have been broken. All experience, whether subjective or objective, is on the same plane of acceptance, and all experience is acceptable, because the sole binding of experience is the form of recurrence and variation and the substance of the human sensibility. Its content is automatically self-limiting and at the same time expansive because it is the history of the human sensibility, and like the notes of music the sensibility has immanence; it speaks without needing to be explained.

In this way Joyce wins a strange distorted victory, (particularly as we contemplate *Finnegans Wake*), wrested by a superhuman effort to solve the problem of knowledge in his art. The question posed itself. What is the world? The world is what is known. How do we know the world? Listen to the voice of the knower and record it. What is the knower? The knower is the world speaking in all its voices. But that kind of comprehensibility was ultimately Finnegan's dream, more intellectual nightmare than dream. In a dialectical irony, a great coherence was almost indistinguishable from incoherence, and the greatest omniscience from solipsism. For *Ulysses* we can say otherwise. Poised before its own extreme development, with the subject still alive and distinguishable from the phenomenological stream, and the tension which is the sense of life itself still intact, *Ulysses* is truly a great intellectual and artistic adventure. For that success, I believe, Joyce, like Stephen, might be grateful to that humble life saver and bringer, Leopold Bloom.

IV | THE METAPHYSICAL COMEDY

E. M. Forster once said that if God would tell the story of the universe the result would be a fiction, implying of course that the story of the universe would be plotted and have meaning. But what if God told his story for a universe whose meaning had radically descended from the standards of fiction, which had no teleological purpose and in which he did not intervene? The result would be very much like the fiction of Joyce, who meant something pointed when he has Stephen Dedalus say that he couldn't love God but would like to join his will with His. In the context that surely is not the submission of the moral will, but rather the submission of the intelligence to things as they are. The inability to love God implies in fact that motives have been separated from knowledge; it is knowledge without assent. Certainly if the universe has no program in the traditional anthropomorphic sense, to join one's will with God would in fact require leaving the normative human imagination behind. This Stephen rather brutally does in terms of all the ethical and metaphysical commitments offered to him. Such a creator then, as he says, who enjoys contemplating what he has created, is manifested by the completeness of his knowledge and not by a purposive intervention in the problems of his creatures. Since his creatures, being human, continue to act "lovingly," that is, in terms of a purpose which matches their concerns, the result is a universe which is comic.*

In each of the stories of *Dubliners*, for instance, there is an ironic relationship between the inner sphere of consciousness

---

* Although Stephen in his cryptic discussion of his esthetic theory in *The Portrait* says that the tragic emotion is static, arrested above desire and loathing, it is obvious that its stasis is of a different kind and emotionally more compromised than that of comedy. He says, for instance, that "Pity is the feeling which arrests the mind in the presence of whatsoever is grave and constant in human sufferings and unites it with the human sufferer. Terror is the feeling which arrests the mind in the presence of whatsoever is grave and constant in human sufferings and unites it with the secret cause." The God whom Stephen cannot love but with whom he would unite his will could not easily be conceived from that standpoint. *United with* the sufferer and with the secret cause of his suffering, but helpless in both knowledge and power to affect that secret cause, the God of tragedy would surely be a lesser God than the God of comedy.

Stephen's esthetic principles seem to lend themselves best to a theory of comedy. This is supported by Joyce's remarks in his Paris notebook of 1903, at the time he was developing the ideas which were later to be used by Stephen in *The Portrait*. "All art which excites in us the feeling of joy is so far comic and according as this feeling of joy is excited by whatever is substantial or accidental in human misfortunes the art is judged to be more or less excellent: and even tragic art may be said to participate in the nature of comic art so far as the possession of a work of tragic art (a tragedy) excites in us the feeling of joy. From this it may be seen that tragedy is the imperfect manner and comedy the perfect manner in art." As the editors point out the term "joy" as he uses it here is meant to describe the esthetic pleasure, "the luminous silent stasis of esthetic pleasure" as he later phrases it in *The Portrait*. (Ellsworth Mason and Richard Ellmann, eds. *The Critical Writing of James Joyce*, Viking, p. 144.)

and an outer circle of neutral awareness. In "Ivy Day in the Committee Room," written with perfect impassivity, the story of Parnell, the Irish political romantic, is retold to the accompaniment of "poks" from the beer bottles placed on the hob. Parnell is a grotesque shadow as we watch the drab scene, its seedy participants, and hear the slight report, the blab of insignificance in the universe as the heat drives out the corks from the bottles. The contrast is not simply between the local scene and the heroic figure of Parnell. What carries the story further than a supercilious irony is that its real interest is the legend making human mind, expressed for instance in the very vulnerable poem which Hines recites. We see Joycean terms; the scene of the commonplace, more vulgar than brutalized, and the contrasting imagination of the characters, itself infected by the commonplace, but achieving the delicate balance of comedy and pathos in reaching for what the human imagination considers ineffable. It is to the accompaniment of such bad poetry that the human race tries to exceed itself. It is remarkable to recall how much of *Ulysses* was written in the versatile imitation of "bad" writing.

Irony, we might say, is the way in which an omniscience entertains itself, but it is also the way in which it proves itself. The mad and paralyzed priest in "The Sisters" laughs in the privacy of the confessional, but as he laughs he knows some secrets. In "Ivy Day in the Committee Room" the vague shifty priest briefly appears, mistaken for an actor, a failure both as priest and actor, perhaps because he knows the breach between illusion and reality and knows that he is the unemployed servant of illusions. For the artist-priest who would refuse complete unemployment something remains. The defeat of illusions or the failure of action can be transcended in laughter. Laughter on its highest level is not easy to understand, but surely in some sort it is the relief afforded by the lucidity of consciousness, a relief which waits upon intolerable difficulty or certain failure. The comedian thus escapes the mere pathos of a commitment to action by making his commitment to perception. Under the Joycean rule life is a failure, but art is a success, particularly if it takes form as a comedy.

Joycean art, as we know from the first, implies a search for the illusion if not the reality of omniscience. We might illustrate a serious omniscience in the comprehensiveness achieved by classic tragedy. In that mode, a kinesis, a particularity in human experience has so magnified itself, by the conviction of passion supporting it, that the sense of relevance is complete. The presumptions and conclusions of tragedy tell us that the hero is representative, and that the truth of life has somehow been absorbed on the microcosmic stage. Perhaps in an Aristotelian sense, it has been possible to so magnify a man that he has won the right to speak for everyone as he addresses himself to God, the universe, or to his fate. The basic premise which makes tragedy possible is that the protagonist has an understanding capable of interviewing the universe and approaching its secrets.

Joyce founded his vocation on a state of religious disbelief and metaphysical alienation which in its terms and its own excess, apart from temperamental factors, was opposed to the tragic vision. The vulnerability to bathos or to nihilistic incoherence would be certain to repel him deeply, particularly as we keep in mind his great ambition to master the materials of his art. It seems inevitable that he should have written a comic epic. Limitations are purged by the spirit of irony, and the survey of limitations communicates the effect of a completely perceived world. At a sufficient distance, omniscience renews and establishes itself; it does so by holding in arrest the debate between the human consciousnes and the meaning of its experience, by rising above the debate itself and surveying its terms. The comic spirit knows but will not explain, understands but will not intervene in the action it portrays.

A comic omniscience suggests that it "knows everything" (that seminal ambition of Stephen Dedalus) by knowing disparities and incongruous analogies. It links in its knowledge Leopold

Bloom and the hero of the *Odyssey*, Henry Flower with the Lotos Eaters, Bella Cohen with Circe. When we look at Bloom closely, with at the same time a firm awareness of multiplicity and quantity unbounded in dimension, his movements are as vulnerable to comedy as those of Gulliver observed by the Brobdingnags. The agent in a comedy acts as if he knew his world and could control it. But he is wrong, as the comic episode reveals, and in a comic agnosticism, denying anthropomorphic familiarity with the universe, all men are clowns in a broad comedy, about to trip and fall in their mistakes. Nevertheless the comic perspective is an alternative to madness, or the uncontrolled disintegration of a reasonable universe; it is the response of intellectual power after all, which even while it features the reverses experienced by the human mind, achieves a special kind of victory over circumstance.

In *Ulysses* every scene, object, and person is a particular, or the part of a whole so large and extended that it has a comic smallness when considered separately, which Joyce insists on doing in the interest of *quidditas*, or the thingness of art's object. Minute details are immensely important to Joyce because it is only in their "epiphanic" realization as well as their accumulation and recurrence that the sense of the universal can be achieved. However, the crucial weight of significance is not with the microcosm, as it would be in tragedy, but with the macrocosm. The singular instance is an illustration or repetition of a larger principle, and not the enactment within itself of the complete drama of life, as in the religious ritual of the mass, or in archetypal tragedy. Joyce's omniscience, we might say, is not spiritual but intellectual. He has traded the priest's power over matter for that of the scientist, who makes no effort to penetrate its mystery at once, but catalogs its manifestations patiently. Leopold Bloom was fated to be the creature of history and the unit of a quantitative mass, and not the exclusive agent of dramatic concern, where, as in the religious analogy, God or the creator intervenes directly in the fate of the individual being.

Now God has a kind of quantitative, collective concern for the human race, and an uninhibited curiosity, for his joy is contemplation and observing multiplicity and change. This is a way of describing the naturalism and historicism of Joyce's point of view, a description more valid it seems to me than interpretations of the monomyth and symbolic universality. To think of Bloom seriously as the avatar of Odysseus is to beg the question of the point of view. The point of view is comic, and has its own way of dealing with analogies. We might add that under sophisticated extension, naturalism inclines toward comedy, rather than the flat histories of conventional literary naturalism, which when they are not tendentious on behalf of a neo-scientific or political doctrine, tend to drift into inanity. Inanity is the threat of Joyce's own writing, but he welcomes it, he transfigures it and makes it epical, as in the closing episodes of *Ulysses*, and it becomes the material of his naturalistic comedy.

There are many kinds of comedy in *Ulysses*, as broadly physical as in any vaudeville, and as subtle and verbal as one could expect from the wittiest genius of an age of literature. Essentially, however, we can say that the comic theme is a comedy of the mind, projected in its ineptitude against an enormously magnified resisting field of events. This is the comic action which involves both Stephen and Bloom, Bloom more than Stephen because he is an active man, concerned with real goals and intent on knowing and judging everything in his experience. The comic force is in the principle of subjectivity itself, as we see it in the novel, endlessly at odds with the external, which has the solid unreceptivity of the floor on which the clown takes his pratfall. The comedy plays itself out within the field which separates an aloof omniscience, a power which is all mind and nothing else, and the concreteness of things and events. The comic predicament is to be engaged with reality with an inadequate strength and an inadequate consciousness. To escape from comedy requires an escape from life.

Considering Stephen in *Ulysses*, one would think that as he is brought back from his neutral power and self-sufficiency at the close of *The Portrait* to a renewed engagement with life, his bad luck is his inability to be absorbed in it completely. Captured in life again, his urge toward freedom has become a troubled and trivial paranoia. His largeness of understanding has become a personal indifference; Daedalus back on earth finds life petty. Life may have grandeur to the creator who sees *all* of it in a timeless arrest, but to the particle in the stream there is only blindness and futility in its buffeting. If there is any vital force left in Stephen it is that of his bitterness, finally a nihilism which would crush the "bawd and butcher" god and end all time in "its last livid flame."

We find that when a subjective awareness is truly reconciled with experience, it is achieved by a silencing of the mind. In that respect the one active member of the world of *Ulysses* who comes closest to knowing is the one with the least pretension for knowing. Molly Bloom as she lies in bed with her sensate consciousness is total in action, total in being; because she is so much body, knowledge cannot separate from it. She is immanence itself, a being without judgment or understanding of itself, and her final affirmative word, her simple "yes," says nothing and everything. Her only rival is the great neutral consciousness which wrote the book. Stephen in *The Portrait* escaped from comedy, that is, the subjective limitation, by transforming himself into such a disengaged consciousness. Molly Bloom escapes comedy by refusing mental extension, by concentrating in her moment of being. In the perfect dichotomy between the mind which "knows everything" but cannot be incarnated in action or life, and the reality which knows nothing but is itself life, we perceive the intellectual dilemma which dominates the modern imagination, and its most resourceful spokesman is Joyce.

All this invokes an artistic as well as philosophic dilemma. The massive concreteness of Molly's presence, or analogous agents in the novel like Bloom's ubiquitous soap, all the epiphanies of the thingness or whatness of life which Joyce so much loved, are designed to give anchorage to what has become a universal consciousness, the sensate music of reality. This has no limits in expansion and thus is in danger of dissipating itself in space, a phenomenological record surrounded at both ends by inconsequence. One might contemplate the totality of verbal consciousness, as presented in the Oxen of the Sun or maternity hospital episode, with awe, but it is an awe quickly succeeded by indifference, because so distant a perspective and so inconclusive a narrative reduces all its elements to equal significance or insignificance. The neutrality of such omniscience is so strong that its expression would not seem to be worth the effort; the anecdote is too long and too laborious to be a good joke and mere curiosity would be exhausted in a quarter the length.* This, it seems to me, more than its difficulty of access, is what makes *Finnegans Wake* a lesser work than *Ulysses*.

In the latter it was firmer in Joyce's purpose to combine the two perspectives of an omniscience, the particular and the universal, without losing his hold on either. It might be argued that Stephen in *Ulysses* is his characterization of the man who in his hunger for omniscience has condemned himself to futility of spirit, and knowing everything has lost interest in everything he knows. We can say that the opposition between general comprehension and particular being is itself the dramatic theme of *Ulysses*, personified in each case by Stephen and Bloom and developed in the comic cross-purposes of their attempt at communication. That effort has no resolution until we are absorbed in the sentience of Molly Bloom as she lies in bed, and with her, we have, so to speak, given up the effort at comprehension altogether.

If it were Molly rather than Bloom who complemented Stephen and engaged with him in the novel, we would remain

* Richard Ellman quotes Joyce's remark in reference to *Finnegans Wake*. "Now they're bombing Spain. Isn't it better to make a great joke instead, as I have done." (*James Joyce*, Oxford, p. 706).

dissatisfied, for both Stephen and Molly seem unable whether together or apart to strike the note of human verisimilitude that we need. Molly is after all so immediate in being as to be almost indefinable as a personality, lost in the stream of sensibility of which she consists, and Stephen, whether he is embittered in the rather puerile vein of *Ulysses* or transcendent in his artist's vocation as in *The Portrait*, communicates a special and even pathological version of human experience. Considering Stephen and Molly as hopelessly apart, representing life and the mind which contemplates life, we have, if that is all we are given, a frozen world terrifying in its bleakness. The comedy of an affair between Molly and Stephen, if Joyce had carried out Molly's light fantasy, would have been an exercise in the grotesque.

A bridge between Molly and Stephen exists and it is Leopold Bloom. The artistic fate of *Ulysses* depends on Bloom and how he is taken. If he remains simply the object of reductive Olympian satire, the sensual average man exposed in every detail of his limited life, then every other aspect of the work loses its major force, the brilliant achievements of verisimilitude, the verbal genius, the intensity of Stephen's attack on the universe and its God, as well as the profound immanence of life radiating from Molly. A nihilistic epic is inconceivable; the monstrosity would be interrupted at some point, either by its readers or its creator, made arid by indifference. Nor is the novel written in the Promethean mood, as the conventional outcry of the aristocrat of spirit in an imperfect world. Stephen is not the hero of the work, nor does he command our strongest interest. The spoiled priest, the passive romantic, has an uninspiring quality as drab as that of the elusive actor or priest in "Ivy Day in the Committee Room." His defiance is a sullenness of spirit, his pride has turned sour, and his witty intelligence is that of the immature genius, the *enfant terrible*, whose antics depress us for their self-indulgence.

Ulysses is a great comic epic, and as such it defines value in the midst of a relentless drama of humiliations. The point of view from which *Ulysses* is written is not angry, as a Swiftian anger might support satire, and if we see nothing but abuse for Bloom we would not even have the stimulus of sadism in reading it. However, accepting Bloom as the true hero of a comedy, the sadism quickens and is valid, for we must observe that Bloom's victimization, and his humiliations, have meaning. They are part of a purgative truth, they are the stripping and cleansing of intellectual comedy. It is Cervantes rather than Swift who suggests a parallel.

Though battered in the comedy, Bloom as its hero keeps our interest and rises in it. Circe has made him a swine, but he has his holy root of mundane humanity; he refuses to stay in the muck and recovers, and immediately as he recovers we see him bent over the body of Stephen, comically "saving" him. He is really irresistible, his voice, his breath, everything in the aura of his commonplace being rises upward and escapes negation. It is Bloom's survivability, his strongest, purest trait, which makes him the hero of the comedy, and in the end gives him the dignity of assured existence. We cannot dismiss this man or his fate, that is what comedy tells us after the most severe questioning. The moment in comedy which is crucial, we might say, is the moment when the clown gets up from his fall. It is his bearing then, mysterious as it is to elucidate, which completes the comic insight, just as in tragedy the catharsis must depend on what the tragic hero reveals in himself. The affirmation in comedy is pure, absolutely stripped of pretensions, because it survives at the lowest level of faith in the human subject.

Bloom's comic dignity rests on his repeatedly exhibited will to live. Through everything he exhibits his power to react, to consider, to imagine, to suffer, to endure. Above all he is the curious man, his curiosity surviving with his every tired thought in the long episodes at the end of the day, and his curiosity transcending every inept superstition and homily of his very human brain. That curiosity and the equally inept sympathy which moves from him to others in all his wanderings makes

Bloom a considerable person, a man indeed, quite definitely differentiated from his soap, his hat, his Keyes ad, and the general thingfulness and timefulness which bury him during the day. In the mechanism of things around him, in his own mechanism of flesh, we recognize the essential non-mechanical Bloomness in him. This always makes him rise, a new savior "shot from a shovel," the incarnate man distinguished from abstract matter and the time process, which in this quite naturalistic form of redemption, still rule him.

The comic image of man begs no relief from either cosmic or petty humiliations, nor from the limitations of natural being, but for that very reason, purged by such humiliations, we are the more powerfully reassured to find that a man is not a phenomenon like any other, and reduced to the significance of any other. If we have faith in this hero of the commonplace, it forbids enthusiasm, but nevertheless it is deeply steadying, it calms the heart, as Stephen in *The Portrait* knew when he passed the odor of the stables. The last image we have of Bloom is to see him paring his toenails, preparing for bed. Isn't this his victorious posture in the obscure and illimitable universe which has just been described around him? We remember briefly that creator God who sits outside his creation paring *his* nails. It becomes a gesture of immunity and acceptance, the creature reconciled with his created being.

We may understand from Joyce's work that comedy has its own form of catharsis. Its anti-climactic and mock-heroic program has equalizing results. With the most refractory materials it achieves the cathartic balance of knowledge and feeling; extreme disparities and confusion itself have been unified in a lucid consciousness. Irony itself is lucid, it is judgment gaining mastery over impossible contradictions, as irony may be the resort of those whose urge toward omniscience has revealed their ignorance and whose urge toward unity has revealed the incoherence of the world.

But beyond irony, Bloomism itself, the commonplace substance of experience, is accepted in the comic catharsis and transformed. It becomes an affirmative truth because it has earned its validity by passing through our skepticism, as well as our ridicule and contempt. By the tolerance of the comic spirit, the oppressive hero worship or idealizing faculty of the mind has been cured, and that cure may be nothing else but the cure of despair. Nihilism is the enemy of comedy as well as tragedy, though in the intellectual comedy that Joyce writes, nihilism has every chance and is allowed to do all it can to reduce our hero to insignificance. Bloom persists and Bloom finally wins our allegiance to his being, which is our own familiar truth. In the stasis achieved, the new, lucid, and tempered consciousness in comedy no longer remains divided between the heroic and the mundane, the imaginative and the real, the living and the dead. In that reconcilement we are reminded of the conclusion of "The Dead," where Gabriel, another agent of the commonplace, a comic figure essentially, unites in spirit with Michael Furey, and arrested above the earth feels a forgiving wisdom, like the snow falling on everything and everyone.

Hemingway
and the passive hero

The distinctive writer is an obsessed man and he deals in his work with an immense effort to clarify that obsession. Hemingway has felt more than most writers the force of an obsession, and its finished form and significance explains his durable reputation. He has recorded a favorite myth of our time. Reconstituted from the whole body of his work, this is the story of the wounded hero, by turns a man of sensibility and man of action, helpless and strenuously active. We gather that his hero has been hurt by something but it is not always clear what has hurt him. This is not entirely a defect of intellectual clarity; he has imagined an abstract enemy whose effect is precisely in its protean and escaping identity.

Jake Barnes, Frederick Henry, Nick Adams are wounded in the war, but the war has limited characterization. What is behind the war? Society, history, nature? Vaguely all of these as it is expressed in that quiet excoriation by Frederick Henry in *A Farewell to Arms*.

> . . . Now Catherine would die. That was what you did. You died. You did not know what it was about. You never had time to learn. They threw you in and told you the rules and the first time they caught you off base they killed you. Or they killed you gratuitously like Aymo. Or gave you the syphilis like Rinaldi. But they killed you in the end. You could count on that. Stay around and they would kill you.

"They" are the great context of action itself, diffuse as it is threatening, which forces itself upon the protagonist, for which he has no responsibility, where he is the passive victim.

Sooner or later the Hemingway hero expresses a grievance. We observe stoic action and fierce experience but at the center there is a moral and intellectual weakness; his characters reveal a startling softness of sensibility in the midst of violence. If the people in *The Sun Also Rises* are "lost" we are never quite sure why they are lost, and the vagueness has something to do with the poignance of their suffering. Poor Brett, they say, "she hasn't had an absolutely happy life, Brett." There is more attention to the condition of unhappiness than its cause, and this lays the work open to the charge of sentimentality, a charge frequently made by Hemingway's critics. It is true, I believe, that many of the characteristics of Hemingway's writing can be understood as a compensatory drive against the threat of sentimentality. However, the knowledge of his work as a whole helps give it intellectual strength. If we think of a trilogy composed of the short stories of *In Our Time*, *A Farewell to Arms*, and *The Sun Also Rises*, we derive a more or less sustained theme which is nothing less than metaphysical in its conscious implications. This is demonstrated at significant points in the form of what we might call naturalistic shock.

For instance, the boy Nick Adams sees his father perform a Caesarean operation and the Indian husband consequently commit suicide. "Why did he kill himself?" "He couldn't stand things, I guess." The appropriately titled "A Very Short Story" gives this epilogue for two lovers separated by the war. "The major did not marry her in the spring or any other time. . . . A short time after he contracted gonorrhea from a salesgirl in a loop department store while riding in a taxicab through Lincoln Park." Death and sex are the agencies of naturalistic shock, reaching their peak in the war scenes and stories. The climax might be the death of Catherine Barkley, who is perhaps Hemingway's major figure of naturalistic pathos, destroyed by love itself in its biological force. The disillusionments in Hemingway are the classic ones for love and death, but they have their special harshness in the stress on naturalistic fact, and their specific poignance in that the reaction to them below the hard surface is soft, the idealizing sensibility of a boy. It is in the juxtaposition of these extremes that his writing reaches its characteristic vividness.

Hemingway's themes of disillusionment are therefore in the tradition of ironic realism, those dramas of rebuffed subjectivity characteristic of the work of Flaubert and Joyce, who are the masters of the school. The images of defacement are defiant and sharp in the early scene in *The Sun Also Rises*, as Jake wanders about his life's milieu in Paris. Georgette, the prostitute, who "with her mouth closed was a beautiful girl" goes out for the evening with the castrated man who introduces her to his friends as his fiancée. She ends the evening dancing with the homosexuals who have arrived accompanying Brett, the glamorous aristocrat abandoned to a promiscuous life. Brett is the ikon for all male adorers, but she gives herself away continuously in desecrating situations, most particularly when she goes away with the forlorn outsider, Robert Cohn. Expressing romantic protest, the actors further their own hurt and help destroy themselves, as Mike, the bankrupt, does in his drunkenness, as Brett, the spoiled heroine, does in her careless affairs. They demonstrate to the world an inverted revenge against the world's injury.

In that complex Hemingway's people are obsessed by their wounds. But this has an important aspect which goes beyond grievance. The Greek count ("one of us," Brett says) pulls up his shirt to show his scars, and the scars mean experience. They are his true medals which entitle him to membership in the aristocracy of suffering. This particular conversion of terms has basic importance for the understanding of Hemingway's work. Experience is painful, it has its various dimensions of pathos and protest against a corrupt, violent world, but at the same time it is initiatory. It is the requirement for honorable membership for those who would transform themselves from victims of illusion to the heroes of reality. In that sense we understand that natural experience is the object of both attraction and revulsion for Hemingway's characters. Experience is pain, but pain is redemptive as the ticket of admission to the select world of those who "really know and have their lives."

This may help to explain the recurrent ambiguity in Hemingway which leads a movement from nihilistic despair to a celebration of natural experience. His characters may be wounded in the force of nature and see its darkness, but they also find intense compensations there, and natural pain and pleasure are the gods of experience.

The drive in his work is for incontestable experience, a search we might say for the elusive "reality principle." This demands the style of violent disclosures, the dramatized surprises of truth. Often his people are suffering from nerve shock, a numb state of distress through which only the sharpest sensations penetrate. His stories seem to be explorations of the nervous system at primary levels of disordered sensation, projecting the clicks, tension, and throbs of the network itself. But preceding that stage of incoherence, the mind is filled with the vestigial paraphernalia of social mythologies and private illusions. These have to be swept away. The confusion of thought and sensibility has made the consciousness desperate for a pure experience. Therefore the famous mindlessness of his characters under stress is not only the effect of shock but the means of recovering immediate reality. His "dumb ox" characters (to quote the somewhat unjust epithet of Wyndham Lewis) are not proposing idiocy so much as repudiating the false mind, and the apparent inanity of style expresses the real sophistication of a wounded sensibility. It is an impressive writing style after all, and it has its own rhythms. In one effect it seems to imitate the stages of illness, the shock of suffering, the blurring of consciousness, and eventual convalescence when reality is accepted again, but in simple childlike aspects like taking new steps after a long time in bed. So in "The Natural History of the Dead" reality is felt violating the vague Platonic sensibility. Upon the latter the plain style is murderous in effect, but that victory won, the stark language continues to express the hunger for uncompromised experience.

"Big Two-Hearted River" points to the theme. "Nick felt happy. He felt he had left everything behind, the need for thinking." Krebs in "Soldier's Home" comes back from his war shock and is sickened by involvements. "I didn't want any complications, intrigue, talk when it came to getting a girl," and he thinks of "the time long back when he had done the one thing—the only thing for a man to do . . . (and it) was lost through talk and lies." Wilson says to Macomber after his initiation into courage, don't talk and spoil it, and Brett never finishes her sentences, "talking is bilge." Thinking and talking denote a corrupted consciousness in the first place. On the other side, consciousness is pain. Nick after his wound tries to keep from thinking and resorts to counting sheep, remembering details of trout fishing, the pure action. Frederick Henry recites the names of cities and places for relief.

This is a metaphysical view of consciousness. The inarticulations in Hemingway communicate the great tension of the unknowable for characters whose concept of the unknowable has been enlarged to the point of breaking the mind itself. Behind the natural histories of pain and death there is the metaphysical darkness. The *nada* asserted in "A Clean Well-Lighted Place" needs its relief in the well-lighted places of physical fact and sensation. With such poignancies the radical

skepticism and intellectual pathos of Hemingway's writing make themselves felt.

The clean place is the good place where Nick goes in "Big Two-Hearted River." He walks through progressively wilder country as though searching for pure sensations, and when he camps finally, "He was very tired, nothing could touch him, he was there in the good place." He needs to become very tired and hungry, as though this were the way of stripping consciousness and reaching the purged experiences of eating his dinner and sleeping. He crawls into his tent and is very comfortable; this suggests the regressive movement in Hemingway, the search for a boy happiness. The style itself is regressive, as if to imply the declarative, uncomplicated sensibility of a boy.

It is important to stress this reductive movement. The revelations of pure experience do not open out to a universe of light but rather to a corner of safety in a world which remains largely undefined and threatening. The stress on physical sensations in Hemingway hardly ever has the value of a true sensuousness. Reality in its shock, consciousness in its despair, communicate a desire for narcosis, obliteration in some specialized sensation, and this is the quality of most of the hedonistic experience described in his writing. In the story, "The Gambler, the Nun, and the Radio." Frazer asks the quasi-Communist why the opium of the people should be taken from them. Bread, drink, education, religion, politics are all opium. He might have added sport and sex. And he asks why the people should be operated on without an anesthetic. In the same way the old man in "A Clean Well-Lighted Place" takes his drinks in the bodega as literally the alternative to his suicide.

In The Sun Also Rises when the fiesta is over, the passions emptied, and all actors gone, Jake is left alone with his sunbathing, his food, his wine. He knows a frustration which cannot be examined; he gets blind drunk in the first phase of his reaction to Brett's affair with Romero, and finally in the collapse of

Brett's world with his own, he eats a wonderful enormous meal in Madrid with Brett watching. Thus the hedonism of the defeated is not really pure. It is a protest, a lament, and an expression of license. The typical mood is that of the fiesta, the central climax in *The Sun Also Rises* which is no true orgy, but rather the great American binge where the effort is to break controls and lose consciousness. "Everything became quite unreal finally, and it seemed as though nothing could have any consequences." As it is presented, the moment without consequences is not so much a heightened sensibility as it is a drugged state. What is appreciated in it is the fact of irresponsibility, the freedom of sensations rather than their quality. Bill Gorton and Mike Campbell, two people who definitely "belong," are both drunk when they are introduced in the novel. This is a personality essence or perhaps a personality substitute, expressive of their charm, their pathos, and their freedom. If there is passion in the experience of these people, one feels it curiously empty, it has energy but no content, the freedom is defiant, the exhilaration has no joy. Direct adolescent aspects of this sort are expressed in "The Three Day Blow," where Nick and his friend dumbly drink the afternoon away, against the context of Nick's barely mentioned problems.

The break from responsibility is essentially an aspect of the reality trauma. Jake Barnes represents the man interrupted in life and spoiled by his wound; his striking dimension in the novel is actually his passivity. This is a general essence in Hemingway's protagonists; they are outsiders, newspaper reporters, expatriates, *déracines* fighting someone else's wars, all people who act either by indirect, private motives or exist simply as observers. At the extreme Hemingway's man is stalemated completely. When he suffers he cannot define the issues or alternatives except that he knows he has been betrayed by all previous prescriptions for action. When he is driven he is driven by blunt instruments, visceral compulsions and blank causalities.

Even in the late work, *The Old Man and the Sea*, with its modifying affirmations, the sense of compulsion and divided consciousness is sharply expressed. "How do you feel, hand?" the old man asks his cramped hand. "I'll eat some more for you." The body is treated as second person, at a distance from a frozen or reduced consciousness.

* * *

Where does a writer go for hard substance after he establishes what seem like the crippling premises of a traumatic reality and a spoiled consciousness? The threat of a flabby melancholia is upon him and he must disgorge sentimentality. If he sees his people totally injured for belief and action what shall he write about at all, without repeating the numb abbreviated pathos of such a story as "A Clean Well-Lighted Place?" We understand here the interest in the short story which lends itself to the emphasis of aborted actions and motives. However, action is the staple of Hemingway's fiction; he has no interest in developing the complications of the sensibility itself, nor to extend the moral and spiritual issues of defeat. Nor is defeat the single issue. Like any writer with an authentic creative imagination, he keeps the will to wrest some aspect of victory from defeat.

Accordingly one might say Hemingway discovered sport as his positive theme. It is a subject to contrast with life, literally *play*, with its own possibilities of interest and drama. Sport after all belongs nostalgically to the boy world and it, too, is an opium, not reality so much as the game played with it. At the same time it was a lucky find for Hemingway, (apart from its natural issue from his own temperament and life activity) in that he was able to use sport as a metaphysical image, conceiving life as a game which tests character and behavior. In using sport he avoids direct commitments; it is ostentatiously non-serious. On the other hand it has both the purity of motive and the purity of form which action has lost, and therefore writing freely about it, one might draw a symbol with its own serious meaning, invent active heroes and even make moral judgments.* In other words sport is Hemingway's literary mythology.

Sport revives heroism in the only sphere where heroism is possible, and where action is not doomed to failure or disgrace. The moment of value in sport is transient but vivid. The action is a gesture, a performance, a willing creature of art. The fisherman, the bullfighter, the boxer achieve the greatness of posture in the Hemingway metaphor for life, defining it as the moment without consequences.

Let us say a metaphor for life as it should be lived. The boy prepares for life in his games. The Hemingway hero retreats to games, in order to enact the virtues and regain the nobility which life has lost. If life is formless and meaningless, sport is not. It ritualizes action, it discriminates, it dramatizes; the significance is clear, victory is possible.

In this manner much in Hemingway seems to be an effort to find values discriminated in a world which has lost its marks. Even the self-conscious hedonism, when it isn't defiance and when it isn't narcotic, is the assertion of a kind of taste, a concentration of appreciations which counterweigh the absence of other values. The larger actual values which are discriminated in his fiction are implicitly aristocratic virtues, closely and essentially related to the virtues of sport. They do not have ethical range and if anything they contradict large areas of conventional morality. In the stress on the sport hero, they signify the effort to surmount fear and passivity and to distinguish the champion from the crowd.

In the group that forms itself around Jake and Brett in *The Sun Also Rises* we can see an inchoate aristocratic principle struggling to find itself. They are not so much "lost" as they are busy defining themselves in selection from the rest of the world. The Greek count is one of us, Brett says; he has had the careless

---

* Symbolism is the natural means of a writer dealing with a refractory reality, whose complex aspects resist evaluation. Surely modern symbolism has this force behind it.

adventures and the wounds. Brett herself, it is said, is built like a racing hull. She belongs to an actual aristocracy, English, of course, as Mike does, and in every sense she stands out, absolutely self-confident, and the innovator of manners. "She started all that," someone says, referring to the women's short haircuts.

It seems sometimes to be the spirit of exclusion searching for a basis. To a large extent the group defines itself negatively, and the character of Robert Cohn seems to have been invented chiefly to manifest the traits which deny membership. (In basic respects he is a "square" in the contemporary jargon.) Cohn is the soft romantic and his sin is that he is greedy for life, when the posture of the initiated is of course a sharp disillusionment upon which they base the poignant savoring of experience. A crucial point about him is that he does not get drunk; vulgar optimist, he lives in the future, he does not know the moment without consequences. Expecting Brett's arrival at Pamplona, he gets himself a haircut and shampoo, whereas the casual air is mandatory in the face of either possible happiness or suffering. Worst of all he corrupts judgment; he should know how unsuitable he is for the heroine of the clique, Brett. She is to be reserved for the true hero, Romero, the bullfighter.

Brett says of Cohn, "I hate his damned suffering." In the world of the defeated, there can be no *display* of suffering. To suffer is to complain, to presume a good end or success in life. It expresses the naiveté of the subjective principle, whereas those who know reality conform with its uncompromising aspects, with accents only of courage and pride. The soft virtues, hope, compassion, remorse, are irrelevant, or worse, a contemptible weakness in nature, or worse yet, leading to the greatest sins, cant and self-delusion.

In the story, "In Another Country" the community of those who have the truth, who have faced death in battle, is the ideal gang which excludes everyone without that experience. In the same sense, the *aficionados* of bullfighting are a club where a similar mysterious knowledge is the membership requirement. There was a "secret between us" Jake says. Robert Cohn cannot stand bullfighting, Brett reacts well immediately. The ultimate in aristocratic discriminations, expressed in talks between the *aficionados*, Jake and Montoya, leads to Romero, the hero of the values.

The climactic fist battle between Romero and Cohn becomes almost symbolic, as if an old conflict between pagan values and the Christian-Jewish conscience were re-enacted.* Cohn with his trained boxing skill, keeps knocking Romero down, and Romero, in his blazing courage, keeps getting up. Finally Cohn collapses in remorse and begs forgiveness. He is the broken man at the end of the novel, but in a large sense what has broken him is his sense of the amoral life about him, a violence in which he cannot function. He begs forgiveness from everyone and it seems like a gross irrelevance and sentimentality. Romero on the other hand would willingly kill Cohn in their battle, without a scruple. When violence is offered, violence is answered, and to the end, without mercy.

The value system focussing on Romero seems to be a combination of aristocratic virtues with a pagan naturalism. Perhaps it is Nietzsche who stands in the background, quarreling with the subjective ethics of the old tradition. The desire to be forgiven and loved, the ethics of self-restraint, proposes

---

* The treatment of the Jew in modern writing takes its tone from existent moral crises, as the image of the Jew always has perhaps, and it would be interesting to pursue the theme in a reading of Pound, Eliot, and Joyce, as major examples, and variant as these writers are in their imaginative concepts of the Jew. The range is from unrestrained polemic in Pound, to fastidious moral revulsion in Eliot, and to major comedy in Joyce, accompanied by a peculiar Olympian affection. The problem of the Jew apparently becomes linked with both the rejection and the clinging to an old conscience. The Jew, old rabbi of the world, suffers in resurgent moral ambivalence, as nature searches for its freedom, as the conscience cries treason against itself, or as moral values struggle to survive. Value maker as well as value breaker in the myth of the West, the Jew lends himself as target for either avenue of attack which the modern dilemma of values opens up.

humility to those who have already lost their pride; its irrelevance is monstrous in the world of nature. There is no factor of truth in it, its spokesmen are self-deceiving and soft. A man who wishes a truth sanction must draw his ethics from nature as well as his reviving vigor. It is a war ethics, a hunter's code.

The restored hero regains that which has been torn away from him, his virility. Natural reality, which first frightened and subdued him, will be the field for his victory, and by its own terms. Macomber is frightened by the lion and thereby, in symbol and reality, defeated in his life; but his redemption comes when he can kill the lion and be a man. The heroic value is virility because it suggests the mastering of reality, the spirit of dominance which is masculine. The climactic challenge to that power comes appropriately in the figure of the woman. Women like Mrs. Macomber and Brett, unsurrendered, unsatisfied, need the domination of men, as reality demands the exercise of the heroic will. Jake, the lost hero, gives Brett, the defaced woman, to Romero, a true, athletic man. Romero is Jake's sexual surrogate, and as he can tame and kill the bull, so he can take Brett easily and inevitably. Brett like the bull has been the center of natural danger, the cause and object of passion, of suffering and maiming. Romero thus provides a contrasting experience for the defeated men, the deformed and the spoiled, the drunken Mike, the sentimentalist Cohn, the wounded Jake, etc. He wins and masters the woman everyone wants, herself inadequate as a woman. And although Brett must leave, for fear of corrupting this natural saint, this is one experience she leaves without disillusionment, as a sacrifice, deciding not to be a bitch as she says, praising the true values.

Beyond sex, though linked to it, it is death which is the chief challenge of nature, and it is death that he dominates when the protagonist revives as hero. As Hemingway said in his creed as a writer, he wanted to write commencing with the simplest things and violent death was the simplest thing of all and the most fundamental. From the time his boy protagonist saw the Caesarean operation and the suicide in "Indian Camp," death is the final reality which must be understood and mastered. It is here that sport, in Hemingway's use, becomes not play but meaningful symbol and the road back to truth and moral seriousness. His sports are the sports of nature, hunting, fishing, bullfighting, where nature is the specific antagonist. They are a play which imitates the great metaphysical contest itself; they require killing and at their highest level, the risk of his own death for the sport hero. Thus, briefly, the bullfighter is the hero of reality. The bull is everything explosive and dangerous in life, bull animal, bull hatred, bull passion and death. The fight comes at the climax of the fiesta which is a riot of living with destructive forces set free. "There was much wine and ignored tension, and a feeling of things coming that you could not prevent happening." The reality principle has been released. But above it all stands the bullfighter, risking and taming chaos. In that formal beauty and ritual order, sport has become a religious service; it has given resolution to conflict.

To understand Hemingway in this way is to see him as a symbolist writer transcribing a metaphysical search. It is also to see him at his best, in the aspect which will make his work lasting. The greatest tension in his writing has its source in the alternate hunt for and avoidance of the reality principle, a complex of violent submerging experience. The analogy to *Moby Dick* can be made usefully. The protagonist is wounded by the great whale, yet eternally compelled to hunt him in the double tension of contradictory motives. The motive to find the nature god, as we can call it, is on the one hand compulsive revenge, manifested in Hemingway's work by masks of suicide, the spoiling or wounding carried to limits, a demonstration of metaphysical failure. The other motive is positive, the search for redemptive truth, and strength from truth, by immersion in the reality principle.

Captain Ahab flings his harpoon in a last defiance which is his only triumph, an ironic triumph in the general destruction. He has one of the compensations of tragedy in the sense that character asserts itself against fate to the end. But his testimony is not utterly solipsistic; the human community regards him appalled, his values are countered by those of Starbuck, and his experience has endowed the consciousness of the survivor, Ishmael. The Hemingway hero is also blocked by the power and blankness of the antagonist, but he turns more completely to a salvation in character, as if the recourse were the essentially solipsistic gesture, the action which is its own justification. The premise is that man and animal are both doomed, and there is no alternative or refuge from nature. Thus in Hemingway action is surrounded by blankness at both ends, and therefore action is necessarily art or sport, self-inspired and its own reward. Captain Ahab has passionate reason to complain, hope, fight and die. But Hemingway's hero has the skeptical knowledge in advance which makes him assume immediately the gallant attitude of the sportsman.

At its best Hemingway's work has an almost allegorical clarity. He searches reality at the bottom of sensations, where pain and pleasure begin. Pain and pleasure track the way to revealed authenticity. The climax of sensations is at the peak moment of risk, the moment before death. But what is wanted desperately, beyond pure sensations, is the enactment of *form* at the moment of risk, risk being the element of nature, and form the acting out of the intrinsic values of knowledge and control, a kind of substitute metaphysics, in fact. The bull is the beast of *nada*, characterizing the unintelligent violence of nature, and the bullfighter is the artist of form.

A familiar modern self-consciousness is the key to our understanding of these matters. Art knows itself, and life, as it can be known, tends to know itself as art. This self-consciousness is within the work, with the action divided between actors and spectators, as it is essentially divided between consciousness and reality. Or if there is a principle of fusion, action takes place for *the benefit* of spectatorship, as it does in sport. With a metaphysical or teleological defeatism narrowing the range of possible assertions, Hemingway cannot really get beyond sport, or life as a ritual game, for his affirmative theme. Romero never gets out of his bullfight costume, one might say. He is the hero, but he is the hero on a stage, a possibility compared to life, not identified with it. The true protagonists are Brett and Jake, facing each other in the cab at the end.

> "Oh, Jake," Brett said, "we could have had such a damned good time together."
> "Yes," I said, "Isn't it pretty to think so."

We have had a play within a play and these are the actors off-stage speaking, really the envious spectators, who can only partake of life vicariously, presented by the make-believe of sport.

This has the justice of the real circumstances behind it and of course no other conclusion is possible. Nowhere in Hemingway does the heroic movement go beyond its abortive, doomed conditions. Not certainly in "The Short Happy Life of Francis Macomber," where Macomber dies at his wife's hands at the moment of his private redemption in the sport life. *For Whom the Bell Tolls* provides in some aspects an exception to the main trend of his work, but essentially we might say, I think, that the Spanish Civil War has the attributes of a sport contest whose ultimate results are defeat or irrelevance, and whose issues themselves have little importance in contrast to the private gestures of character made possible by the war. In this case history seems to have supported Hemingway's insight. Action is intensely realized. Again it is the bravery of a small force which is being exhibited, but levied against it is the familiar great vague opposition in which the moral issues themselves are confused or lost entirely. No meaningful consequences can follow the blowing of the bridge and the death of Robert Jordan. Again we look at the action in a closed ring, and the hero is the champion of nothing but his own spirit. Camus' trenchant definition speaks clearly for us here.

> His hatred of death and his passion for life won him that unspeakable penalty in which the whole being is exerted toward accomplishing nothing.[1]

The hero in Hemingway was precisely the hero of the "absurd" at a time so long before it had become part of current literary vocabulary that one is impressed again by the way in which his work has had expressive insight for two generations.

Camus goes on to say that "one does not discover the absurd without being tempted to write the manual of happiness," and, . . . "The absurd man says yes and his effort will henceforth be unceasing." It is not far-fetched to say that Hemingway attempted to write his manual of happiness in his last published fiction, *The Old Man and the Sea*. The note is more tendentious than in his other writing, and Hemingway is at last contemplating his theme to extract its affirmative values, as if to see how "the absurd man says yes." We are not surprised to find that nature is the simply expressed antagonist, sought as far out as possible from the land. However, the old man has no quarrel with his fish like that of Captain Ahab with the whale, and in fact his thinking is as close to pantheism as would be plausible in the fight. The marlin is the fisherman's natural brother. In the great fish the old man sees the analogue of good, a paradigm for life at its best. He remembers, for instance the natural gallantry of the male marlin who stayed with the killed female until it was brought in. In his dream the old man sees the lions on the beach and these appear in their perfection to be something like the angels of a naturalistic heaven. The old man compares himself with the fighting cocks who receive the spur.

> I do not think I could endure that or the loss of the eye, or both eyes and continue to fight as the fighting cocks do. Man is not much beside the great birds and beasts.

1 The *Myth of Sisyphus*, Vintage, p. 89.

In his earlier work, although it has its vitalistic implications and frequently evokes the romantic embrace of nature, Hemingway's sharpest effect comes from an unresolved tension which as I have said was basically metaphysical. The drama divided the respective essences; nature does not communicate itself nor reconcile itself to the human interest, and man is conceived as dramatically beleaguered. There is in fact a specifically human essence; the ingenuity manifested in sport was something like an artifact for the human will and intelligence. At the same time since his philosophic premises were naturalistic, the values of the hero could have no other ultimate origin. Pressed far enough for resolution and stability, they would tend to be reduced to the original ground of conflict. Now in this later work Hemingway seems to be trying to draw more solace from the premises of naturalism, and the effect is to blur his ordealistic or stoic sense of human experience.

The old man is experienced and skillful, but basically his virtue is that he holds on, he endures. This accompanies his gift of strength, famous even in his old age, and these are the virtues of nature, not distinct from those of the fish, his brother. The old man says, "Fish, I love you and respect you very much." . . . "He is my brother but I must kill him." . . . "I'll kill him for all his greatness, his glory. It is unjust, but I will show him what a man can do and what a man can endure." He says, "Fish, I'll stay with you until I am dead." And "Now we are joined together." The battle has become the embrace, a *loving* conflict, and that no doubt was the direction of Hemingway's latent primitivism from the start.

To be posed against nature but to have no principle except that of nature for affirmation, this is the dilemma which faced Hemingway in the effort to resolve his metaphysical theme. It accounts for the ambivalent view of natural reality, the cycles of attraction and repulsion, and the ultimate impasse of heroism. The old man says to the fish, "You are killing me. You have a right. I do not care who kills who." The final position is passive, at the border of death which by a transcendence of personal judgment is not called defeat. It cannot be defeat since the antagonists, man and nature, each have the right, and each win justification whether in death or survival. Where is the lament and where is the praise? Where is the force for action, except the life force which can take care of itself, and has no distinction from everything else in nature? The fish and the man are brothers. And so at the conclusion of battle the hero eats and sleeps. Jake eats and drinks heavily; he endures his life. The old man sleeps deeply, and saying his "yes," tomorrow he will go out to fish again.

If we wished to look further for an emblem of the action we might find it figured in the word "luck"; the old fisherman has had very bad luck for eighty days. Repeated and stressed in the story, "luck" is a word very much like "they," which in the familiar passage from *A Farewell to Arms* was invoked as the unidentifiable source of affliction. "Luck" and "they" are vague words because conflict and suffering themselves have become vague, a turbulence in that nature which includes and therefore reduces all conceivable values. Reality has moved closer and the protagonist has less space than ever for movement in which he can assert will and character. The truth is of course he doesn't have intelligible opposition and therefore no intelligible purpose; the will is only one manifestation, and a small one, of that which opposes the will. Nevertheless by invoking all his strength and enduring his life, a man celebrates his life. And in the distance, as a model for life, the illusion, not the reality of success, the baseball hero, Joe DiMaggio, still flourishes.

The inert
and the violent:
Faulkner's
Light in August

The modern mind is dialectical to an extreme; it looks for division, it dramatizes oppositions. For this emphasis, Faulkner's *Light in August* is a classic of the modern imagination as well as perhaps the most representative of his works. We have in it a series of oppositions which intensify drama to the point of freezing; hard blocks of force are held in arrest as if resolution could never come. The characters have an almost allegorical simplicity of function in conflict, divided against each other and divided within themselves. We think of Joanna Burden with her night and day personalities, physical lust and moral prohibition in exemplary struggle. Joe Christmas can be neither Negro nor white and is violently broken by his mixed identity. In their external relationships Faulkner's characters are fragments of men needing each other to compose the full image. Bunch and Burch are thus complementary phases of the same man, pursued and pursuing, in the life of Lena Grove. In a larger pattern, Joe

Christmas might be seen as the figure for the compulsive body, released to action, and the Rev. Hightower as the spectator, passive mind, a figure for conscience.

In that major duality of mind and body we have the thematic conflict of the novel, concentrated and extended to give it its great structural clarity. All other oppositions are related to it if we see it as a fatal division between natural reality and the moral human intelligence. The subordinate symbols are Negro and white, woman and man, night and day in inevitable antipathy. The Negro and the woman are the root physical realities which inhabit Christmas, burden him and destroy him. They are his temptation and freedom as well as his sin and punishment in the sexual and racial mythology upon which Faulkner draws. We cannot recoil from this, it is explicit in the work. The Negro and the woman are quite simply the savage and primitive source. Against it, within as well as outside himself, Christmas must lead in ageless conflict the male-white principle which defines him, the moral bigotry which hates him. The madman Hines speaks for the theme, cursing "bitchery." That is the word for the blind source from which Christmas springs, where Negro and female meet in a natural coupling. Bitchery is the provenance of woman and Negro, original sin is bitchery, and life is the drama of a fall in which the divisive terms, male and female, Negro and white, invade and destroy each other.

Division is corruption in the world of Faulkner, and miscegenation is its vivid symbolic act. Opposed to this act of violent disorder, we understand an ideal of implicit unity, which is thereby purity. The unmixed blood and culture relate a purity of origin with a harmony of result, and they imply the conscience unified with action. The Negro left alone has a primitive unity and therefore purity of substance. In fact, as primitive, he can function as an idealized moral essence and even perform the role of conscience as Dilsey does in *The Sound and the Fury*. This is a romantic inversion of which Faulkner remains capable even while he writes the tragedies of a broken tradition and a decayed civilized conscience. The white man, in his own order, as he enacted the mysterious sin which was a combination of enslavement and miscegenation, belonged to a system where values worked and civilization existed. So the nostalgia of the myth runs and for us it has no relevance to debate the myth historically. Essentially it is a tragic myth which remembers a hubris of human success accompanied by the flaw or crime which will destroy it. What works for us upon the dramatic field of division are the symbolic forms for an ideally imagined order. Faulkner, related as he is to the romantic tradition, finds this order or unity in two places, in a tradition of the past now lost and nostalgically considered, and in images of the primitive. Lena Grove, for instance, occupies the place of undefilement. She has undebatable origins, she is clear in substance. She stands outside the conflict, and yet she is the primitive source and the goal to which the action returns for a revival of life.

When there is intellectual confusion in Faulkner's work, which is not infrequent, it has much to do with this double allegiance to nature and civilization. The ambiguity is most sharp in the treatment of nature; as we see in dealing with the representatives of primitive reality, we must know how to discern between their roles as restoring or destructive. In this respect Faulkner's work is profoundly American. In the vivid record of American writing we see the conflict of two nostalgias, or a nostalgia and a hope, which we might briefly translate as the nostalgia for a nourishing moral order, a tradition most frequently centering in Europe, and a hope concentrating on the redemptive role of nature in the expanding west, or the expansive future.[1] What gives Faulkner's work at its best its high and rather unique value, is his ability, as in *Light in August* and *The Sound and the Fury*, to reconcile these two impulses and construct from them a dramatic and tragic myth in which nature

1 This theme has attracted the attention of several critics, among them R. W. B. Lewis, *The American Adam*; and Richard Chase, *The American Novel and Its Tradition*.

and the endowed order of tradition threaten each other with destruction and search for the resolution of a restored moral harmony. Joe Christmas is the great cross-breed of Faulkner's fiction, and his bloody career offers the result of conflict between a primitive essence and the disengaged and degenerating moral power. He is the protagonist of tragic miscegenation.

* * *

Where the mixed blood exists there is murder and destruction. Christmas kills Joanna Burden because she is a divided corruption, his own and hers, herself of a vague heredity. She exhibits to him night and day, lust and repression, violent on both sides. When she finally reverses herself permanently, from woman to spinster, grey, tightly bound, sexually dead, she asks him to pray according to the male ruthless code of McEachern. She becomes his absolute enemy, pray or I'll kill you, she says at the last, and the prayer would mean killing to him. She confronts the divided man and would fix his identity at one of its intolerable poles. She calls him Negro and would send him to the Negro college where he would accept the repressive order principle of the white world. This is not to fix his identity so much as to crucify him forever in his conflict.

Christmas' inner division cannot be understood until we look at that major duality of the novel which joins Christmas and Hightower. Has there ever been in fiction a character so reduced to impotence, so dramatically vivid in his passivity as Hightower? Was there ever such cold violent action offered as in the character of Joe Christmas, accompanied as it is by the blankness of his own understanding?

There is an implicit allegory in this novel which says that when action is separated from thought it will tear and slay until the mind awakes. So the imagination thus afflicted deals with itself. Action is violent because nothing but violence can make a claim against unintelligibility and unreason. Only murder can identify such a frozen passive creature as Joanna Burden and awake a mind so betrayed as Hightower's.

It is Hightower who is narrowly the agent of intellect and conscience, and with that Faulkner proceeds to take everything overt in the life of the world away from him. Now ostracized and self-isolating, he has lost his congregation. He has lost his wife (his major failure), being most miserable in his inadequacy for her simple needs; and to his one friend and the only member of a dialogue in his present life, Bunch, he has only retreat and divorce to commend. The image of Hightower, sedentary, flabby, moldering in his unaired house, focuses on the incapacity to live. Yet his mind is alive still, painfully forced to remember the past and observe the present action.

Spiritual degeneracy is clearly the theme in his life. From the beginning of his supposed vocation as minister and teacher, he has been a spirit out of touch with his reality, he has rejected his time. The world for which he gives it up is a mocking secular romance of the Civil War. He chooses the braggart myth of the South in place of his religion, and in that myth we note the stress on virility, physical force and action. It is the compensatory dream of a sedentary, impotent man and it is empty of moral meaning. The spirit of action hungry for its release finds it precisely in the gratuitous event, the unmotivated courage and gallantry of boys in their daredevil ride against the Yankee stores in Jefferson. There is no moral complexity here and no need to disturb the pure image of action with analysis.

Hightower has lived with his mind and spirit turned away from their proper objects, but now Lena Grove and Joe Christmas, alive on the immediate field of action, compel his attention. In the climax of the novel Hightower has the agony of consciousness, he suffers as he knows. What he knows is the life of Joe Christmas, moving dumbly through violent action. He meets him at the tragic climax where knowledge and action meet, moving on separate paths as they have through the novel. Christmas has been the agent, or more precisely, the victim of his own body and his circumstances, compelled by natural force to a destructive and apparently meaningless destiny. In the discontinuity between thought and action, the will is lost, it has no function. After his brutal beating, deserted by his mistress, he lies on the floor of the brothel, "conscious somewhere within him of the two severed wire ends of sentience and volition." As he moves toward the house to kill Joanna Burden, not thinking, as it is stressed repeatedly, "thinking had not begun now," the voice in his mind says, "Something is going to happen. Something is going to happen to me." In his last flight it is to Hightower as a sanctuary of knowledge that he blindly runs, for knowledge is sympathy and only the moral reason might resolve his conflict.

Helpless for a resolution, however, the protagonist of the mind as expressed by Hightower is suspended above time and the action, as Christmas' sensibility is suspended above his body even while he acts. Typically, as a child hidden in the dietician's closet, he watched himself become sick, "Motionless now, utterly contemplative, he seemed to stoop above himself like a chemist in his laboratory, waiting." The sensibility here is not purposive at all. The passive sensibility contains experience in a series of images, drugged states of consciousness. Action does not have its origin in the mind but brings its effects to it, and the division is between the spectator and the actor. The actor is abstract and belongs to the impersonal collective process of history and nature. The spectator is highly personal, his individual consciousness sharply distorted by passions and affected states of being. In the world of necessity only the mind is free, but free only as a receptive agent, for its fantasies, responsive visions, and individual "errors" of perception.

The technical principle in Faulkner accounting for his most characteristic effects is to break the relationship between the consciousness and action and make them work at odds. They are set off by distortion and brought together in a dialectic of risk, guess, dream, and open war. The mind wrestles with experience, escapes it, struggles to reach it, and it is this intensity which is the force of his writing. Hightower, in particular, is the groping and bodiless narrator, reviewing his and everyone else's experience, always in a museum or library quiet, punctuated by the shots and screams as they fade or come closer. The tone of the mind is that of "bodiless voices recounting dreamily something performed in a region without dimension by people without blood."

There is a contrasting narrator in Hines, again in his own way an example of the disengaged mind. His destiny is to go mad, as Hightower's was to dream his life away. In his madness he pronounces a superstitious mythology which explains the violent history from its beginning to a predetermined end. Typical in his Calvinism, he supports predestiny by proclaiming an endless war with "bitchery." He searches for the reality called evil; mad moral prophet that he is, he would purge it by announcing its progress and cursing it. He is the spirit made cruel by its knowledge, whereas Hightower, a spiritual failure made tender by failure, lives in a gentle trance of the past, finding a romantic diversion. The "eunuch Tennyson" in his lap, he builds a child's illusions, forgetting the important metaphysical myth of his vocation.

The suspension of mind above action, the principle dominating Faulkner's themes and his writing devices, means the suspension or distortion of time, for the mind has the time-making function. Action is the central mystery in the human consciousness and it is seen in the variants of subjective distortion. Time is understood in the variants of conscious perspectives. The present calls up the past, the past substitutes for the present, the two conjoin and go apart. The only road to reality is the consciousness, and actually the only moment is the present, the immediate consciousness. To fulfill the sense of reality, one must use a multiple consciousness, variants of the actors and observers, and use the variants of the time consciousness, memory and immediate sensation. That chromatic consciousness, narrating a deeply problematic action from which it is detached, is expressed in all of his important work, *The Sound and the Fury, As I Lay Dying, Absalom, Absalom,* and moves most freely in pace with the action, in *Light in August.*[2]

At the same time the distance between thought and action seems longer in this novel, permanently at odds, as it were. In the dramatic final scenes when Christmas loses touch with the hour of the day, the day of the week, his mind is floating back and forth over his experience in a combining perspective, outside of time. Time is reality, reality is in time, but it is "timeless" time, so to speak. So we see Lena Grove, the autonomous figure of reality, first appear mounted on the slow moving wagon, making its passage, "like something moving forever without progress across an urn." So McEachern turns to stone, mounted on his sculptured horse, in his passionate pursuit of Joe Christmas.

Time is held in arrest in the mind's visions of reality, but it is movement held in thought's arrest. Behind every appearance the wheels are turning endlessly. We notice the recurrent stressed use of the present tense and of the present participle. The view of the continuous verb is of a process that never completes itself. The marked-out past or future are seizures of time by the mind, assertions that time-reality parallels the human sensibility, which does indeed have a past and future. The time-reality as such does not; it moves onward, indifferent to human calendars, and so, ultimately expressive in Faulkner's writing of the way in which it eludes and defeats human consciousness.

The time-reality is "timeless," but the reduced consciousness has a compulsive interest in the past. The present is a chaotic, unselective array of sensations, but the past is an accumulation of events ever bearing forward upon the present as the expression of predestined, if not meaningful, reality. That is why

---

2 Erich Auerbach discusses this aspect of modern fiction under the heading of the "multipersonal consciousness," in illustration from the work of Virginia Woolf. As usual his remarks have great perception and radiating reference. (*Mimesis,* pp. 463–488, Doubleday Anchor.)

nature and history have an equivalence in Faulkner. As a naturalist in a true sense, he has no characters, strictly speaking, but only victims and agents of time-nature, a process stronger than motives and outside them. Fatality moves out of the past and it moves out of nature, and by this Faulkner more than anyone wrote the epics of determinism. As it rules the action, the past also rules the sensibility. What a character knows is chiefly what he remembers. Hightower, the paralyzed man, figures this deeply by living totally in the past, the autonomous mind made so by cutting itself off from present action. "He was born thirty years after the only day in which he seemed to have lived." The story of Joanna Burden has parallel significance. Faulknerian characters, as they are alienated from the present, are tied with an iron bond to the past, usually to a central violent act dominating it, an act both criminal and glamorous. The grandfathers seem to have all the energy and motivation their descendants lack. As they murdered, sinned, wandered in the wilderness, semi-barbarians that they were, they started an inheritance. Their descendants are sterile and virginal, and action in the past arranges the chain of necessity that made them so. Action in the past is all that invites the imagination; they might live in it by choice, they might do penance for it, but they can never forget its significant crimes or its heroic testament, and they carry its "burden" all their lives.

In the technique of Faulkner only the past tells a "story." The moment of immediacy is one of distortion and half-realization in the consciousness. The state of immediacy provides only blunt sensations in the first aspect. The mind remembers and constructs but it feels new events like disintegrating blows. Therefore in the psychologically immediate state there is on the one hand the shock of sensation, and on the other a disjoined level of consciousness, the subjective trance, analogous to the dream. Mental images occur affected by sensations but not grappling with them in analysis, nor are the images analyzed. The mind makes responses, not reports of what is happening.

What is implicit here is the rejection of the anachronistic modes of the traditional mind which assumed empirical validity and worked confidently from its moral and metaphysical presumptions. We have been made familiar in modern fiction with plain reporting, or the objective style, which confesses an inability to judge or evaluate, and wants the truth bulwark of science, no matter how meaninglessly the truth states itself. The purity of reportage can lead it to a catalog of sensations, effective in a bewildering, implicit drama. The neutral style, as in the work of Hemingway, usually has the service of stressing the remoteness of feeling and thought from the reality of the world. Thus the mock technique of science is used to enact pathos, figuring the inarticulate sensibility against the violent, opaque background of experience.

Faulkner stretches the opposition to greater extremes than other writers by totally forcing one dimension into another in alternate phases. When a subjective character absorbs the world, it is entirely his world in mind, blood, and instinct, as might be illustrated by Benjy in *The Sound and the Fury*. In the other perspective the objectification or externalization of the sensibility can be as complete. The sense of automatistic helplessness in action is one of the major effects of Faulkner's work and a chief signal of the originality of his genius. No one went further in suggesting the complete capture of the will, the intelligence, the whole sensibility by overwhelming external force. This power makes its effect by fusing directly with the internal channels of force, so that psychic compulsions and the causality in events seem to be operating in perfect unison.

The singular effect in Faulkner's work is that of his characters as passionate puppets, puppets of themselves, driven by passions which inhabit them like demons, but passions which are essentially instincts or tropisms. For the reason that passion is absolute, it is described by Faulkner as rapt, calm, expressionless, even in white heat. In climaxes his people know without knowing, act without thinking or speaking. McEachern rides to the dance hall where he will find Joe Christmas as if force in space itself will take him where he must go. He cannot tell himself where that is, nor does he need to have a thought of why he is going. At the opening of the novel, the dietician, desperate in her fear of the boy, goes straight to the janitor Hines, aware of his knowledge of Joe's history while he is aware of what has happened in her room, without a word of previous communication. This expression of clairvoyance might be called a naturalistic awareness; one knows as a thing or a force knows, by compulsion.

Experience in Faulkner is suffered, it is ordealistic. Two of his favorite words are "implacable" and "outrage." In these he suggests process in nature, in one aspect immutable, in the other destroying. Seized by subterranean nature, Christmas can run five miles to his prostitute mistress as she waits for him at night in the town. At this extremity motives can no longer be distinguished from action.

Faulkner's "outrage" is a term to denote violence. Violence comes from the outside, it is what rules in necessity, and it is effective as a violation, that is, a seizure *against* the will and sensible values. In the uncontrolled, unwilled world, all action is outrage. Coming from nature, it impinges as a man stumbles and jars himself, as he falls in an accident.

Violence is the ironically appropriate and naturalistically inevitable fate of the passive agent. Crumbling below her rigid surface, reached in her isolation, Joanna Burden falls to unlimited license. She is seduced blindly without apparent enjoyment, and she is murdered in an automatistic act, her throat sliced to the back of the neck. It is violent in proportion to its apparent lack of sensible motivation. In its ultimate trend in Faulkner, action is assault, it is murder, suicide, rape. What is demonstrated is the brutality of nature, sharply evincing its lack of moral sanction or design. What is further suggested is that the human imagination cannot bear passivity or neutrality of value either in itself or in nature. When action surpasses its agent, when it is seen as compulsive necessity, then action as treated by the imagination moves to violent extremes as if to blow itself up.

As for man, where, without its own mind, nature rules against the human mind, the chief virtues—if there are any virtues—are in strength and endurance. The assertive protagonist is a stone or a whirlwind. Joe Christmas is whipped endlessly by Mc-Eachern and refuses to cry out. Byron Bunch travels all night in order to pray all day in his Sunday services. Since motive is not intelligent but compulsive, motive cannot be persuaded, it must be broken. So Hines and McEachern find their principle of action and so Christmas reacts. Think of adding intelligent communication between these two and Christmas and we see how deeply the principle works in this novel. Lena Grove on her agelessly slow wagon moves endlessly to her object without knowing her object. She rolls on forever, blankly persistent, defenseless, but durability itself. Movement substitutes for motive, intensities and powers substitute for qualities. The image of man is heavy, columnar, graceless, like much modern sculpture. Behind both is the same estimation of the block-like force of nature.

The ordeal which approaches tragedy in Faulkner's writing is located in the drama of an amoral, naturalistic force which has captured the sensibility of man. The moral intelligence undergoes a continual shock, generally resembling the paralyzing disillusionments of Quentin Compson in *The Sound and the Fury*. The deepest effect is in the demonstration that the intelligent consciousness and compulsive action are separated from each other in desperate imprisonment. There grows a starved need for a reality which is non-illusory and still intelligible. Somewhere at some point there must be a fusion of meaning and action. It is this in part which endows primitivism with its force, conceiving a unity which precedes the mind's alienation from reality. Therefore the Negro and the woman, pure in physical substance, in their rich and terrible depths the pre-mental source of life, are the attracting foci of experience. They are a ferocious revelation of reality, ferocious to the degree that the mind needs reassurance.

However, in Faulkner primitive nature acts in ambivalence and can damn as well as save. It must be revealed but its revelation explains with the mythic force of original sin, the alienation of mind and spirit which is the theme of the novel. A natural crime, expressed by slavery and the Civil War, appears in history, and determines the tragedy in contemporary events. A deeper violence and tragic source is found in "bitchery," the primitive sexuality figured by the miscegenation of white and Negro, repulsive and pre-human as the mating of animals. Faulkner's Southern imagination, haunted by its experience, makes these two symbolic experiences, enslavement and miscegenation, the source of tragic suffering. When Joanna Burden and Joe Christmas, white woman and Negro, meet, the two themes fuse. Joanna Burden in her abortive, sterile life is the relic of the Civil War and her violent abolitionist ancestors. All of Christmas's experience is crossed by the sign of "bitchery." He is born the blighted creature of miscegenation. He vomits when, seven years old and uncomprehending, he witnesses the scene of intercourse from the closet in the dietician's room. He vomits again when he is told how women menstruate. His active sexual education is conducted by a prostitute, with whom he falls in love in the adolescent ordeal of disillusionment. Christmas is revolted by sex as he is revolted and persecuted by his own nature and his sources. The sex act is utterly uncompromising as the intervention of material nature in the sensibility itself, a power before which the mind has always quailed. At the same time, seen as it is, it suggests the violated ideal of love, as transcendent as its source material is base and reductive. Thus the "original sin" is sexual, the substantive pattern in a reality trauma for which the human spirit looks for compensation and relief.

Christmas has inherited nature but superimposed on the naturalistic theme is the Calvinist drama of damnation and predestination. Rising up against the sign of bitchery stands the revolted moral man, the bigot, the hater of nature. Hines and McEachern are creatures of the mind, as Calvinism might be understood as a program of the mind in revulsion from nature. We see the role of Christmas more clearly when we examine these antagonists arrayed against him. Opposed to him first is Hines, absolute in his definitions, terrorist in his means. He hates what he calls evil, and the dualism in which he fights endless war is brought to its sharpest simplicity. His knowledge is superstitious and his judgment pure prejudice. This is the fearful religious mind, the revulsion from nature reaching to madness, and the breach of mind and matter carried to an extreme.

McEachern is not mad, but he is stubborn in his hatred of what Christmas represents. He lives by an anti-natural rigidity. His life is pure form, devoid of instinct or random impulse, but as compulsive as the counter-action of the young boy. In simplistic psychological terms the superego is at war with the id, and the ego (this can be very expressive for the dichotomies already observed in the novel) is crushed out of existence by forces so extreme and unreconciled. There is no trace of reasoning or a process of judgment in McEachern. His content is mental and abstract, but his ideas are habit forms; a moral fatality has been planted in him as deep as instinct. His faith, his judgments are not his choices, they are his history.

In the major oppositions of the novel this is seen as the male principle, an abstract order prohibiting nature. Torn by his divisions, Christmas actually comes to welcome the fierce punishments of McEachern. From him he knew what to expect, the created form, the intelligible life, the light, and he prefers it to the dark, the woman, with her dangers and betrayals. His spite must vent itself on the woman, even as she comes to him with comfort and sympathy, as Mrs. McEachern does after his beatings, but in so doing representing the treachery of the passions and the body.

When the lynch mob finally faces Joe Christmas its members express again the cruel Calvinistic dualism of Hines and Mc-Eachern. This is the way Faulkner explicitly sees it. The conflict within themselves drives them to crucify him and each other, with hatred, without pity. "Pity for him, Christmas, would admit self-doubt." The moral imperative acts in blind urgency against instinct in the *manner* of instinct. In that dichotomy, the mind repelling nature in absolute fear, Joe Christmas is driven further toward destruction, lacking the means of a moral communication and reconcilement.

The ultimate executioner is Percy Grimm, a major figure in this allegory of moral conflict. He is a purified police principle, the abstracted force behind the law. His appetite for violence is fed by the punishing power; he is not primarily, however, representative of the lynch mob, which is a term for aroused social terror facing the natural outlaw. Grimm is there to keep order, as he says, to police the world. He has no mind, and a very narrow sadism for feeling, but he acts for order. The social principle made mechanical becomes militaristic, enforcing discipline without interest in values. The important symbol for Grimm is his military uniform. He does not think much about Christmas's crime, he wants an orderly process of punishment in the first place and the certainty of punishment in any case, and thereby he is the example of the morally unredeemed and mechanized conscience.

In the final episode Hightower stands helpless, surrounded by the implications of moral and spiritual degeneracy, as Grimm achieves the execution of Joe Christmas. Later, his head bandaged, sitting in deep resolving reminiscence at his window, he sees the two faces of Grimm and Christmas, joining and turning on a wheel, that symbol of time and process in the novel. To understand what has been happening conclusively we must ask what is the relationship between these three men. We must stress again the division between Hightower and Christmas, the one as outcast spirit, immobilized and sterile, the other as the black substance, the rich flow of life itself, outlawed from spirit. The death of Joe Christmas is a testament and appeal from the breach of spirit and nature.

The two faces on the wheel are a supreme violent duality of blind matter and blind inhibition separated without the resolutions of the moral intelligence. Grimm and Christmas are complements of a debased substance, force meeting force in passion and repression. A third force is needed, that of the moral will and spiritual sympathy. First there must be knowledge as Hightower is capable of knowledge, and finally, a redemptive sympathy, summoned by Hightower's vision of the "crucified shape of pity and love." Grimm, Christmas, and Hightower together close the issues at a point suggesting something possible for survival and morally meaningful as tragedy. Specifically in the theme we have followed, the only available moral consciousness in the novel has been awakened from sleep by two excruciating actions in reality, the death of Joe Christmas, the birth of Lena Grove's child.

In his death Christmas has finally met a moral awareness. He runs finally to Hightower, not knowing why he runs, knocking him down in fact, neither fighting nor surrendering. But driven and unconscious as the action is, the meaning is very clear. The only possible umpire between Christmas and Grimm, the only alternative to Hines, is Hightower, and behind him, "the crucified shape of pity and love."

* * *

What Faulkner has done in this novel is to express sharply the obsession of modern fiction with natural reality, and the search for its tolerable and accommodating meaning. Essentially he asks us to take our terms from a traditionally tragic, specifically Christian resolution. The moral consciousness finds its accommodation with nature in the mystery of resolved tragic antinomies, expressed by Christ's crucified shape. God who is mind-spirit, enters the body, suffers it, in order to inhabit it, a habitation made possible by the moral results of a reality which has been endured. Giving Joe Christmas his name makes its point, though to be sure he is a half-Christ, victimized in the flesh and history, and his death becomes a testament only when Hightower's consciousness suffers it as such. Hightower, a fallen-away spirit, perhaps a god-angel who had given man up, comes back to endow the active life of matter, dying as matter, with redemptive meaning. However, it wouldn't do to over-emphasize this or take it in its full terms. The novel supports itself with these meanings, but does not completely fulfill them. Tentative and nostalgic, more a matter of pathos than conviction, Hightower's insight is that of a broken hero, divided even from the essential act of sacrifice (that is, he is the spectator for it) which should have been the fusion of action and knowledge. Hightower remains the searching consciousness, he hears the cherished echo of a tradition, he points to it, but divided in function with Christmas as he is, and in the absence of all communication between them, the effect is closer to the piety of conscience than tragic illumination. The role given the mind and spirit is the power to bless, to redeem in consciousness and forgiveness, but not to take possession of action and reality. The high force is nature's force and the ambivalent moral intelligence (always ambivalent if it must accept and not subdue nature) has had a peculiarly modern reconciliation with it. Except for what the analogy with the crucifixion is worth, it is not a transcendence so much as a surrender or accommodation. Nature, as figured in the long rolling wheel of Lena's wagon, recovers in itself, and is intrinsically the whole of life. In the Christian sense, then, there is no transcendence. Christ, the god who is mind-spirit, enters the body it is true, but only as consciousness, not as full power. For this effect the martyrdom of Joe Christmas to a death of meaning after the incoherent violence of his life, is culminated only by a question offered to Hightower. He, the man of spirit, is not much more than a bandaged conscience brooding from his window on the scene of life.

We could say that Faulkner has written the tragedy of modern naturalism, that is, he has created a peculiar but compelling amalgam of passive determinism with the traditional function of the tragic and religious spirit. The sense of life which he records truthfully makes it impossible to present Hightower as anything more than the disengaged conscience, an intelligence that observes. Here we might say the full cycle of tragedy leaves the stage and requires the spectator intelligence to express its pity and fear. The action itself remains an enigma; suffering is the response of the sensibility, but does it have relevance, is it inherent in the order of nature? We understand clearly that the suffering of Christ was a metaphysical drama in the universe itself, as was for that matter the experience of the classic tragic hero. The gods felt it, understood it and were in fact changed by it. Hightower's consciousness, affirmative as it may seem to be at the end, remains lonely and helpless, gesturing in the direction of an incoherent world whose mystery remains intact, whose purpose is its own. Man adapts to it, or translates terms in his own mind for adaptation, but in the end, he remains outside, a puzzled, defeated agent who is capable only of pity, and the embracing gestures of his moral consciousness, which are threatened by comic irrelevance.

So one considers Hightower with his sleeves rolled up, receiving Lena's child. So we consider Bunch, Hightower's pupil, but active in the pursuit of life, who both for his ineptitude and insistence on living, is reduced to a role in comedy. Characteristically, as I have observed in the discussion of Flaubert, it is the comic theme which has the last word, but in the process moves beyond comedy to a more ambiguous function. It is Lena Grove, the impassive heroine of the folk comedy which parallels Christmas's ordeal, who must inherit the tragic seriousness which Christmas's death releases. She bears her child at the symbolic point of junction and it is Hightower who receives that birth as he receives the burden of Christmas's death.

Lena, as much as Christmas, is the agent and object of a pursuit. She sits on the creaking, pre-determined wagon, riding to her comic goal, Burch or Bunch, but sure of her purpose, serious in her real destiny. Lena contrasts with our theme of a breach between knowledge and reality, for she is a concentrated reality which needs no knowledge. Her quality is a "tranquil unreason," herself the child of nature. She accepts the fatalism in events beyond her knowledge or choice, she gives them her assent, she smiles and is at home, everywhere. She is not a self-sufficent force, she pursues a man, but she has the confidence and self-containment of nature. She accepts the inevitability of Bunch though he is not the man she has followed. She cannot be swerved or changed by disappointment. Her confidence in finding Burch, naive at first, impressive at the end, becomes clear in its meaning. The essence is the same, the particular man has changed, but only as if by so much as a single letter in his name. Her relations with Hightower and Bunch are manifold in significance. When she finds Bunch, he is a strangely transformed Burch, hungry himself for life and somewhat the surrogate for Hightower, the active principle for the latter's passive moral sensibility. He comes from his strenuous religious and working life, bare and austere as it is in its moral imperatives, to find Lena, the fecund object of his need.

Lena is the true protagonist of nature, whereas Christmas is split in his white and Negro substance and in his self-revulsion. She, like Christmas's mother, carries an illegitimate (but "natural") child. When Lena feels a birth pang the earth stirs within her. It is a Negro hut where the baby is born and Hightower, after the birth, goes outside to look toward the other hovels and senses their "rich black life." In a conversion of terms, Negro and woman, the sources of "bitchery" and damnation, are the life sources offering reconcilement. The primitive threat has become a primitive redemption, and nature triumphs, though only by the recognition of mind and spirit.

Here then in the celebration of life which seems the recompense of tragedy, the deep note of passivity follows us to the end. The effective principle in Lena, and in the union of Bunch and Lena which closes the novel, is not so much the intentional will as it is the crude (and comic) capacity for survival. Action does not start in the intelligence or imagination, but in the natural vitality of substance. Lena leads, Bunch follows. His role clarified by his association with Hightower, Bunch with his own ineptitude and clumsiness of desire follows after, whereas Lena moves by a rich strength and predestination. He is man in nature, so to speak, relatively fumbling and impotent, at odds with what he wants, rewarded at intervals and in her own good time.

"I have come too far now be dog if I am going to quit now."
"Ain't nobody ever said for you to quit."

Character
as reality:
Joseph Conrad

I

In "Heart of Darkness" Conrad conceives the human enterprise
as a kind of cardboard reality against the background of nature.
The Europeans represent the pathos of civilization, mocked for
its ingenuity as when we see the rusting carcasses of machinery
in the Congo jungle, and mocked for its aggressions as the guns
of the white men's ships point and go "pop" into the darkness.
Their cause is only an "imbecile rapacity"; they are led by the
"flabby weakeyed devil of commerce." The characteristic moral
somberness of Conrad here stresses the triviality, meanness and
inconsequence of the human adventure in the natural world.

Yet the ironic theme finds a contrasting quality in its own
extremes. Such an extreme is expressed by the bookkeeper, who
as Marlow finds him in the midst of the heat and lassitude of
general defeat, wears his immaculate collars and keeps the uni-

form and gestures of his trade. The bookkeeper sits on his stool, sharing his hut with a dying man brought in from the wilderness, and he complains for the distraction which makes him commit errors in his accounts. This grotesquerie, if it isn't madness, is admirable for its unimaginative persistence in living, defined as an occupation, so to speak, a humble and routine task. Certainly the posture is not heroic. The manager of the jungle outpost, it is observed, has come to lead the enterprise not because of his ability but because he survived whereas others died. His commonplace health was the secret of his success, and Marlow adds, "perhaps he survived because there was nothing in him." Nature rewards neither intelligence nor great faculties, but simply a vulgar talent for survival.

Marlow, and Kurtz before him, has voyaged past a margin of intelligible values, into a darkness where the human genius founders and nothing has use except the capacity for endurance. The search for innermost and outermost reality which is the dramatic frame of this story, reaches an abyss which tells men nothing but shows them the shape of their own illusions. The ultimate reality is "an implacable force brooding over an inscrutable intention." That is why Kurtz, lost before him in the darkness, has become chiefly a voice for Marlow, remembered for an idealistic eloquence which is now heard simply as rhetoric.

We feel, as we respond to Conrad's own verbal music, a melancholy which communicates the illusionary effect of language. When we hear the words in the long ruminative accents of Marlow, for instance, we also feel the encircling silence. His periods roll against their own echoes, as though the world were an empty space filled only with the human voice, disembodied in the end like Kurtz's voice.* In this sense Marlow is an in-

---

* Conrad wrote in a letter to Garnett, Sept. 16 1899: "All is illusion, the words written, the mind at which they are aimed, the truth they are intended to express, the hands that will hold the paper, the eyes that will glance at the lines. Every image floats vaguely in a sea of doubt and the doubt itself is lost in an unexplored universe of incertitudes."
We can appreciate the unity of style and theme in Conrad if we remem-

dispensable agent in this story, as he is elsewhere in Conrad's work, for he plays the crucial role of a consciousness in a field of action which resists meaning. We find this stress on the ruminative spectatorial figure significant for our theme. Knowledge takes precedence over action, though knowledge is the onlooker, and the true protagonist is implicitly the analytical modern intelligence.

Marlow's search is in symbiotic relationship to Kurtz' more extreme ordeal which has ended in silence. The search is to find Kurtz and thereby know himself, as he goes further and further beyond institutional or "rhetorical" supports, past the "monkey tricks of civilization" into the wilderness which is dark. The darkness is a metaphysical and moral incoherence and it is here that the ultimate ordeal of consciousness takes place. It is an ultimate ordeal because the supports of meaning are gone; the reality he faces here is empty.

Despite some of the atmospheric hints and allusions, the corruption of the white men and of Kurtz in the wilderness is not complexly demonic or exotically immoral. Kurtz is not a Dr. Faust who has sold himself to anti-human rites and experiences; though he has participated in the practices of savagery, that is not the chief aspect of his degeneration. We know from observing the white men along the route toward Kurtz that their major afflictions are disease and a monstrous apathy which has made them shadows. Kurtz has gone further, to the limit of self-knowledge, and his death is an expression of final awareness as he exclaims, "the Horror, the Horror."

---

ber this preoccupation with illusionary meaning. Otherwise we might be struck by a sense of melodrama in his situations and floridity, if not rhetorical unction, in his language. The recognition comes again that style in modern fiction labors to suggest the gap between intelligence and reality. Thus such writers as Hemingway and Camus stress the pathos of difficult meaning by the harsh concreteness of reportage or the numbness of sensibility, whereas Conrad (like Joyce in some of his stylistic maneuvers) stresses the voluble subjective monologue of the human voice, "floating vaguely in the universe of incertitudes."

But the Horror, which can be only obscurely communicated to Marlow, is really the compact revelation of a vision which is utterly nihilistic. "He was alone, he had kicked the earth to pieces." Being alone, he had looked into himself and into reality and had gone mad. Marlow speculates at one point that Kurtz had surrendered because there was something missing in him. Looking into himself he had found he was really hollow at the core and looking into natural reality he had found it a corresponding blank. At this point Conrad sets the ground for his moral theme, when Marlow observes, "he did not have what saves you, what brings a man back up."

To know what is missing in Kurtz we look to Marlow, who comes back from the wilderness, having gone almost as far as Kurtz. Marlow says, a man (stressing a manly courage and endurance) does not collapse in the face of Kurtz's revelation, nor does he let himself go so far as to embrace it. A man knows or guesses what Kurtz knows and restores himself with something. What is it? We very much need to know in this story; it arouses a demand for moral insight. Marlow says in his own voice, a speech which takes up Kurtz's lost rhetoric, that what saves a man and brings him back up is the "idea at whose shrine one worships."

There is nothing grandoise about Marlow's idea; no moral sublimity is expressed in it. Reduced to its essence it might be seen as his occupation, significantly the navigating of a ship in difficult water. The tattered book on navigation which Marlow finds in the wilderness is the key. Read and cherished by its owner, the mad Russian outcast, it is really the bible of civilization, plain, pragmatic, expressing the labor of survival. The ultimate concern is with survival, but not in the reductive terms expressed by the company manager, whose health is his blind natural luck. Rather the principle of survival is morally sophisticated, like Marlow himself. To navigate the ship involves labor and sacrifice, it embodies a definition of character. What a true man falls back upon there in the darkness, where the structure and the certainties of life have disappeared, is a capacity for faithfulness to the occupation of a man, that is, the craft, the discipline in nature which defines a man. The loyalty is not to a transcendent vision or command, but as Marlow says, "the devotion to an obscure, back-breaking business."

Stripped to its basis, this is a conscience without ideas at all really, without structure or pretense. The concept is that of a moral first choice, made before values themselves are defined, and its essence is a loyalty to man in the condition we find him, in his illusionary enterprises, obscurely formed and even more obscurely destined. In this sense Marlow navigates his ship loyal to an enterprise which is mysterious, surrounded by an unexplored wilderness, in search of a man whose identity is a deeper mystery and whose moral value is not merely ambiguous but suggestively monstrous. The idea of loyalty is a distillation of the conservative instinct, a sober, obstinate affirmation without reasons, expressed by devotion to one's metier, tradition and social commitment. It is a morally sensible conservatism, not complacent or obscurantist, which has emerged from the ordeal of disbelief. Realistically what has been affirmed in the wilderness is that human values have only themselves upon which to depend. At the last outpost of the voyage into reality, when human knowledge and belief are stripped bare like the decaying litter of the trading post, a choice remains. This is the choice of loyalty, the sense of honor which pulls a man up—and back to the human community which claims him.*

It is evident that loyalty receives its severe test and is itself exhibited nobly not in the context of a faith but that of severe doubt. The moral order in its last crisis requires an affirmation which is not supported by images of belief but by a tenderness for images which have become apparitions in an empty world.

---

* (Conrad's remark in his 'Familiar Preface' to A Personal Record) is clarified sufficiently in "Heart of Darkness." "Those who read me know my conviction that the world, the temporal world, rests on a few very simple ideas; so simple that they must be as old as the hills. It rests, notably, among others on the idea of fidelity."

In "Heart of Darkness," for instance, Kurtz has become a shadow in the knowledge of everyone in whose life he played a role, particularly his fiancée. That young woman, called with stress the "Intended," is perfectly innocent and illusioned, and it is evident that for her the real Kurtz is absolutely unknowable and cannot exist without changing her own essence completely. The close of the story, as Marlow visits her at her home in the setting of a western European city, is not an irrelevance nor an embellishment of pathos. The girl's illusions are grotesque, but irony is not the chief point of the scene, nor does Marlow make any effort to share the truth with her. Marlow pays his respect to her illusions, not in themselves as substance, but in the aspect of the life-giving capacity for illusion. The "Intended" has filled a void with resonant images; these are not as important (to Marlow) for what they reflect of Kurtz's reality as for what they reflect of her own. Marlow refuses to disillusion the girl for a profounder reason than its obvious and useless cruelty. He occupies an elevated moral stance in the end, far higher than that of the girl herself, and it would seem that his role is to protect her innocence. But in a sense he is protecting his own or all human innocence, as though affirming that the voyage into the darkness is a universal fate, the test of faith is universal, and the decision to return and be loyal to what the human light provides is crucial. In this story, so immensely significant for understanding Conrad's work, what is suggested is not that the function of the enlightened man is to protect specific human illusions, but rather the task of making them "real" by accepting them as motives. Values are intended values, reality is an intended reality; the function of life is to work for them. That perhaps would have been the role of a returned Kurtz, if he had been able to return, like Marlow, redeemed from his vision of the Horror. We understand this better if we refer ourselves at this point to other work by Conrad, "The Secret Sharer," for instance, where the task of Captain Leggatt is to purge himself of ambiguities and contradictions and define himself finally (we might say create himself) in the form that the world needs and in which he *wills* to know himself. In "Heart of Darkness" because of the roles assigned to Kurtz and his fiancée, and the spectatorial role of Marlow, we see a stress upon the faculty of illusion as such in its aspect of innocence and vulnerability. In *Victory*, a later work where the theme carries itself forward, it is seen rather as a great strength.

II

In *Victory* Conrad examines his principle that the beginning of an intelligible, inhabitable world is an arbitrary motive in man, expressed without support from intelligibility in nature, rather against an indifference which reads like hostility. The motive is loyalty to the strange fact of shared habitation in the universe. Lena and Heyst on their island, are surrounded by "the devouring sun, the intense blaze of the uncovered sea." "I am here," Lena says, "out of the sun," and for Heyst it is like an escape from the heat and pressure of the day to find her. She says in this passage quite clearly, "If you were to stop thinking of me, I wouldn't be in the world at all." To exist requires a communicated thought; it is not romantic love so much as necessary response which makes her existence and keeps it from separating into the elements of sea and sun. Insofar as men exist intelligibly they are like Lena with Heyst, "Swinging between the abysses of earth and heaven in the hollow of his arm."

We stress that it would be a misreading to think of this as the theme of "all for love and the world well lost." Rather it is the world well found, where love is the strongest if not the first human gesture which fills the void. In Conrad's view their love has interest not so much in the psychology of passion as in the problem of moral communication and shared identity. We are rather surprised by the form that love develops in the first place, when Heyst takes Lena to his island, helplessly, because there was nothing else to do, because she needed him and he was committed to that need. The only point of entrance, in fact, into Heyst's self-sufficiency, the disengagement which he had prepared all his life, is his sensitivity to a strong need, as we have seen in the case of his disastrous involvement with Morrison. The characteristic which Lena and Morrison have in common is the way in which their vulnerability and open suffering make a claim which must be answered.

What comes between Lena and Heyst is "the fatal imperfection of all the gifts of life," the "incompleteness not altogether overcome." And Heyst says, "What more do you want of me— the impossible I suppose." Again these words sound as if Lena and Heyst were romantics, the label chosen for Lord Jim in his own story. If they are, it is in Conrad's special meaning of the term. In a universe as empty as the sea which surrounds their island, to dream of union and to trust knowledge seem as extreme as yearning for perfection. Lord Jim dreamt of becoming a hero but the minimum he really wanted was that men know him and trust him. In Conrad's world, with men knowing their isolation and threatened by extinction, the minimum equals the maximum; it is the stake for which men fight and for which they must attest their lives as Lena and Jim do.

"The fatal imperfection of all the gifts of life" is that none of them are given except in an act of faith. The world itself exists in an act of faith, and it is threatened by the latency of distrust, the doubt that demolishes everything. The malicious voice of Stromberg intervenes between Lena and Heyst, but his voice is not a particular evil, it is general in the world and it rises to malice only in the encouraging soil of skepticism which brought Heyst to his island in the first place. Heyst is accurate in saying of the calumny produced by Stromberg in Lena's mind, "She only half disbelieves it." The half is inescapable; it pertains to a tragic limitation of knowledge.

The structure of suspense in "Heart of Darkness," Victory and Lord Jim involves the problem of knowing the true subject, human life and human character, in the heart of a mystery. The objects of this suspense, Kurtz, Lord Jim, Heyst, are men who represent problems of definition to themselves and to all observers, particularly that man of great curiosity, Marlow. Thus in the early passages of *Victory*, Heyst is introduced in contradictory aspects, from the point of view of various observers, as Spider Heyst, Hard Facts Heyst, Enchanted Heyst, Utopist Heyst. Doubt is universal because it springs from a metaphysical dilemma. Who is Heyst? The question wanders like his own existence through empty stretches of the southern sea, through obscure and inconclusive enterprises, to his small and deserted island. Doubt is universal and metaphysical, but distrust is a moral issue. The question then is translated to a moral drama, and in that process we see Conrad's imagination at its essential work.

If we examine the elements of the story we see that Heyst has acted on the premises of his metaphysical skepticism. It has led to a questioning of values, a doubt of himself and others, and a revulsion from life which has isolated him on his island. His distrust is confirmed by the corruption in human nature represented by Stromberg, Jones, and Ricardo. But these after all are close cousins to himself; they merely project the premises of distrust into action and in them it becomes malice, slander, and violence. The gentlemanly Jones is a creature of fine tastes and fine revulsions, and we see him as a distorted mirror image of Heyst, now become a cynic with an appetite for pleasure and action. Action for Heyst is degrading, for action would reduce any distinction that remained between himself and the others. Specifically it would mean, in the crisis on the island, stooping to the level of Jones and Ricardo to deal with them in the manner required to save Lena and himself. He speculates whether he was capable of throwing Lena as a victim to them simply to save his dignity, and it almost appears that he is. Looking at Jones and Ricardo he says, "You people are divorced from all reality in my eyes." To himself he says,

"They ought to have aroused my fury. Nothing is left but disgust."

The combination of his moral sensitivity and his skepticism has paralyzed him and this directs the catastrophe at the end. He surrenders to a climax of distrust when he listens to Jones, now appearing clearly as his demonic alter-ego. They both in their imaginations see the same sordid love scene between Lena and Ricardo. In a sense Heyst is right and his vision is plausible, for she has descended to the level of action, on Ricardo's terms, and from the external view the two would seem to be in the same world, as Ricardo insists and convinces himself that they are. There is more to this than a smoke screen of suspense with which Conrad indulges himself and the reader. We are led to think that action is always mysterious and ambiguous, the proper object of distrust. In the test, Lena is a martyr to action, moving toward it out of the darkness of uncertain knowledge and faith. For she has known the limitation too, looking at Heyst "with infinite concern for him whom she could never hope to understand and whom she was afraid she could never satisfy."

For Lena, action is a leap of the spirit across the void of knowledge, challenging the mystery of what she is herself doing with Ricardo, challenging her own problematic identity, and the problematic identity of Heyst. Things have gone too far for Heyst. The combination of his suspicion and circumstances have so complicated the truth that only an heroic absolute assertion could overtake him in his withdrawal from the world. We have been led to believe that Lena is in somewhat the same case; Stromberg's slander has done its work, though she is less inclined than Heyst to assign tangible values to what she has heard. Her action at the end and her consequent death are a martyring demonstration against this impasse of suspicion. We understand it as the basic moral presumption, equivalent in its way to a metaphysical gamble for the existence of God. So Lena gambles for the existence of a man she loves and can trust. By her action, she wills that Heyst should exist, that she should exist in relationship to him and feel "she was no longer alone in the world." In her death she demonstrates to Heyst that he had not been alone in the world; this is her "victory" even though it crushes Heyst with guilt, and the sense of his missed opportunity for living.

This is one of the most expressive climaxes of Conrad's writing. In a world deserted by metaphysical meaning, a moral meaning takes its place, faith substitutes for knowledge. The knowledge of reality is blocked on all sides, by the dark margin of the natural world, by the dark center of the human soul. The search for conviction may end in Heyst's paralyzing skepticism or in the void which is the "Horror" to Kurtz. But the world may be reconstructed in the moral experience, which is like a gamble against total risk in its initial or ultimate gestures. That stake may be offered in the last stages of disintegration by the act of loyalty which Marlow asserts in "Heart of Darkness," or it may be offered by Lena's act of faith, which is the dominating will that the moral reality should exist. It exists in the first place in a kind of inevitability, which Heyst can't understand and resists with his intelligence and his temperament when it confronts him in the claim made on him by Lena and Morrison. Nevertheless he must respond; the human need is like an empirical first fact which appears against the background of the enigma of the world. That reality, the mutual response of need in men huddling together in the universe, is the moral fact which is the basis for the intelligible structure of life. When men are together they gamble on the sense of reality they give each other. Conrad often expressed what experience is like when men are truly alone. We remember the suicide death of Martin Decoud in Nostromo, the gregarious skeptic whose life evaporates when he is forced into isolation on his castaway island.

> Solitude from mere outward condition of existence becomes very swiftly a state of soul in which the affectations of irony and skepticism have no place. It takes possession of the mind, and drives forth the thought into the exile of utter unbelief.

After three days of waiting for the sight of some human face, Decoud caught himself entertaining a doubt of his own individuality. It had merged into the world of cloud and water, of natural forces and forms of nature. In our activity alone do we find the sustaining illusion of an independent existence as against the whole scheme of things of which we form a helpless part. Decoud lost all belief in the reality of his action past and to come. On the fifth day an immense melancholy descended upon him palpably.

More directly to the point we remember the fatal scene in *Lord Jim* when Jim jumps from the *Patna*, and drifts on the empty ocean with the cowardly exiles, the ship's officers who have deserted the ship with him. It is significant that Jim has jumped under the guise of a man already dead—the third engineer, George, who has just died on deck of a heart attack while the others are crying from the lifeboat, " 'Jump, George. We'll catch you! Jump.' " It is Jim who jumps at the last minute, and in doing so he takes on the identity of the dead—he has made the morally negative gesture and deserted the sleeping human life on the ship.

A silence of the sea, of the sky, merged into one indefinite immensity still as death around these saved, palpitating lives. . . . "I didn't think any spot on earth could be so still," he said. "You couldn't distinguish the sea from the sky; there was nothing to see and nothing to hear. Not a glimmer, not a shape, not a sound. You could have believed that every bit of dry land had gone to the bottom; that every man on earth but I and these beggars on the boat had got drowned!"

III

Lord Jim is Conrad's clearest effort to relate a species of metaphysical reassurance with the achievement of moral character. When Jim jumps from the *Patna* he falls into a metaphysical void, a state of non-being equivalent to his loss of moral identity.

The allegorical implications are emphatic. There is the parable of the ship, the *Patna*, an almost derelict vessel carrying mankind, the pilgrims, who live on this voyage as all men live,—"urged by faith and hope of paradise," and "desiring to pray and serve God." The ship, worn by time, always on the verge of dismemberment, exists as civilization exists, in an ironic security, in the ultimate threat of the sea. We remember the litter of trade and civilization on the shore as Marlow follows the river into the "heart of darkness." The men of the *Patna* are facing death on the sea, on the verge of losing all the structures of meaning before they actually lose their lives. In this ordeal there is only a great suspense and a great fear, the God these men would have served isn't there, the hopes they have pursued are illusory. The question is what do men then do, how do they act and in terms of what values, and what is the consequent idea of themselves which remains?

Jim has been ideally formed as a man, the product of a rich tradition which has given him a full character. In this confrontation the essence of character is understood to be the power of dominating the circumstances of life with the consistent principle of one's being which defies the inconsistency of events. At this point we see that Conrad is almost unique among modern writers for his treatment of character. Without confusion, with a strong sense of the dramatic possibilities, he returns to an essentially classic definition of character as opposed to nature rather than a part of it. We know that nature represents in Conrad's view a darkness in which consciousness and purpose are lost, rather than the rich source of meaning if not inspiration from which human nature has its being. The point is that human character hasn't the equivalence of human nature. Conrad's interest is in the circle of meaning which is circumscribed and maintained by men, a civilization which is individual and general, the soil and substance of character, and which stands out against the outer darkness.

When it looks as if the *Patna* were going to sink in a few

moments, what seizes the white members of the crew is the great fear which is the last ordeal of character. We must understand the metaphysical stress of this fear. It is not merely an instinctive, biological fear—at least not with Jim as Conrad describes the event—but it is the fully imaginative despair of the formed character before the void of its own extinction. It is into this void that Jim jumps, at the mercy of the final weight of impulse or instinct. His consequent despair is the greater, not less, in survival, as Jim, in describing the event for Marlow, remembers how he sat on the tossing gunwale of the boat, longing to return to the death that had been marked for him.

Although he survives, his great fear and the moral abdication he made by it has destroyed his sense of personal being as effectively as death. Jim has faced and been forced to join "the unintelligent brutality of existence" and now is a man struggling to recreate his identity as though without any help at all, out of nothing. We can be sure that a naturalist writing at the time that Conrad produced his novel, a Zola or a Dreiser perhaps— would have paid less attention to the moral problem and more to the psychology of fear and to the transcendent actuality of death. They would have regarded nature and necessity in such awe that the novel could have only been an extension of this moment or a series of variations on its theme. But to what we might call a contrasting humanism in Conrad, instinctual, grappling fear was a surrender of humanity and not a natural reality to be regarded as definitive.

As Conrad tells the story, Jim's character or his human reality is a sharp alternative to the biological response which produced his fear. The effect of surrender to it was a deep humiliation, so deep as to be obliterating. The broken character feels disintegration in shame, and the living character is held together by ideals or values which are reflected in pride. We are reminded again of Dostoevsky's *Notes from Underground*, useful as it has been in pointing to the implications of the naturalistic theme in modern fiction. The key response of the "man from underground" to his own naturalistic insights is a deep and resentful sense of humiliation, and this consideration of his role in the universe is the clue to his pathology. The metaphysical drama becomes stirring when the question of human dignity becomes involved in its issues; the Job-like protagonist questions the superiority of a human principle to mechanistic process, the role of God's interest, the problem of justice.

These issues are confined in Conrad's story to an essential moral humanism. Without any metaphysical supports, or the reliance on super-nature, the test is whether the human principle can transcend the aimless violence of nature. We stress the condition, with an *unsupported strength,* for it is that limitation which provides the strain and exhilaration of Jim's story and makes Conrad one of the great spokesmen of modern literature.

The lost souls, who fail in the metaphysical crisis and disintegrate in nature, are the self-preservers who jumped from the ship with Jim. The fat captain is a monster of mere flesh and the instinct for survival. He is as shameless as he is physically gross, but the chief engineer, a more complex being, eventually goes mad from the experience, which is a way of describing the dissolution of character. To surrender to the fear of death is the same thing as surrendering to natural being, essentially, despite its atmosphere of exotic horror, what Kurtz had done in "Heart of Darkness." The officers of the *Patna* accept the condition of savagery. In contrast to them Jim hesitates; between staying with the ship and its passengers (as the code of the sea very strictly demands) and jumping into the boat, he is frozen in the conflict between the demands of character and the demands of nature. He jumps as a result of the thin but absolute over-balance of his fear, and the consequence is a moral defeat which he must spend the rest of his life redeeming.

We are made to understand that it is as natural as life to fear death. The French officer, one of the important minor characters who ponder Jim's experience, says in his conversation with Marlow that fear is universal, all men are born cowards. The conflict is irrepressible because character is an idealization superimposed upon the given natural elements of life. To understand this better we have offered to us, to contrast with the image of the fat, self-preserving captain, the brilliant young captain Brierly, who serves on the examining board which judges Jim. Brierly is drawn as the perfectly idealized man who lives as he imagined himself. Brierly has never made a mistake, his surface is without a crack in it, and he is capable only of the severest judgment of Jim's behavior. In his revulsion he represents exactly the terms from which Jim has departed, but in his eventual fate he further mirrors Jim's experience. In a postscript we learn that Brierly himself disintegrates suddenly and completely and commits suicide. Without supporting detail, Conrad merely tells us that Brierly was finally forced "to examine his own case." Knowing finally his own depths (by thinking a great deal of Jim's case it is implied,) he is unable to bear the discrepancy. We remember that the full confrontation of reality can be a horror. Brierly's idea of himself is like Kurtz' rhetorical eloquence; it is hollow for having evaded the essential truth. When this knowledge comes he is not prepared for it and so must collapse. "Hang ideas!" Marlow says early in the novel, in considering the problem of courage; what is wanted is "an unthinking and blessed stiffness before the outward and inward terrors, before the might of nature. . . ."

The words of the French officer are a further admonishment to the idealism or "romanticism" of both Jim and Brierly. Man is born a coward, the French officer says, courage doesn't exist except by habit or example, even as the demand of one's metier, but then, stonily pulling himself up before the possibility of misunderstanding, he points out that "honor" is real, honor does exist alongside natural cowardice. This is not defined but in the context it does not need definition. Honor is a term like fidelity which does not invite analysis, because it means simply, in the appropriate military sense, an esprit de corps, a loyalty to the human combination, the premise for all values. As the French officer says, to imagine what life would be like without it is impossible.

The French officer in his blunt stoicism retreats from the mystery of an intellectual justification for human values, even that of his own heroism in finally towing the *Patna* to shore and succeeding to the role that Jim had abdicated. But in his own words as well as his actions he controverts nihilism. His refusal to think is deceptive; it only magnifies the problem. What can support an absolute opposition to something so absolute as the natural fear of death? The simple man, like the French officer, says, "This is too fine for me, I don't think about it." Those who think, like Brierly, are already at the brink, incapacitated by what they see. But a judgment, a consideration, and a decision are implicit in the French officer's action and his words. Analysis might perhaps find an empirical morality or a racial utility in sacrificial risk, but men like the French officer cling to something else, more compelling, closer to an absolute. Honor is the postulate by which a man permanently puts aside the considerations of nature in favor of the considerations of whatever may be his creed as a man. This has support not so much in its own analysis as with the definition of its alternative. As the officer says, life is worth nothing when honor is gone. This slogan is no longer a cliché; it has rich meaning when the urgency is harsh enough.

The term "honor" contains the essence of a moral understanding in the dilemma which Jim faced. If the self is a natural self, then character, which depends on honor, is a struggle to transcend oneself. That struggle in Jim is exacerbated but also keenly illuminated by the fact that he is a "romantic" in Conrad's own use of the term. In Conrad's play on words, to be human is to be romantic, and Jim's humanity is exaggerated in the sense that like Brierly, he has stretched to the breaking point the tension between his natural being and the image of himself which he serves. He has always thought of himself as a man born to be a hero and the episode of the *Patna* has its sharpest initial pain for him, obscuring in fact the real failure, in his missing the opportunity for heroism. Since the *Patna* and its pilgrims happened to survive, he no longer thinks of the bleak silent heroism he would have won by dying unpraised with the pilgrims, but he thinks of his missed chance for glory. Perhaps his failure was precisely his need for an empirical justification for heroism, either in some chance of success in saving the pilgrims or in receiving the appropriate praise. He insists over and over again that if he had thought there was some chance of the ship's lasting beyond the crucial minute, he would have swum back to it from the lifeboat. This naiveté misses the point entirely. What was asked of him was the blank sacrifice of his life, without the prospect of a usefulness to others, much less a reward to himself. Nevertheless Jim's thirst for heroism is a needful stress, for we see that character and heroism are related and of the same essence. They are a matter of opportunities and missed opportunities; they are not given by nature but are things achieved, kept, or lost.

What he progressively feels, beyond his missed chance to be a hero, is rather his radical isolation. He is cut off from himself and other men and he is without a name, for the latter depends on the way one is considered and considers oneself. As a result everything in Jim is now concentrated on achieving a form to fill the void. In this sense he is a "romantic," because of his wish to escape the destroying insight of the *Patna*, and "become loved, trusted, admired, the legend formed around his name." But a man cannot be a legend, any more than he can remain within the limits of naturalistically circumscribed reality.

Jim's life is a profound manifestation, because as Marlow and later Stein, that sophisticated student of life, see him, he exists at the agonizing point of unbalance. Stein generalizes the case for us. Everything in nature has accuracy and harmony in a balance of colossal forces, but only man is not a masterpiece, only man is out of tune; disturbed and disturbing in the world, he does violence in search for unfulfilled ideals. Man in nature is unique as a romantic, as Jim is a romantic, and the only cure for it is death. Marlow agrees, "Yes, strictly speaking, the question is not how to get cured, but how to live." Stein gives his concluding judgment: "The way is to the destructive element submit yourself, and with the exertion of your hands and feet in the water make the deep, deep sea keep you up." . . . "To follow the dream, and again to follow the dream. . . ."

Drowning or living, tragic or successful, it is that tension between aspiration and reality which gives Jim the vital spring of his life. As Stein says, "What else is it that for you and me makes him exist?" It is the great cry for existence in Jim which gives the poignance to this, the most sympathetic if not the greatest of Conrad's works. The effort in Jim is to give full utterance to his life, to be voiced in those final words "whose ring if they could be found would shake heaven and earth."

The repeated use of the term romantic in this dialogue between Marlow and Stein is an effort to sum up Jim's case. In its own way it reflects the obsession with romanticism or the romantic experience which touched its high note in Flaubert's work and which characterizes the critical spirit of realistic fiction. Here again we have the drama of a man divided between a natural reality, for which anthropomorphically congenial terms have been utterly lost, and his irrepressible imagination, which creates the images of egocentric fulfillment. "A man that is born falls into a dream like a man who falls into the sea," Stein says. Jim is a better swimmer than Emma Bovary but he lives in a more demanding and complex dream. Emma has a tangible existence which is presented on a level separate from her consciousness, but Jim would seem to have nothing beyond the acute struggle between his images of value and the dark immanence of reality which challenges them. More perhaps than any other protagonist of modern fiction he presents the story of a profound human struggle to maintain a coherent consciousness.

The great theme is this: a man struggles for his coherent

existence in the face of an essentially incoherent order in nature. As we see Jim in the last episodes, trying to detach one part of his nature from another, one part of his life from the rest, he is a man in the naked emergency of the struggle of consciousness, trying to be reborn. His chance comes in Patusan, an isolated and primitive world, where a new beginning might seem possible. He need have no past, and it is there that Jim can create himself with his own strength. It is an heroic achievement, one that has a resounding ring in the modern imagination, as if for once a man could master his fate and dictate the terms for his social and natural life. Jim's success is the more vivid as its fragility remains apparent and its doom seems certain. He has achieved it in transient passage, in a segment of time and in a tiny corner of the world isolated from the rest. As he says, to leave Patusan would be harder than dying. As a parable of living it has sharp poignance, surrounded at both ends by a past which contradicts it and a future which will obliterate it, surrounded in space by a world which totally ignores it.

In another aspect the fragility of Jim's success is attested by its dependence on human communication. Divided as he is from an essential part of himself, he is the more dependent on recognition from the outside. He says, "I must feel every day that I am trusted." This is not merely a particular flaw, the neurotic dependency of a man who cannot truly accept himself. In the implicit view of life we take from Conrad's work, this is the basis of every achieved identity, and every coherent consciousness. It is both made possible by communication between men, and tragically limited by it, as communication is limited. Jim wants trust because trust defines character and demands its consistency. But every act of trust is under risk, it is in danger of misunderstanding, because like character it is superimposed upon an undetermined reality. In this sense the people of Patusan trust Jim but do not know him. In its last emergency trust is an act of faith which requires martyred sacrifice to make itself pure, as Lena demonstrates in the conclusion of Victory.

The love affair with Jewel, as twilight lit and flickering as any of Conrad's love stories, accentuates the theme. They were "like a knight and maiden meeting to exchange vows among haunted ruins." Jewel is a white shadowy figure and her obscurity stresses her subjective existence for Jim. Love is legendary, created out of ruins in a struggle with reality; as Marlow says, dream and reality fight in every love affair. Love is the climactic travail of subjective experience striving to make itself real.

Jewel's love generates in her a great fear and a sense of impending tragedy. What she calls the threatening "thing" is Jim's oppressive nightmare communicating itself to her. She implores Marlow to vouch for Jim's actual identity. He can't, nobody can. To live is to make the great effort to know, which finally reveals what is unknowable. Jim has simply told Jewel that the world outside has rejected him. She asks Marlow in passionate protest, "Why does the world not want him?" The answer is mysteriously but rightly, "Because he is not good enough." The judgment is general not particular at this point, as Marlow adds for illumination, "No one is good enough." No one is real enough, stable enough, strong enough to meet the ideal principle either in her mind as a lover or in the world's mind which always judges in terms of ideal principles. Jim must be compared as he exists in the legend of a lover, and as he is, a limited, inconstant, unrealized being.

To be not good enough is an echoing phrase, at the center of Conrad's theme. Marlow gives poor comfort to Jewel with generalities, but as the conscience of the reader, he may know more than this at the end. The sequence is not finished until Jim's death and his death has more meaning in it than the final silence put to his voice trying to utter his identity. This needs to be said while further accounting for his second great failure and the catastrophe it causes. As we examine the closing action we are fully absorbed into Conrad's carefully designed point of view, tentative and strained as it appears in Marlow's consciousness. It is not possible to form a definitive judgment of Jim's fate, least of all for the people close to it. Conrad marshals the versions and reports of Jim's death, joining the struggling judgments of the subordinate characters with the reminiscent narrative of Marlow. The novel is a triumph of sustained tone, and the tone is that of Marlow—of speculation and reflection, of doubt and multiple consideration, of a melancholy deepened by compassion. This is the tone of the skeptic activated by moral judgment. He wonders, is Jim a rare man who has achieved moral dignity, who has met the great test at the expense of his life? Or is he rather the pathetic creature of illusions, obsessed by fantasies of guilt and fantasies of noble courage, divided between two dreams of failure and success? Does he have the human sickness, as Stein says, separated from the harmony of nature, which does not question either the real or the possible?

To stress the pathos of Jim's case, seeing him lost in a self-destroying dream and unable to unite the separate elements of his being, would be to stress a patronizing compassion, modified by Jewel's legitimate bitterness over his desertion at the end. It would suggest the advice of a therapeutic psychology that he should have faced the truth squarely, acknowledged his early and late failures, and brought the world with him to a forgiving realism of judgment. It is clearer within Conrad's design to see Jim's conflict climbing from pathos to tragedy. Even the admonishment from Stein is anti-tragic, when he describes how a man might avoid drowning by letting the great waters of his dreaming consciousness bear him up. The ordeal of tragedy is to test the depth of the water. As Stein clearly says, in all nature which is a success, only man is a failure, whose likely fate is drowning. Jim's existence was designed to exhibit the limits of fate. As tragedy it towers in the background of every partial success.

In the context it would not be anything but sentimental to imply that for Jewel or the people of Patusan, the whole truth about Jim would have been acceptable, that her love and their trust made no absolute demands. As Jim knows, this is self-deception. In the trap in which he has been caught, the demand has become absolute. As he says to her, and he is not being grandiose, if he should fail to confront old Doramin for judgment, "I should not be worth having." There is no escape, not even in the forgiving power of love, for a man in conflict between his failures and the image of himself for which, in the end, he must give up everything.

For the greatest human failures there are no definitive solutions. They are rather austere inevitable phenomena which spring from a dilemma too profound to be fully described and for which prescriptions, if they are offered, only subtract from the dignity of the tragic point of view. Jim's culminating failure has been rooted in his whole life, but is the direct sequence of the affair of the *Patna*. He releases Brown and his sordid band of outcasts, essentially resembling the motley deserters from the *Patna*, because he cannot deal with his earlier guilt. Jim identifies himself with the adventurers who have invaded the peace of Patusan; unable to face them directly or deal with them simply, he allows them to escape because he wishes them to disappear. We remember the similar inertia in Heyst when he faced Jones and the invaders of his island. Jim is still his secret's victim and Brown in his shrewd and reductive psychological insight brings it out. But in letting them go, he has allowed treachery, cowardice, and destruction to be liberated in the world, like the bad contents of Pandora's box, and this has its inevitable consequences. Again we recall the *doppelgänger* relationship between Heyst and Jones in *Victory* and between Marlow and Kurtz in "Heart of Darkness." This is not so much the duality of good and evil as the contrast between man morally formed and man unformed. Jones, Kurtz and Brown come from the mean chaos of nature and the others are forced to share in them. Identified with Brown as he is, Jim has caused the death of his best friend and has betrayed the people who trust him. It is clearer, looking at Brown, or remembering Jones, that the dark secret is not something that one easily comes to household terms with, that requires only confession or repent-ance for its release. Rather it is a haunting reality that refuses to be purged either in common sense therapies or in the tradi-tional climaxes of dependence on God. The sense of evil in Conrad is tragic, therefore mysterious and unassailable, and its occasion seems deeply inevitable within the scheme of the universe.

However, if defeat in tragedy has over-awing implications, so do its austere compensations. Jim's death has a special kind of heroism which he did not anticipate in the long regretful dreaming of his life which was the interlude between the *Patna* and Patusan incidents. By accepting death and judgment at the hands of Doramin he proves that in the face of all apparent denials, even the disbelief of those who witness his death, he can remain faithful to the idea of himself and to the people for whose good opinion he lived. He says, "I must stick to their belief in me." This is a demonstration of irony, for their belief is gone and will not be salvaged by his offering. The situation is an ironic return to the problem of the *Patna*, where heroism seemed offered as only a gesture to himself.

The bareness of the gesture is stressed by the fact that at the end Jim's sacrifice is a pure act of will, the arbitrary moral gesture, because nature is impervious to moral gestures. In the crucial case, the moral community itself will remain uncon-scious and unrewarded for the gesture. If it depended on recognition and reward there would be a limitation drawn on the area of moral action, but character, in Conrad's strong dramatic insight, is absolute and ends only with life. The re-vengeful bitterness and suspicion which surround Jim's last action are a symbolic moral confusion. With the facts available to support it, that confusion surrounds the scene of moral action, ready to invade it at all points. Perhaps, in the diminished prac-tical and rational significance of his act, all Jim can achieve here is the bare claim to remain in touch. The conclusion rather simply is that a man cannot run away from the commitment which is his character. By this we understand again that a man does not find being in his bare natural existence, nor in his ideal character which is never really achieved, but as martyr to the struggle between the two. His death is a sacrifice to the cause of character; failing to hold it in the eyes of others, uncertain of it in his own eyes, he carries it forward to the last act possible for himself, he dies to attest the effort, which is the whole point.

When Marlow's narration is interrupted after describing his last visit to Jim and before he learns the end of the story, the case had been presented for a triumph, apparently the story of a man who had regained himself and recreated his life on his own terms. One of his anonymous listeners, as if in prophecy of the end, objects. This observer would not admit that Jim had mastered his fate. For him Jim remained the romantic egoist, isolated in his image of himself. It was self-created, self-perpetuated and built upon a hidden contradictory secret. What made it hopeless and something like a mental disease was its fatal isolation. He had been cut off from his necessary supports. This sober member of Marlow's audience asserts that character, or the mastery of one's fate, required a racial, historical basis— "a strength at our backs." This is clearly stated and is the heart of the conservative principle which weighs so much in Conrad's thinking. "A man is rooted in the land from which he draws his strength, the faith together with his life." And "Woe to the stragglers. We exist only as we hang together." In this plausible concept character is a mold; it pre-exists the individual in the presence of his own people, his own language and tradition, and it survives only in connection with them.

This has the value of only partial insight, though the conclusion of Jim's life does so much to support its truth. It does not perceive the essential case. As Marlow says, in answer, "The point, however, is that of all mankind Jim had no dealings but with himself, and the question is whether at the last he had not confessed to a faith mightier than the laws of order and progress." The moral drama reaches beyond a dialogue between a man and his inherited values. The ultimate and universal case is in the dilemma of the straggler. Behind the racial and historical supports which conceal it from most men there is the blank border which has no explanations or affirmations to make, and which tells a man that whatever he may be in the social intelligence which identifies him, his beginning has been a zero in silent space. It is the true threat of an end, a crisis like that of the *Patna*, which reveals that beginning. Jim's pure, unsupported effort to recreate himself is representative of the initial action whereby the species made itself human. It is the first movement without any discernible help or instruction which says, "I am." The naked effort to assume a moral consciousness is all that Jim affirms in his death, but in that sense it is the greater heroism; he dies in the first step which creates the ideal fiction, that socialized romance which gives intelligibility to ordinary lives.

Behind the whole drama in the first place is of course the problem of reality. Conrad's metaphysics is dark and skeptical. The natural world as soon as it is approached on the margin of the civilized order is a mystery, and when the effort is made to uncover it, the result is to discover the mystery in oneself and perhaps set free the chaotic forces which disintegrate all sense of meaning. Like Kurtz, it is not so much a horrible degradation, or moral disgrace, which faces Jim at the heart of his own mystery but rather the nihilism of nature. In Conrad intelligible reality is identity, that is, something wrested from chaos and darkness; it is the purely human. Reality is character, there is no other reality; it has a profoundly moral basis because it is a reality which depends on the human code and most of all on the primary act of human communication. The skeptical naturalism in Conrad's thinking is as persistent and perhaps more fully realized than in the work of other modern writers; his sense of the solipsistic threat is as keen as that of Flaubert or Joyce. There is something classically inspiring, however, in his stress on the moral effort to transcend solipsism which contrasts with the neo-scientific effort, masking as the neo-esthetic, which characterizes his much more influential peers. Perhaps the implicit humanism of Conrad's work will one day be accepted as the more significant vision. He says, quite simply, there is nothing else except what we do ourselves, or have had done for us by human ancestors. There is only the human enterprise, even in its ruins, like Heyst brooding over naturalistic and historical defeat on his deserted island. A light shines for the skipper Davidson when he passes the island to tell him that Heyst is still there. That light is again reflected in its austere and flickering reassurance from Lord Jim's existence, as when Marlow says goodby to him for the last time, and the figure in the white suit disappears, "the white figure in the heart of a vast enigma."

The naturalist theology
of D. H. Lawrence

The modern artist inherits before everything else the problem of his own sensibility. As an artist he knows that his vocation requires a vitalized perception of life. As a modern artist he makes his career with a continuing suspicion of conventional knowledge and the conventional sensibility. Since the period of romanticism it would be fair to say that the artistic sensibility has lived in something like a state of permanent revolution. In a sense the artist was at the center of a quarrel between those who cast the greatest doubt on an orthodox, rationalistic sensibility, and those who cast more suspicion on the private consciousness. The major effect perhaps was to place both in great insecurity, with the artistic sensibility free to draw a sanction where it chose.

When we consider the work of D. H. Lawrence we must observe the lively endurance of that aspect of the romantic tradition which positively affirmed the private sensibility. Whatever the doubt thrown on the capacity of the subjective intelligence to enclose the world, it was the ultimate knower of that world. The consequence was that the greater skepticism was focused on the official knowledge of collectivities, the vestigial arts, moralities, and religions in which by formula illusions standardized themselves. Perhaps more telling was the fact that the artist had to conceive himself as the rival of the scientist, the purveyor of the only form of collective knowledge which had unchallenged prestige. If it was the value of the sensibility as such which was at stake, as in art, then it was obvious that the richer, vital sensibility was the individual sensibility. In fact, in its aspect as the "creator," this instrument was set permanently at odds with an established collective sensibility, an incrustation of values and beliefs which had become institutions rather than truth. (In a real sense, the modern artist has to substitute for a church.) The dramatic loss, of course, was the attrition of a collectively accepted metaphysics and the super-reality of a God whose immanence touched all minds. The world persisted by habit. Without faith, convention is the skeletal structure of principles which survive, and which are used to keep a world of discourse and action alive. In a word, the sensibility in a true sense is dead, and conventions become the detritus to be swept aside in its re-awakening.

His art for D. H. Lawrence, like so many of his contemporaries and predecessors, was first of all a destructive process. He had to ensnare the conventional sensibility, attack and shatter it, if necessary confronting a void in its place. But Lawrence, of all modern writers, was the one least afflicted by defeatism and nihilism. His writing was controlled by an affirmative revelation; no one can mistake Lawrence's motive to teach and spread a gospel. His mission was nothing less than to restore the value of life, and his first goal was to rediscover or re-awaken the primary human sensibility. As he says in his characteristic essay on Fenimore Cooper, "To open out a new wide area of consciousness means to slough off the old consciousness. The old consciousness has become a tight-fitting prison for us, in which we are going rotten."

Searching for a new sense of life, Lawrence drives to penetrate consciousness at its source. He enters the physical body but does not stop at the brain, or at the nerve endings, but goes deeper to reach what we might call the visceral sensibility, where the awareness of life is found at the vital centers. This is Lawrence's base of strength for his quarrel with an "old consciousness," a consciousness which has conquered the exterior senses and the brain and must be overthrown by a violence from within.

A story like "The Blind Man" is explicit in illustrating our initial theme. Maurice's blindness is a blessing because at the start it gives freedom from a cerebral or visual sensibility. "He seemed to know the presence of objects before he touched them." Maurice has "the sheer immediacy of blood contact." His victory has been total over the fragmentizing superficial sensibility represented by his antagonist, Bertie. Bertie is one of Lawrence's sick people. He is dead at the center, and this is expressed characteristically in the manifestation of his sexual incapacity and his excessive mental consciousness. Bertie can't bear the natural communion of bodies; he shudders at physical contact, and when he is forced to touch Maurice's wounded eyes he feels he is undergoing destruction. This has its own sense of being true, for the structure of his personality, which is a superficies of eye and mind, is being broken. Bertie's consciousness is a false existence, one which defends him against his own truth and that of others.

Lawrence's fiction moves from sardonic humor to rage against the perversion of life by the false sensibility. As a whole Lawrence is repetitious in his themes, but never more so than in this respect. A more extreme portrait than Bertie in "The Blind Man," Mr. Massy in "Daughters of the Vicar" is a creature formed in the mind and composed essentially of mental functions. He is a formula of convention, intellect and rational Christianity; although his life is given up to the performance of good deeds, yet he is inhuman in proportion to that effort. It is not his goodness which makes him inhuman, but the pervasive quality of abstraction in it and all his thoughts and actions. In this view Mr. Massy, as a pre-eminently rational man, has been manufactured; he is what he is supposed to be by the dictates of reason and convention. His goodness is chiefly decorum, his justice abstract, his success determined chiefly by external standards. He is essentially the manipulation of his own being, now in its vital nature either desiccated or buried behind its mask.

What is evident here is a dramatic distinction between character and nature, as meaningful for the topics of Lawrence's writing as the distinction made by Conrad, but of course reversed in its standpoint. To Lawrence character is the mask or artifice which substitutes for nature and therefore denies a valid life. To Conrad character is the saving artifice or human construct, which in the midst of the threatening void of nature offers a meaningful life. The contrast is absorbing and in its polarity we may observe the significant intellectual struggle which lies within the modern search for values.

The inherited concept of fallen natural man, so strong in the Protestant West, must play some role in this sharp division and old debate, but it would be perhaps as plausible to point to a sophisticated elaboration of the distinction between the animal and the man inherent in the modern biological and social sciences. In dealing with nature and human experience, a rationalistic naturalism is ultimately as dualistic in implication as the traditional Christianity which defined an opposition between material nature and spirit. The dominant historical empiricism of the nineteenth century asserted that civilization and mental life are the fulfillment of undeveloped possibilities in organic matter. But in its view all organic distinctions are distinctions of growth; the key issue was the relation between the stages of growth. What meaningful or value-bearing relationship could there be between a modern man and a crayfish? What could there be between him and his hominid ancestor of pre-historic life? And further and conclusively, what could there be between him and his own cellular, instinctual substance? The relationship was necessarily one of guarded, patronizing study and control, the relationship of master and slave essentially, with the threat of a reversal implicit, or rather predestined, in the natural cycle. The myth of science is profoundly dualistic after all; we see it expressed by the early story of Frankenstein and his monster, by the contemporary image of the scientist liberating the energy to destroy the world, or the deeper modern mythology of the wars between the superego and the id. As a prophetic and religious writer, Lawrence is enrolled in those wars, but dedicated to a synthesis of value which would reconcile vital being with the consciousness which inhabits it.

An early story of violence gives the landscape of battle, with emphasis upon the war between master and slave. "The Prussian Officer" presents a neurotic confrontation between the passive orderly and his sadistic officer in which the allegory is one of tight military control threatened by an inner explosion. The tension preceding the crime, the murder, the flight of the murderer are the symbolic actions for the breakdown of the cerebral consciousness and its controls. We are reminded of a typical crisis psychology in modern fiction; Joe Christmas in *Light in August* and Meursault in *The Stranger* are examples. Violence expresses a war between a structured, formal, if not conventional consciousness, and an internal sensibility which forces a breakthrough.

The larger action in "The Prussian Officer" is on a level below the articulate consciousness; remarkably few words are exchanged and very few overt issues defined. The boy on the one hand seems open and liberated, he moves naturally, and expresses his physicality with every feature and gesture. The very heat of the body thus communicated is a torment to the captain for it awakens the repressed vital sensibility within him. He is rigid where the boy is loose, bound tight in the discipline of his body while the boy is soft and vulnerable. They move in attraction and repulsion on the level of organic violence, and though we imagine the captain's mental control, the narrowing of focus puts the conflict in terms of abstract physical states, hard versus soft, cold versus warm. There are only two people in this world locked in engagement, and the struggle is skin to skin, bone to bone. The body transcends everything in our view, and we must read the psychological complexities in the shadowy pantomime of the body.

Narrative structure and style are dictated accordingly. The dramatic rhythm of the story describes the buildup of tension, the climax of release and the wasted, stupefied state of emptying. The following episode should be quoted at length to stress the pattern.

> He rode all the evening, then came straight into supper. His orderly was out. The officer sat with his long, fine hands lying on the table, perfectly still, and all his blood seemed to be corroding.
>
> At last his servant entered. He watched the strong, easy young figure, the fine eyebrows, the thick black hair. In a week's time the youth had got back his old well-being. The hands of the officer twitched and seemed to be full of mad flame. The young man stood at attention, unmoving, shut off.
>
> The meal went in silence. But the orderly seemed eager. He made a clatter with the dishes.
>
> . . . .
>
> The orderly took his hands full of dishes. His master was standing near the great green stove, a little smile on his face, his chin thrust forward. When the young soldier saw him his heart suddenly ran hot. He felt blind. Instead of answering, he turned dazedly to the door. As he was crouching to set down the dishes, he was pitched forward by a kick from behind. The pots went in a stream down the stairs, he clung to the pillar of the banisters. And as he was rising he was kicked heavily again and again, so that he clung sickly to the post for some moments. His master had gone swiftly into the room and closed the door. The maid-servant downstairs looked up the staircase and made a mocking face at the crockery disaster.

The officer's heart was plunging. He poured himself a glass of wine, part of which he spilled on the floor, and gulped the remainder, leaning against the cool, green stove. He heard his man collecting the dishes from the stairs. Pale, as if intoxicated, he waited. The servant entered again. The Captain's heart gave a pang, as of pleasure, seeing the young fellow bewildered and uncertain on his feet, with pain.

"Schöner!" he said.

The soldier was a little slower in coming to attention.

"Yes, sir!"

The youth stood before him, with pathetic young moustache, and fine eyebrows very distinct on his forehead of dark marble.

"I asked you a question."

"Yes, sir."

The officer's tone bit like acid.

"Why had you a pencil in your ear?"

Again the servant's heart ran hot, and he could not breathe. With dark, strained eyes, he looked at the officer, as if fascinated. And he stood there sturdily planted, unconscious. The withering smile came into the Captain's eyes, and he lifted his foot.

"I—I forgot it—sir," panted the soldier, his dark eyes fixed on the other man's dancing blue ones.

"What was it doing there?"

He saw the young man's breast heaving as he made an effort for words.

"I had been writing."

"Writing what?"

Again the soldier looked him up and down. The officer could hear him panting. The smile came into the blue eyes. The soldier worked his dry throat, but could not speak. Suddenly the smile lit like a flame on the officer's face, and a kick came heavily against the orderly's thigh. The youth moved a pace sideways. His face went dead, with two black, staring eyes.

"Well?" said the officer.

The orderly's mouth had gone dry, and his tongue rubbed in it as on dry brown paper. He worked his throat. The officer raised his foot. The servant went stiff.

"Some poetry, sir," came the crackling, unrecognizable sound of his voice.

"Poetry, what poetry?" asked the Captain, with a sickly smile.

Again there was the working in the throat. The Captain's heart had suddenly gone down heavily, and he stood sick and tired.

"For my girl, sir," he heard the dry, inhuman sound.

"Oh!" he said, turning away. "Clear the table."

"Click!" went the soldier's throat; then again, "click" and then the half-articulate:

"Yes, sir."

The young soldier was gone, looking old, and walking heavily.

The officer, left alone, held himself rigid, to prevent himself from thinking. His instinct warned him that he must not think. Deep inside him was the intense gratification of his passion, still working powerfully. Then there was a counter-action, a horrible breaking down of something inside him, a whole agony of reaction. He stood there for an hour motion-less, a chaos of sensations, but rigid with a will to keep blank his consciousness, to prevent his mind grasping. And he held himself so until the worst of the stress had passed, when he began to drink, drank himself to an intoxication, till he slept obliterated.

· · · · · · ·

The orderly had gone about in a stupor all the evening. He drank some beer because he was parched, but not much, the alcohol made his feeling come back, and he could not bear it. He was dulled, as if nine-tenths of the ordinary man in him were inert. He crawled about disfigured. Still, when he thought of the kicks, he went sick, and when he thought of the threat of more kicking, in the room afterwards, his heart went hot and faint, and he panted, remembering the one that had come. He had been forced to say, "For my girl." He was much too done even to want to cry. His mouth hung slightly open, like an idiot's. He felt vacant, and wasted. So, he wandered at his work, painfully, and very slowly and clumsily, fumbling blindly with the brushes, and finding it difficult, when he sat down, to summon the energy to move again. His limbs, his jaw, were slack and nerveless. But he was very tired. He got to bed at last, and slept inert, relaxed, in a sleep that was rather a stupor

than slumber, a dead night of stupefaction shot through with
gleams of anguish.[1]

Implicitly the rhythm in this narration is perhaps sexual,
certainly it is an organic pattern which supports the dramatic
dominance of the vital organs. Actually Lawrence's fiction is
episodic in structure rather than dramatic. His stories don't
point toward a pyramidal conclusion, but rather make cyclical
patterns of tension and release in a series like that of natural
recurrence.*

The style, as expressed in this passage, opposes the dominance
of mental control. The characteristic effect of Lawrence's writing is an apparent spontaneity in the inventive flow. His language seems to move without molding and consideration. The
syntax becomes transparent, energetically declarative, staccato
in brevity. We notice the absence of complex, conditioning
phrases. The language and syntax reflect action and immediate
experience, stripped free of the secondary mind as much as
possible. The climaxes of action are actually accompanied by
climaxes of inarticulacy, like the "click" in the soldier's throat.

Sensation itself is stunned by violence. "He felt blind"; "His
face went dead." Or to further touch inexpressible immediacy,
the climaxes of style transcend sensation metaphorically and
mingle the sensibility with the natural world. The officer's
blood "seemed to be corroding." His hands "seemed to be full
of mad flame," or again, "The officer's tone bit like acid."

We see that the style and the point of view serve the cause
of dramatic immediacy, and yet it is one of the curious effects

1 "The Prussian Officer," *The Tales of D. H. Lawrence*, Heinemann,
pp. 14–17.

* Lawrence makes his own comment briefly in the prefatory note to
Women in Love. "In point of style, fault is often found with the continual,
slightly modified repetition. The only answer is that it is natural to the
author; and that every natural crisis in emotion or passion or understanding
comes from this pulsing, frictional to-and-fro which works up in culmina-
tion."

of Lawrence's writing and not the least compelling, that he should keep himself very much alive in his work. Lawrence's way of breaking through the screen of authorship is to present his own consciousness, liberated with that of his characters and seeming to move only at the direction of events. His gift as a novelist was a sensibility incapable of detachment. We might say that Joyce and Flaubert remove the embarrasing intervention of the author by not allowing themselves to be detected in the work, while Lawrence will not allow himsef to be detected apart from it. If he preaches against the mind's pictorial version of experience—and against analysis—his own practice is in harmony. The sensibility he gives his characters, for instance, is a poetic sensibility brought to excess. It removes abstract distance entirely, subject fuses with object, object penetrates the subject. When we see a woman among flowers, she is not merely observing them, she is absorbed by them, or rather, they have entered her consciousness and have become, as flowers, a part of her sensate being.

Slowly she went down one path, lingering, like one who has gone back into the past. Suddenly she was touching some heavy crimson roses that were soft as velvet, touching them thoughtfully, without knowing, as a mother sometimes fondles the hand of her child. She leaned slightly forward to catch the scent. Then she wandered on in abstraction. Sometimes a flame-coloured, scentless rose would hold her arrested. She stood gazing at it as if she could not understand it. Again the same softness of intimacy came over her, as she stood before a tumbling heap of pink petals. Then she wondered over the white rose, that was greenish, like ice, in the centre. So, slowly, like a white, pathetic butterfly, she drifted down the path, coming at last to a tiny terrace all full of roses. They seemed to fill the place, a sunny, gay throng, She was shy of them, they were so many and so bright. They seemed to be conversing and laughing. She felt herself in a strange crowd. It exhilarated her, carried her out of herself. She flushed with excitement. The air was pure scent.

Hastily, she went to a little seat among the white roses, and sat down. Her scarlet sunshade made a hard blot of colour. She sat quite still, feeling her own existence lapse. She was no more than a rose, a rose that could not quite come into blossom, but remained tense. A little fly dropped on her knee, on her white dress. She watched it, as if it had fallen on a rose. She was not herself.[2]

In the same hunger for a naturalistic immediacy, the sensibility moves in a stream; it has fluid rather than architectural form. Emotions for instance are immediate and strong but they have no descriptive finality. They are not meant to be calculations of attitude or character, but reflections from the passing dream of sensate existence. Lovers characteristically move between the extremes of emotion, and consistency is not their problem. An expressive passage is the description of the early days in the marriage of Will and Anna Brangwen in *The Rainbow*. Only Lawrence it seems could manage such quick transitions as the following:

His soul only grew the blacker. His condition now became complete, the darkness of his soul was thorough. Everything had gone: he remained complete in his own tense black will. He was now unaware of her. She did not exist. His dark passionate soul had recoiled upon itself, and now, clinched and coiled around a centre of hatred, existed in its own power. There was a curiously ugly pallor, an expressionlessness in his face. She shuddered from him. She was afraid of him. . . .

The change follows in two rapid pages of narration:

He rose and went out of the house, possessed by the evil spirit. It tortured him and wracked him, and fought in him. And whilst he worked, in the deepening twilight, it left him. Suddenly he saw that she was hurt. He had only seen her triumphant before. Suddenly his heart was torn with compassion for her. He became alive again, in an anguish of compassion. He could not bear to think of her tears—he could not

2 "Shadow in the Rose Garden," *The Tales of D. H. Lawrence*, Heinemann, p. 130.

bear it. He wanted to go to her and pour out his heart's blood to her. He wanted to give everything to her, all his blood, his life, to the last dregs, pour everything away to her. He yearned with passionate desire to offer himself to her, utterly.

Both hate and love have more accurate emotional definition in Lawrence than literary conventions usually allow. However, it is not the rapidity of transition of extreme emotions so much as their quality of an absolute seizure which is characteristic, and illustrates Lawrence's sensitivity to immediate experience and his refusal to condition it according to the self-conscious restraints of character. Character in Lawrence, we must finally observe, is extremely volatile, and it is questionable whether character in the conventional literary sense exists at all in much of his writing, particularly *The Rainbow* and the short stories. Character opposes itself to the flux of natural experience; it tends to be restrictive and a definition of fixed judgments. In a word, character is an abstraction, and the level of experience which interests Lawrence precedes all abstractions.

The actual power on Lawrence's writing is Dionysian in the sense Nietzsche made current; the personality breaks out of its mold and mingles in the vital stream of being. The dramatic process is a breakthrough, the intellectual and social sensibility is swept aside, and the structure of character is dissolved and replaced by something else. We understand this external emphasis on character better if we remember the highly socialized English background of most of Lawrence's work. His people are made to confront distinctions which define them from the outside and condition their value, those of class predominantly. Thus in "Daughters of the Vicar" Alfred, in loving Louisa, faces the social abstractions which keep him inferior. Lovers thus separated know their chief enemy, the censoring inhibiting force of the exterior sensibility. The vitalism of the body has then a revolutionary role. Sex is the great liberator which truly declares men free and equal for its revolts against the abstract distinctions which condition personal value. It substitutes for political liberation, but we may go further with Lawrence and say that it substitutes for a metaphysical liberation, like that principle of Christianity which promised men an ultimate divine equality. The vital force is in all men, all those not yet killed by abstraction, and it is the source for them of a redemptive self-justification. The value so discovered at the very basis of living is absolute, it is subject to no dependencies or conditions except its own release into action.

I think we can see here why a deeply convinced and clearheaded religionist like Eliot would call Lawrence's work diabolical. There is no threat to divine theology like that of a naturalistic theology. Both are concerned with the transcendence of a temporal secular identity. The immortal soul released from the body was a shadow of its old self—presumably what it felt chiefly was its unity with the divine substance. Similarly the incarnate body is released *below* the distinguishing features of the personal identity. Its important existence is in universal natural substance, understood as ineffable. Passion is the instrument of a naturalistic grace, and its violence is directed essentially at character, which occupies the seat of judgment, choice, and limitation. In an ironic sense we must observe that character replaces the role of the body in traditional supernatural theology, where it is the body that is the mark of separation, the fall from divine unity, and it is the body which must be surpassed to regain it. In Lawrence we can say that character is the mark of the fallen man, insofar as it is the climax of a self-consciousness, founded on the sense of separation and the responsibilities of private choice. Therefore passion is opposed to character; it means its death. It wants to erupt into the great formless stream of experience where the human agent is absorbed beyond his powers of resistance or judgment. The vital sensibility is profoundly passive and ultimately selfless; that is why it can offer an apotheosis for the personality that approximates the religious.

The Rainbow, written at the height of Lawrence's maturity,

gives perhaps the most extended demonstration of these principles, particularly the submergence of character in the great
stream or tide of life which carries the generations of the
Brangwens. When climactic passion arises, persons become
secondary, definition is blurred, as when Lydia Lensky receives
Tom Brangwen as her lover. "She did not know him, only she
knew he was a man come for her." He feels the same imperson-
ality; "He was watching her, without knowing her, only aware
underneath of her presence."

The passion which seizes Will Brangwen in his love for Anna
is his fatality. He sees her and she is his, he knows. It is a
divinity which seizes *him*, he does not choose or search for it.
The quality of a religious revelation is as explicit as it can be
in this passage:

> Will Brangwen went home without having seen his uncle.
> He held his hot face to the rain, and walked on in a trance.
> "I love you, Will, I love you." The words repeated themselves
> endlessly. The veils had ripped and issued him naked into the
> endless space, and he shuddered. The walls had thrust him
> out and given him a vast space to walk in. Whither, through
> this darkness of infinite space, was he walking blindly? Where,
> at the end of all the darkness, was God the Almighty still
> darkly seated, thrusting him on? "I love you, Will, I love you."
> He trembled with fear as the words beat in his heart again.
> And he dared not think of her face, of her eyes which shone,
> and of her strange, transfigured face. The hand of the Hidden
> Almighty, burning bright, had thrust out of the darkness and
> gripped him. He went on subject and in fear, his heart gripped
> and burning from the touch.

This is a compulsion, a graced passivity; our attention in the
process has been lifted not only from Will's power of choice,
but even his particular sensibility in the experience. We are
directed to a larger design of force which has been brought
into circuit with him.

In these deeply characteristic passages we read the language
of animism, a new anthropomorphic communication with

nature which penetrates the solipsistic barrier and releases human awareness from subjectivity. We remember in this confrontation of lovers, the ecstatic and convincing scene of Will and Anna harvesting corn together in the moonlight. In that scene the moon is a force like magic, the moon *is* passion, and absorbed with it is the sharp hiss of the mingling corn.

> There was only the moving to and fro in the moonlight, engrossed, the swinging in the silence, that was marked only by the splash of sheaves, and silence, and a splash of sheaves. And ever the splash of his sheaves broke swifter, beating up to hers, and ever the splash of her sheaves recurred, monotonously, unchanging, and ever the splash of his sheaves beat nearer.
>
> Till at last they met at the shock, facing each other, sheaves in hand. And he was silvery with moonlight, with a moonlit, shadowy face that frightened her. She waited for him.

The divine being will have immanence; so nature has immanence in proportion to the concreteness and immediacy with which it reveals itself. Within the confusion of questioned abstractions, the sense of life itself begins to depend on the proportion of actuality or "thingness" in experience, as we have seen in other expressive examples of modern fiction. As we considered it in the work of Hemingway, for instance, the compulsion toward concreteness is a way of stabilizing an insecure mental consciousness, or the path of healing for troubled minds. In Lawrence the effort goes further in its implications. The concentration upon the physical scene makes a dramatic arrest of the conceptual mind and drowns it in sensate consciousness. The ordinary tools of description and analysis won't do, and we find ourselves eventually in an area of mystery.

The point is that the hunger for immediacy or concreteness in Lawrence defines itself clearly as the search for a metaphysical or absolute security in experience. The physicality of experience is divinized, it extends its intensity to a transcendent meaning. The vital sensibility is not really animal and half-conscious, though it might simulate that condition, but it is really as Lawrence expresses it a poetic sensibility, if not a religious one, which strives to express the intangible and include the largest area of implication within the direct scene. This area out of shadow is seen by the third eye of vision, as Lawrence calls it in his long story "St. Mawr." The third eye denotes the profundity of the vital sensibility, a level of knowledge which exceeds the dimensional vision of the intelligence. All the senses compile themselves into a sixth sense, or the third eye, in the attempt to penetrate immediate being, which in the end appears as mysterious or mystical as a supernatural essence. Whatever the sensibility may be, vital, rational, or spiritual, it has the need to extend itself as well as purely realize itself in particulars. The purest unextended moment of sensation would be a pinpoint approaching blindness. If extension is refused in ordinary conceptual terms, then it may occur in symbolic or metaphoric terms, where images touch the shadowland of universal essences. The sensibility thus extended might use terms like "darkness," "flame," and "deep," so characteristic in Lawrence's language, or finally in a surpassing image, it may resort to the oxymoron, like "the flame of darkness," tropes which bear the familiar usage of mysticism.

We have seen therefore that by the avenues of passion and sensation, the vital sensibility moves toward totality or the absolute in Lawrence's apocalyptic writings. We realize its neo-religious function when it transcends the barrier of personal knowledge and identity. The threat of solipsism has been overcome in proportion as the self-defining limits of the cerebral sensibility have been surpassed. Thoughts distinguish between mine and thine but passions and sensations either combine with their rivals or destroy them. When the vital rather than the intellectual centers of the sensibility are touched, the way is open for asserting that experience is unitary and that consciousness is the equivalent of being. So far then the modern intellectual dilemma can be said to have led one writer, Lawrence, to his own form of vitalism and primitivism.

It was predestined that Ursula Brangwen, the focus of the family history of the Brangwens, should have found botany her one meaningful study at college. In the midst of the sham of her general education, Ursula looks into the microscope and sees the living cell. She has approached the starting point, the irreducible life, and in it she sees the essence of her own being. "To be oneself was a supreme gleaming triumph of infinity." The naturalist theology thus gives its revelation. The cell is a metaphor for immanent being, the point of arrival beyond classification, analysis and complication of function. Since the cell is irreducible (as it appears to Ursula at any rate) it has the indispensable attribute of the divine. It has been found in the microscope while previously it could not be seen. The revelation of unitary being is finally featureless and a mystery. The cell which Ursula sees has perfect immediacy and clarity, existing in the little circle of light under the microscope, but its true being comes from the "dark." It is a messenger from the "underlife," in Lawrence's language, whereas the "overlife" consists of illusionary forms. The conventional sensibility of the mind lives in the world of forms, and has in fact created them. But the inner sensibility, the vital consciousness, is in touch with the "dark."

This then is the experience to which a conversion leads Lawrence's favored characters. Ursula says, "The angels of the darkness were lordly and terrible and not to be denied." She is prepared to meet the lords of darkness when Anton Skrebensky comes back from Africa, with the darkness of the continent about him. The dark points to a sexual achievement at last, the culminating awareness of the vital sensibility.

The sexual union presents the consummation of a naturalistic theology. Like the divine union it bears with it a promise and a threat, for the drastic offer of fusion with universal being is also a threat of personal extinction. It is here that Lawrence's naturalistic creed has its greatest difficulty of resolution. With his scrupulous insights he projects a deeply intense conflict, the veritable agony of union, as his lovers confront each other. The ambiguity of success in love, in fact the continual cycle of success and failure which Lawrence stresses, reflects a deeper metaphysical ambiguity. The paradox of division and unity in the self's engagement with the "other" is the continuing paradox of theologies, but the more so in Lawrence where the two terms are closer to equality. After all, in the ancestry of anthropomorphic religions, one did not question the superior enclosing strength of Godhood as one approached the crisis of a union with it. The complications, in contrast, are severe in the religious union of lovers. Ursula, who soon takes an aggrandizing ascendance in her relations with Anton, feels that "she was perfectly sure of herself, perfectly strong. The world was not strong, she was strong. The world only existed in a secondary sense. She existed supremely."

It is characteristic in such cases that one is never sure that what has happened is a conquest or a submission, whether the ego has absorbed totality or been swallowed up in it. If Ursula exists supremely, then how does Anton exist? Certainly among Lawrence's lovers success rarely seems mutual and simultaneous; when one seems victorious the other seems to have been overcome, when one seems to have contained the world, the other feels he has been swallowed up in it. For some, like Anton Skrebensky, the lords of darkness come like destroying angels. It happens therefore that at the climax of Ursula's demand, Anton fails her, as so many men and women fail in Lawrence. The darkness is a fearful thing; its consummation seems allied with death, and if it may be that a new existent self may rise from it, its cycle requires a preliminary extinction. The mystery in any case remains; what identity can survive the passion which transcends the personality? In what way is existence contained in the undefined darkness of natural being?

The power in Ursula is destroying, from Anton's point of view. He feels himself in his own shape external, apart from her, and in the overflowing of natural power he must be annihilated. We must try to do Lawrence intellectual justice here. It is not merely a case of cannibalism where the strong overwhelm the weak, or of erotic megalomania where the strong appetite must find its food. The weak will certainly be annihilated, but to the profit of no one. Ursula has no advantage in Anton's weakness; he has failed her in the large meeting which is in darkness. He has lacked the passion in himself to absorb her as she absorbs him, and thus affirm his own selfhood while finding his unity with her in the great darkness. This may be the theoretical implication, but nevertheless the fact remains that when we examine closely the actual relations of Lawrence's lovers, even in their successful union, we find a stress of energy on one side (in the effective case, with the male) and a stress of passive surrender on the other, though it is an impassioned passivity. It may be that a meeting of true equals was something to defeat the imagination, particularly on the naturalistic level, and that equality as such is a particularly abstract creed of the developed intelligence.

The point is that nature has no code of controls. Force meets force in action, and it is only a deep naturalistic piety that can imagine a harmonious resolution in forces that are liberated utterly to act for themselves. In the ratio of unequal forces, Anton runs from Ursula, as if to save his life. He typically of course gives himself up to social occupations and accepts a normal marriage. Marriage, Ursula has cried, belongs to the dead "overlife" which she rejects. She wanted to be his "underlife" which is subversive and free. Anton in his flight from Ursula proves that the forms of the rational sensibility are defenses against the radically vital sensibility. The fear of the inner dark, mysteriously solid, yet formless and dispersed, leads people like the younger Tom Brangwen, Winifred Inger, as well as Anton, to find shelter in the outer forms, like outer skeletons, which prop them up and give them shape. But they are doomed thereby to a sort of death-in-life, like Winifred, whose flesh is dead and whose homosexuality is proof of the perversion of vital being.

To be converted in a naturalist theology is not easy or quickly tempting as Lawrence deals with it. It is a frightful invitation which all but the very strong refuse. To achieve a material finality is a prospect more difficult for men than what is promised in a spiritual finality, though it was understood that a soul without strength or redeemed virtue could not bear to see the face of God. Nor is one given relief by the postponement of heaven. Salvation is offered immediately, to be taken or not, in primary matter, in primary energy, and in the primary darkness of passion. For the revelation we remember the scene which closes The Rainbow and determines Ursula's final break with Anton. The trampling wild horses which almost kill her embody that violence in the flesh which is transcendent substance. "She was aware of their breasts gripped, clenched narrow in a hold that never relaxed, she was aware of their red nostrils flaming with long endurance, and of their haunches, so rounded, so massive, pressing, pressing forever till they went mad, running against the walls of time, and never bursting free. Their great haunches were smoothed and darkened with rain. But the darkness and wetness of rain could not put out the hard, urgent, massive fire that was locked within these flanks, never, never." Like this the root and confirmation of being is found. But to know it is to risk dismemberment.

Every theology must deal with the fear of death, the passing from a conceivable form of being into the inconceivable. The natural religion has its own way of making death conceivable. It is precisely in the transition between death and life that the moment of being is transcendent and vitalizing. This is promised in the actual cycles of growth. Ursula's greatest moment has been a germination, not a fulfillment, and it has required the casting off of the old husk of her life.

She was the naked, clear kernel thrusting forth the clear, powerful shoot, and the world was a bygone winter, discarded, her mother and father and Anton, and college and all her friends, all cast off like a year that has gone by, whilst the kernel was free and naked and striving to take new root, to create a new knowledge of Eternity in the flux of Time. And the kernel was the only reality; the rest was cast off into oblivion.

The more convincing vision for Ursula is the rainbow itself, arching over the corrupt and weakening life of the world she knew, but confirming the promise of eternal change and renewal. The arc is the symbol of eternity in the flux, the redemptive sign of the God in nature, the God of changes.

The rainbow expresses the arc of connection, the circuit of unity, and that reconciliation of life and death which is the metaphysical success of religion. The religious analogy appears directly in the very expressive chapter entitled "The Cathedral," as Anna and Will Brangwen visit the cathedral at Lincoln which Will Brangwen so much loves. The arches of the cathedral exist in parallel with the arch of the rainbow. Both embody consummation in the climax of eternity and both share their roots in the great procreational darkness.

> Here in the church, "before" and "after" were folded together, all was contained in oneness. Brangwen came to his consummation. Out of the doors of the womb he had come, putting aside the wings of the womb and proceeding into the light. Through daylight and day-after-day he had come, knowledge after knowledge, and experience after experience, remembering the darkness of the womb, having prescience of the darkness after death.

The rainbow is the more conclusive symbol, however, closer to eternity and closer to the natural arc of life. The church was built in the same pattern, but symbolically, with protective limitations. Anna Brangwen is ready to go beyond it. "The altar was barren, its lights gone out. God burned no more in that bush. It was dead matter lying there. She claimed the right to freedom above her, higher than the roof. She had always a sense of being roofed in."

The church has left a great deal out, Anna further observes, as she notices the "sly little faces" of the gargoyles which mock their own structure. The ultimate roof was after all outside. Will Brangwen joins in Anna's response at this point, and they share disillusionment. "He thought of the ruins of the Grecian worship, and it seemed, a temple was never perfectly a temple, till it was ruined and mixed up with the winds and the sky and the herbs."

A temple is never really a temple until it is ruined—and nature's temple appears above it. This is a succinct way of presenting Lawrence's natural theology, that is to say he felt a prophet's need to accomplish the ruin of temples. However, it must be noted in this significant statement of Lawrence's thinking that he deals with the traditional church with a fierce tenderness, uncompromising in rejection, but unlike the attack on other institutionalized abstractions, like the industry which Tom Brangwen serves or the debased university which Ursula attends. A believing church is a housing of life which leads to divinity; that is, whatever it failed to include or denied, it at least unified experience and found incarnate value in it. In that regime the works of man, his institutions and ideas, were ideally considered to be part of the works of spirit and therefore connected with immanent meaning. It could be said that spirit traditionally was the intervention between the intelligence and matter, it was both a final ideal reality and the intelligence expressing it. In the terms of our general discussion in these essays, it was a consciousness which penetrated and inhabited external being. When the concept of spirit died, when "God burned no more in that bush," the anthropomorphic effort lost hope, and consciousness and reality came to their typically modern alienation. What was left were the vestigial ruins, the complicated and now useless elaborations of an intelligent civilization which no longer had the clear motive to further elaborate itself and achieve ideality. A church might be the structural image of a spiritual reality. If it were not that it would seem to be an excessively overgrown protuberance in the process of racial and organic survival.

In other words the intelligence is a function, whereas spirit and matter are definitions of substance. One might say that when the intelligence, opposing itself to mere physicality, wished to find value or meaning incarnate in itself, it had to invent the concept of spirit. The affirmative naturalism of Lawrence, however, dismissing a role for super-nature, suggests that matter is its own spirit. The result was to invert the traditional value of conceptual insights, the works of the intelligence. The latter were not really formed originally to serve organic life, but rather to master it in the service of the higher reality which the spiritualized intelligence conceived. The natural theologian then finds the true god enslaved to a cerebral sensibility which, rather than being adapted to the resurrected divinity of nature, is by its history and development organized to oppose it.

Thus with the death of spirit, the intelligence lost its service in a teleological synthesis. More than that of course, the development of the modern intellect was itself the apparent cause of the disappearance of the unitary consciousness which was spirit. The rational intelligence which triumphed was analytical, not synthetic, pluralistic and not unitary, and most crucial, it confessed itself to be the limited agent of the organic life and physical universe it observed. Spirit or soul had immanence in a conception of the important world as spiritual, so that the individual and conscious spirit was a manifestation of total spirit inhabiting the world. Without the addition of spirit, the intelligence had only descriptive or analytical functions. It was not itself either a part or the whole of immanent being, but rather the mirror of it. When matter or organic life thinks, its thought is less than its own being, and only a specialized and quite peculiar function of it.

In Lawrence's natural theology then the intelligence becomes deeply suspect, because its activity disperses immanent being or immanent consciousness, rather than concentrates it. If nature has replaced spirit as the significant substance of the universe, then immanence must be in nature. It must be questioned and made to speak in its own way. If the mind fails to make a revelation then the blood must speak or the vital organs, and the awareness which is in them will be the entrance into resolved and unitary being.

It was inevitable that Lawrence should eventually write a specific gospel, taking in fact Christ, the great exponent of spirit become incarnate, and leading him to a path of rediscovery and reversals. In "The Man Who Died" the resurrection of Christ is the theme, and it is a naturalistic resurrection; that is, he does not pass in transcendence into a geometric stable heaven, but is resurrected into literal life, his physical being on a physical earth. The story tells us that when the first Christ was crucified, he had willed his own death in the increasing spirituality and abstraction of his message. His spiritual sensibility had made its effort to transcend physical being for the sake of reveries of form and abstractions of value. As he says now, with his new insight, he had "wanted them, (his disciples) to love with dead bodies. Perhaps Judas loved me in the flesh. I willed that he should love me bodilessly, with the corpse of love."

In offering the abstraction of love he was offering death to men and to himself, and it was right that humanity should crucify him. They would do it again. He says, "I was murdered, but lent myself to murder." The abstractions of consciousness, the spiritual consciousness more than any, are alienations from reality. Christ says, "I would embrace multitudes, I who never truly embraced one."

It is into the abstract void that Christ passes when he dies, and from it he must be resurrected. However, his resurrection cannot be completed until his sexual union with the priestess of Isis. The absorption into physical being is completed in the sex act, and it is only this which can take the last traces of death out of him. Osiris, the dying God, is reborn in a fertility rite.

This new Christ speaks in a new testament for naturalism. Sex is the ritual communion, life is made incarnate in value, and this revelation heals the wounds of death. But the moment of union has no extension beyond itself. It does not persist as in a marriage or in permanent mutual possession. The lovers meet and then go their two ways apart. "I have sowed the seed of my life and my resurrection," Christ says. Sex is a metaphysical appetite, not a mundane pleasure and need. Christ has exorcised death and met his own immanent being and justified it. What more is there he could claim from the woman? To claim more is to claim too much. Earlier in the story Christ had instructed himself. The fear of death had made men mad and they bully each other with their intellectual and moral allegiances because of the egoistic fear of their own nothingness. The compulsions of love and marriage which they lay on each other are the measure of that bullying. The great enterprises of law, morality, and custom are tyrannies of the will and intelligence which would impose a unity on life. But they move in the wrong way, from the outside inward, from the whole to the particular, the many to the one. The natural, non-combative means of achieving unity are from the inner being, below the will, below intelligent judgment or spiritual abstraction. There at the vital center the fear of death is relieved, because consciousness has touched immanent being, and the need to bully others is stilled.

In "The Man Who Died," one of Lawrence's summary works, he has given us the parable of false and true salvation. In "St. Mawr," also a late story and a summing up, he gives us the genesis of evil—and describes the basis of what we can call a naturalistic morality. The dominating character in that work, Mrs. Witt, becomes an image of perversity and evil. Her vital hunger, which is unusually strong, has not been appeased and her life has become a quarrel of the will, the mind and the nerves. These are frustrated external organs trying to replace the function of the vital centers. They are always poisonous and over-active when so enforced.

Thus Mrs. Witt is megalomaniac in her pride and will. She is the agent of the great bullying which starts with the fear of extinction. She wants a man who is a combination of Abraham Lincoln and the Czar, who is everything at once. Mrs. Witt worships intelligence and is its creature, and the intelligence is pre-eminently the weapon of the centrifugal and destructive ego. She is constantly the psychologist for instance. She subdues people by analyzing them. Her aggression, her angry disenchantment, her detached contempt express themselves in her mind's curiosity, but what the intelligence excavates is already dead and raises an infernal stink—as Lawrence puts it.

For all this when she expresses her love to Lewis, she is only repellent to him. He says in ringing words, "No woman who I touched with my body should ever speak to me as you speak to me, or think of me as you think of me." Strong figure that she is, Mrs. Witt has insight to accompany her perversion in living. As she says about Lewis, whom she loves, he is just an animal, he has no mind. But she also says, "I never wanted to touch the hair of those with mind." The horse, St. Mawr, is supremely mindless and therefore contains the secret. "There seems to be no mystery in being a man, but there is a terrible mystery in the horse." Mrs. Witts' daughter Lou, in her own more poignant frustration cries, the age-old cry of romanticism, "I want the wonder back again or I shall die."

The mind in its exile is the theme, the mind which knows its own limits and stops short of mystery. The mind can't, like St. Mawr, "get our lives straight from the source." It can't be helped, the mind is an outsider, the eternal spectator. It can reason *about* but it cannot reason *in*. For Mrs. Witt, as she says, "Life is a series of newspaper facts." Concentrated in the brain, consciousness exists independent of life, and living itself is numb. In her desperation Mrs. Witt can only hope, "If death hurts enough she'll know she was alive." Again we see the clue to the genesis of evil. To cause violence, or to experience violence, the need at any cost is to authenticate the sense of life.

To think by analysis is not communication then, it is the opposite and sets subject apart from object. The break in communion between the person and other persons, and between the person and immanent reality, has a simple consequence. Life becomes a state of war and its characteristic emotion, as Lawrence stresses it in Mrs. Witt, and as he perceives it elsewhere in his writing, is anger. Anger exists when the subjective consciousness cannot break out of itself, and when the ego's only touch upon the world is through the mind and the will. The will is human impulse acting from the wrong end, conflicting with other wills, attacking the world in striving to possess it by aggrandizement, or as it may be, demanding to be possessed in violence. In Lawrence it seems that destructive violence is not the product of the vital sensibility. Violence is the expression of the alienated sensibility, it is the force for communion acting corruptly through the will and intelligence. Outside the nucleus of immanent being there is the whirlpool of alienation and paranoia in all the crucifying forms of the social relationship.

In a summary figure, the evil released in Mrs. Witt is like that of the reversed horse and rider in the story, the horse with his strength at the wrong end and perverted. Frustrated to the point of madness, knowing only her isolation and her own unreality, Mrs. Witt cries at the end, "Conquer me O God before I die." What god to conquer her but the god that is hidden in everything, the great god Pan, "looking out of the everlasting dark." But this god the megalomaniac solipsistic intelligence, lacking the third eye of vision, cannot see.

The problem
of action

The issues confronting this approach to modern fiction are the
dramatic issues of the novels themselves. They are the questions
which ask how we know, how we can value what we know, and
how we can act in terms of what we value. The figure at the
center is the human actor, but we have to concern ourselves
with the manner in which he may properly be called the actor.
In the literary view his effective role may be submerged in the
scene, he may simply present the background. He may be only
the fragment of an action, producing a cause for action in others,
or exhibiting the effect of action by others. In every relationship
of events his role in action has degrees of fullness or intensity.
It may be that the character in fiction will not seem qualitatively
a part of action at all but of something else which might be
called movement. To be reduced entirely to movement would

be difficult, so long as he keeps a recognizable human nature, but degrees of action in contrast to movement can be a matter for observation. For instance, a reflexive movement like withdrawing one's hand from the fire is less an act than withdrawing it and cursing the fire, and the latter less an act than extinguishing it. We assume then that intelligence and choice have roles to play in action, and that the sense of action has strength to the extent that the relationship of intelligent choice to events is clear.

In the naturalistic view of life, at its extreme, we can say that action is less like itself and closer to movement. The fulcrum of force is no longer in the personal intelligence but evasively located in the whole area of force composed of the biological process and history. The individual is no longer an agent so much as a manifestation. He represents deflections of energy from the great map of force which contains him. The relationship of intelligence to action is thereby shorted, and concepts of value, which need to distinguish human motivations from the generalized force in events, have lost their support.

Kenneth Burke gives us a most succinct and useful definition of our basic term.

> Action involves character which involves choice—and the form of choice attains its perfection in the distinction between yes and no (shall and shalt-not, will and will-not). Though the concept of sheer motion is non-ethical, action implies the ethical, the human personality.[1]

Action implies the ethical—a crucial concept which leads us back to religious metaphysics, where the ethical principle suffused all events and activated all movement. The concept of man as actor has historically taken its strength from the teleological assumption that all acts swayed the scales of judgment.

1 *The Rhetoric of Religion*, Beacon Press, p. 41.

Man as actor regarded the world as mastered by the same power that mastered him, impelled by the same interests, moving to the same destiny. The essential point was that his will, or ethical judgment, affected destiny. This was a mystery but it also was a most deeply intelligible structure in which the temperament of man had central place and could move freely, explaining itself and the world simultaneously. At the extreme of primitive anthropomorphism an analogy was equal to an explanation, a metaphor could supersede empirical or literal knowledge. So long as this was true the human consciousness had ultimate correspondence with the reality of things and events.

An action in its ideal intention and success, moves toward the relationships of order. The actor is at the center of an arc between effective motives and effected results. The deeper the motives are understood to be related to the systematic order of the world, and the deeper the relationship of results to that order, the larger the arc of action is drawn, and the stronger is the felt rational and moral energy within it. When emphasis is placed more heavily on either motives or results, with an imbalance of stress, the moral energy within action can be expected to decrease proportionately. When further, motives are replaced by causes, mechanical, instinctual, or simply generalized in the plane of force which contains the actor, the dramatic arc we have transcribed for action simply disappears in the large stream of movement, and the moral energy of the person dissolves with it. The passive mood, as I have described it in these studies of the modern literary imagination, is the consequence of the dissolved arcs of action, which have rested traditionally on the forms of anthropocentric faith.

It is therefore reasonable to ask, as many have asked, whether the enterprise of human culture, which depends on the moral energy of action, can survive without the exercise of some form of the anthropocentric imagination. The essential meaning of the term, modernity, as I have used it here, focuses on these questions. How is it possible to describe the interfusion of the human interest (and actions) within the rationalizations of the world order? Is it even possible for the human mind to accept its own hegemony in the world of substances and appearances, and if not, how can the human agent act with the faith necessary for a true action? The paradox is that the modern intelligence does not know enough to give an ultimate rationale to action, and yet knows so much more than the actor on the scene needs or even wants to know. For instance, it cannot define a final event which confirms the motives for action, but it can give an oppressive sense of limiting causes and limiting substance which undercut motives. It is not remarkable that literature, which describes the attitudes toward action, has moved between the extremes of stoic quietism and enthusiastic primitivism. These are the extremes, but perhaps the more typical standpoint is that of the mode of irony, which proceeds from the intellectual sense of superiority over oneself as actor.

It has always been normal to rebel against reason, but what is the case when the rational intelligence itself keeps a patronizing independence from the actor and his action? It is hardly a war but a breach in the personality and in culture when intelligence is separated from the vital life process. The vitalist or primitivist might indeed preach revolution, but apart from that extreme, modern thought tends to an aristocratic sense of guilt and diffidence before the rightful claims of nature. What we could call the reactionary standpoint is to feel a mixture of contempt and ironic detachment while regarding the naturalistic comedy. On the one hand we see the indecision and lack of confidence, if not outright self-abasement, which has been made habitual in the modern exercise of intellect. Or else we see the greatest arrogance of an intelligence which has transcended its own practical functions. This appears as something finer but complete in the words of Albert Camus. "And real nobility (that of the heart) is based on scorn, courage, and profound indifference." [2]

To fight to maintain the integrity of consciousness, even if it requires disbelief or neutrality in the crises of action, seems a sympathetic cause. The oldest instinct of human nature must cling to the necessity of admitting the truth, because every lie or illusion indicates itself as a kind of biological flaw, like poor hearing or seeing. So lies must call themselves truths to be accepted, and they can be regarded as self-preserving only while there remain believers. They become in that instance the rationalizations of power, as in the argument of the Grand Inquisitor. That endlessly stimulating passage in Dostoevsky's work tells how the man of intelligent disbelief acts when he has the responsibility of power. It is a modern portrait of the large intelligence committed to action; forced beyond self-delusion, it is resigned to hypocrisy and the manipulation of belief in others.

The major intelligence may then rather seize upon its self-respect through negation, which becomes an inverted means of moral expression. The modern mind has been busy in demonstrating that all power-assuming knowledge, including that of divine power, is subject to criticism; therefore the intelligence tends to assert its strength or maintain its purity in the act of disproving. The power to say no is perhaps the most majestic of all. Thus the intelligence becomes a kind of perverted oracle; it has no great affirmations to make, but its mission is to unveil great illusions. What remains from the religious hope for a transcendent power and knowledge is simply a transcendent knowledge, like the godlike power to say there is no God. It

---

2 *Notebooks, 1935–42*, Alfred A. Knopf, p. 140.
(It should be pointed out that this entry was written in response to the start of the war in 1939. However, it is precisely such radical events which put the test and express the breach we have been describing. We recall Joyce's remark on the bombing of Spain. "Isn't it better to make a great joke instead, as I have done?")

was inevitable perhaps that transcendental motives should turn to the abstract intellectual hegemonies of art and science. The language of the religious spirit was after all a language of the human imagination and intelligence. The impulse to transcend the sphere of abortive action, the worldly sphere, remains as the residue of the religious striving. It turns to a self-transcending knowledge, which proves itself most often by its power to criticize homocentric illusions.

The religious metaphysics set up a dichotomy between absolute and limited realities, between the spiritual and earthly awareness, but only with the intention of bridging them. The two worlds met in promised salvation; the spirit raised a fallible reality to the level of spirit. To a passionate religious imagination like that of Dostoevsky it meant leaving nothing behind, not a shred of skin and identity, but the stressed personal actuality of life restored and made perfect. This recognized the dialectical relationship between imagination and reality and followed it to synthesis, and it is the offering of that synthesis which will always beckon powerfully from the religious tradition.

The problem of action and the problem of mind, as I have treated them in this discussion, follow from the break in the religious synthesis. Can action have the root of its motives in the "other world" of the unlimited imagination? Can thought have the sincere faith of its relevance to events, actual and becoming? And what is the view of action which remains when the answers to these questions make life appear an impasse?

I have tried to inscribe some relevant responses to these questions in the preceding chapters. The imagination will find the theatre of action it can accept, and it will find its heroes too. The writing of Flaubert and Joyce made the artist the only hero of his own work; he becomes the hero by his power to acknowledge chaos, or to translate into the artifice of form a life reality which resists every success except that of contemplation. The artistic intelligence raises itself above the level of its subject in order to be immune from corruption by it. Identifying with that authorial consciousness, the reader assumes the amoral perspective of the self-sufficient intelligence, like the dominant amorality of the scientific intelligence, which deals with experience in order to increase itself. The implicit protagonist strives for the virtue of appreciation or the virtue of knowledge, but these stand beyond the active virtues and vices which are the *subjects* of knowledge. No species of literary identification could be more self-flattering than this. A heroic personality has been achieved, for its clear vision and daring omniscience, but it has a great fallibility. It does not really exist *within* the work, but is rather the intelligence enclosing it. If that sort of heroic consciousness is pushed into action by the mere momentum of life, it in turn becomes the object of a constantly self-transcending intelligence. Joyce's system of ironies included this insight too in the example communicated by his intelligent butt of the intelligence, Stephen Dedalus. In the same sense Flaubert as much as confessed that the only way to rise above *being* Emma Bovary was to write about her.*

The characteristic distance of the intelligence from its objects, even when they include itself, thus holds us in its implications. Such immunity has intense attractions, that is certain, perhaps equal in temptation to the old career of spiritual contemplation in its own life-renouncing or transcendence-seeking impulse. But surely there is a large difference between looking down and looking up, as if the saint were to observe only mortal error and limitation, rather than the beatitude of heaven. In this perspective, life only suffers humiliation, and its values (motives) diminish with the completeness with which they are known. Such an intelligence withdraws the energy from action, as I've

---

*We have had recurrently in modern fiction the example of the hero transcended by his own consciousness in the autobiographical act of writing. The obvious case is Proust; another is Gide's *Les Faux-Monnayeurs*; Mann's *Tonio Kröger* illustrates a series of artist protagonists projecting their ineptitude. In popular lore the impractical artist and the absent-minded professor are caricatures for the unwordly or "inactive" role of the intelligence.

said; it paralyzes motives, if only by the self-consciousness all motivated men assume. The problem in this speculation is the phenomena of the human intelligence patronizing itself. One has at times the sense that the most sophisticated education of our time is creating an elite of writers, artists, journalists, and scientists (and a host of subsidiary clercs) who are intent chiefly on establishing their membership by the variegated acts of intellectual condescension. In that atmosphere, any act of commitment, voluntary or otherwise, is likely to touch a sense of inferiority, or a vague embarrassment in one who becomes thereby the object of analysis himself. The temptation in defense is to arrogate for such motives, whether regarded as instinctual or pragmatic, an authority which exceeds the intelligence and serves a higher necessity.

At that extreme, an inspired primitivism like that of D. H. Lawrence relieves a great tension and gains consent. Lawrence's drama of values attacks the intelligence in all its postures, contemplative, didactic, skeptical, esthetic, and measures against it the life force which had been subordinated to it. In this view, action and life must be served, particularly at the expense of the self-regarding judgment which breaks the spirit of action. It is in a sense desperation which draws Lawrence to faith in the body's will to action, which was the will to the heightening and fulfillment of life. It was what Joyce himself recognized when, as though exhausted by the labor of drawing life entirely into the consciousness, he signaled his assent to Molly Bloom's primary power. Her recumbent body makes both premise and conclusion to support the madly elaborate structure he had recorded.

Lawrence was consciously a prophet and he proposed a resolution to the dichotomies which tormented his imagination. He could respect only what he felt was the immanent reality of life and devoted himself to finding a consciousness to accompany it, a sensibility of the blood and flesh. Within its naturalistic bias, this was a religious solution, and the emphatic reassertion of the anthropomorphic sensibility in communion with nature. The function of a sensibility was to acknowledge the immanent presence of nature. It needed no bridge of reason or conceptual activity, the bridge of metaphor was enough, and the latter in Lawrence becomes increasingly contracted so that the line between the world and the sensibility tends to vanish, as in the language of a true mysticism.

Mysticism is a word to call up the extreme opposition to the tone and method in the writing of Flaubert and Joyce. Experience in their work is absolutely subjugated by the recording intelligence, and this is true in the most immediate report of Leopold Bloom's or Emma Bovary's sensations. These are perhaps Apollonian effects, whereas experience in Lawrence is Dionysian; it makes a seizure and overlaps the margins of judgment. The fiery fragments of Lawrence's style point to an interior force stronger than consciousness. His protagonists have an almost unbearable physical presence, and in fact their existence is so magnified in focus that we have difficulty in conceiving them properly as characters or in the design of their lives. What most enforces itself is the overwhelming immediacy of a sentient being. But at that point the active personality as such dissolves into a natural immanence. This is as much a problem for true action as with the immobilized specimens of Joyce's esthetic laboratory. Perhaps the abstract intelligence kills, but so does the mimetic sensibility which has pursued immediacy to the point of vanishing into the large essence of nature; this some would call the greater abstraction.

There is a paradox involved in making the vital natural process aware of itself, even if the medium is the most spontaneous poetic sensibility and not the abstract, rational codes of language. To preach animal values is an act of judgment, and makes the vital organs, which used to be called the lower organs, again subservient to a directing intelligence. Ideally they should speak for themselves and any form of the articulate sensibility would be gratuitous. To praise immersion in the vital process as a way of salvation is to preach an idea like other ideas of redemption.

In a sense the problem of action has been solved, as any religion solves it, by offering a final success to motives. However, this has the particularly passive aspect of an animistic, natural religion. In this faith the burden of assertion is diminished; the problem is chiefly one of returning to an original synthesis, one that never changed its course, never separated its elements, but moves in its immutable original perfection. This religious system is actually a religion of necessity. It makes no strenuous demand for choosing between good and evil, but rather asks the agent in salvation to give up his negative compulsions and be himself. It is a religion of letting go, and once the first stage is taken, the great powers carry the program of synthesis to the end. The dramatic force in Lawrence's novels is always the angry quarrel with false gods. Once the breakthrough is gained, we feel the effect of the curious impersonal grandeur of the god Pan acting in his people, absorbing them into himself.

This is the attribute of a monolithic and static naturalist creed. Perhaps its most significant effect in literature is to undermine the subjective sense of freedom in action, though paradoxically, the more extreme pantheistic affirmations serve to mask this principle in the climaxes of passionate affinity and passionate movement. In contrast, the traditional religious metaphysics, which created a distinct personality for God, was intensely dramatic in itself and strongly nourished the dramatic imagination. It conceived man as the unequal but separate dialoguist with God or nature, conceived his interest as somehow communicable in that confrontation, and allowed his imaginative choices a role to play in a dramatic universe that was always in crisis. The sense in the Old Testament is that from the first day God might withdraw his consent from creation. The covenant was a stress of that. In the historic relationship with gods, particularly in Western mythology, human prayers and entreaties were somehow like commands. In Greek drama, for instance, they become appeals to a higher power than gods, the power of a moral fatality in the universe.

The latter is the crucial point; in the traditional metaphysics, power and value were not conceivably separate for long, and if their separation were threatened, the necessary redemption of the world demanded their renewed fusion. Value, a description of the ultimate moral harmony of man and the universe, dominated physical events. Powers, whatever they might be named by magic, science, or religion, served values. The distinctive meaning of modern naturalism is that values serve powers; facts dominate judgment. Values are then pragmatic, adjustive, melioristic but never supreme. But action, in the sense I am describing it, serves only value. Action acts out the human consciousness of goods, and it is a thoroughly faithful action to the extent that goods are supreme over circumstance and events. When power as such is abstracted from value, action to that degree is disoriented from realities. When value to its extreme confinement becomes purely subjective in a real universe of things and process, then action is accordingly haunted by solipsism and its sense of futility. One knows then that the god one serves is a small private god in the brain of man. If he needs to be worshiped, he would best be acknowledged there, and perhaps there he eventually assumes the only godlike prerogative remaining, to have omniscience of the world as it presents itself.

II | THE CULT OF COMEDY

Is it possible to be serious in a world in which power and the mere "thingness" of events dominate values? Such a premise is surely that of the comic imagination. Henri Bergson said what is deeply pertinent for us at this point.

A humourist is a moralist disguised as a scientist, something like an anatomist who practices dissection with the sole object of filling us with disgust; so that humour in the restricted sense in which we are here regarding the word, is really a transposition from the moral to the scientific.[3]

He makes the distinction between what is seriously moral and comically neutral in another passage.

Try, for a moment, to become interested in everything that is being said and done; act, in imagination, with those who act, and feel with those who feel; in a word give your sympathy its widest expansion; as though at the touch of a fairy wand you will see the flimsiest of objects assume importance, and a gloomy hue spread over everything. Now step aside, look upon life as in disinterested speculation: many a drama will turn into a comedy.

. . . .

To produce the whole of its effect, then, the comic demands something like a momentary anesthesia of the heart. Its appeal is to intelligence, pure and simple.[4]

This comic objectivity is exactly relevant to both the theory and practice of Joyce's art. It depends on emphasizing the break between contemplation and action, to achieve not the synthesizing effect of those who "act in imagination with those who act," but rather a stasis in which conception holds action in arrest. The framing principle is not now, in any case, a homocentric faith in the self-justification of action, as in the religious or primitivistic modes. The framing principle is the mode of irony, or what I have described as the comic-esthetic intelligence which rules in the work of Joyce and Flaubert, and for whose gratification that work exists. Irony provides a means of intelligibly contemplating disproportions and disunities, as those between meaning and events, actions and values, motives and results. An extreme and balanced contrast, an ironic contrast,

3 *Laughter*, Macmillan, 1921, p. 128.
4 *Ibid.*, p. 4–5.

has a kind of unity; it is a resting equation. If we extend this to comedy itself, we may say that the comic release is the acceptance of a great difficulty or discrepancy as in the nature of things. In this way a man turns from his own weakness or absurdity, and rising to contemplation in the comic perspective, he eliminates the ordeal of remedial action. He has given himself up to the stasis of the permanently separate, like the infinity of parallel lines, or the intelligibility of the imperfect, as though there were a pattern for the incomplete and the imperfect. Comedy is a kind of meaningfulness provided the absurd.

Self-transcendence, it may be argued, is implicit in the comic mood, and a substitute for becoming a transformed self is to become the not-self, removed in contemplative detachment. It is the viewpoint of the outsider, even though one may be put outside oneself. The pure forms of stoic or unredemptive naturalism tend to become comedies of this sort. The bias is the same, for comedy will accept the dominance of knowing over acting, and, as Bergson says, it puts the emphasis in action upon movement.

> Instead of concentrating our attention on actions, comedy directs it rather to gestures. . . . Action is intentional, or at any rate conscious; gesture slips out unawares, it is automatic.[5]

All distant perspectives are not necessarily comic, of course, but one could entertain the thesis that they tend to become so unless activated by abstractions to which faith is given, whether they be scientific or religious abstractions. The neutrality of vision in Flaubert is ambiguously comic, as we have noted, because the passion for truth is absolute in his work, and commands universality. In a world where everything is absurd, no one laughs. Nevertheless, a problem to be pursued is to see whether the dominant neo-scientific thought of the modern world is not irresistibly pulled toward the comic vision for

5 *Laughter, op. cit.,* p. 143.

imaginative relief from its own intellectual and utilitarian abstractions. In this vein of thought, one might consider that all of *Ulysses* was written on the intellectual basis ultimately to be located in the tedium and befuddlement of the neo-scientific abstractions of the Ithaca episode.

As a response of the "zeitgeist," comedy had had no more perceptive exponent than Kenneth Burke, whose lifetime of writing has been given to the study of human strategies of communication and self-reassurance. His theory of comedy has been Burke's outlet for a strong moral sensibility, so deceptively concealed within his sometimes forbidding structures of disinterested analysis. He has been, in his sense, a "comic" critic, that is, a critic of life and literature from the distant perspective, the "perspective by incongruity."

In an early book Burke put his position clearly. "We have advocated, under the name of 'comedy,' a procedure that might just as well have been advocated under the name of 'humanism.'"[6] The central principle in the "perspective by incongruity" is a dialectical view of action which refuses "polemical, one-way approaches to social necessity."[7] This dialectical understanding evades the positive excess of idealization and the negative excess of reduction.

> A comic frame of motives avoids these difficulties, showing us how an act can "dialectically" contain both transcendental and material ingredients.
>
> . . . .
>
> In sum, the comic frame should enable people *to be observers of themselves, while acting.* Its ultimate would not be *passiveness,* but *maximum consciousness.* One would "transcend" himself by noting his own foibles.[8]

In these germane passages Burke refers to the dilemma of passivity, an effect of the self-observing intelligence bordering

6 *Attitudes Toward History,* Vol. 2, The New Republic, 1937, p. 82.
7 *Ibid.,* Vol. 1, p. 213.
8 *Ibid.,* Vol. 1, pp. 214, 220.

on the comic perspective, but not necessarily equivalent to it. A good deal of our discussion of modern fiction rests exactly here at this border of distinction, as it also rests on the mode of self-transcendence, which we have noted in the effects of stoic naturalism. The latter is in fact the "perspective by incongruity."

In a recent essay, which really is a summary of major interests in all his work, Burke again discusses his "comic" theory of education. Knowledge educates comically, or comedy is the

> protective warning against man's nature, his "natural tempta-
> tions" toward turbulence or the turbulence of his whole
> achieved organic civilization.

In Burke's very clear meaning, this is an education not directed toward salvation, an image of perfection which is not really imaginable, but *against* the apocalyptic holocaust, the damnation which is completely imaginable.[9] The reference is of course to the contemporary crisis of the "bomb." In the same article he offers a rich footnote which presses home to my interest at this point.

> In his *Parts of Animals*, Chap. X, Aristotle mentions the
> definition of man as the "laughing animal," but he does not
> consider it adequate. Though I would hasten to agree, I ob-
> viously have a big investment in it, owing to my conviction
> that mankind's only hope is a cult of comedy. (The cult of
> tragedy is too eager to help out with holocaust, and in the last
> analysis it is too pretentious to allow for the proper recognition
> of our animality.)[10]

This is brilliantly perceptive for indicating the mode of the imagination most suitable for an intellectual era of naturalism, and perhaps Burke's hopes for it have a good chance of being answered. In any case, his design for comedy has in large part

9 "The Definition of Man," *Hudson Review*, Vol. XVI, No. 4, Winter, 1963, p. 512.
10 *Ibid.*, p. 512.

already been answered by actual effects in modern writing. His phrases, which I have quoted, could be used as major texts to describe some of the best literature of our time in the most affirmative moral emphasis which could be made for it. "To enable people to be observers of themselves, while acting"; this is an attractive ideal, and who is to say that the subjective perspectives of modern thought have not made this possible in a way that is revolutionary. "Not . . . passiveness, but maximum consciousness"; that is certainly a lesson to be drawn. A veritable religion of maximum consciousness, to use F. O. Matthiessen's reference to Henry James, is to be found in the most influential modern writing. "To transcend himself by noting his own foibles," is the specifically active moral to be derived from a literature so much at work in making the notations of human fallibility.

These words of Burke are an aid to the imaginative reading of Joyce particularly, as I have tried to indicate at the close of my discussion of *Ulysses*, a comic epic which seems indeed to provide a species of "comic transcendence." Perhaps Burke's concept of "comic education" has been doing the work of the future; certainly the cult has been in existence and its values may have fed us more than we expected. But we have stressed in these chapters how equivocal the effect of modern comedy is, even in Joyce's masterpiece. The burden of consciousness, that "maximum consciousness," and of the foibles we would like to transcend, has perhaps been too strong for comedy as such, though the intellectual frame for comedy survives, typically in the modern classic written by Flaubert, or in the dramas of the grotesque by Kafka and Nathaniel West.*

---

* An extension of this book, and of course it would not be easy to limit extension, would engage with the work of these writers, as well as the obvious pertinence of contemporary exercises in the "absurd" or in "black comedy." The works of Bernard Malamud and Saul Bellow have greater affinities with the more authentic comedy of James Joyce, and it would be interesting to find whether Leopold Bloom was the spiritual father of some of their protagonists.

Burke himself in this passage called up the "cult of tragedy" in making his own choice for comedy. The passage is relevant because modern writing itself wrestles with these choices. I believe myself that one can say more than Burke suggests on behalf of the "cult of tragedy," though the modern history of destruction surely would support his sense of revulsion. There is an immediate deficiency in conceiving the moral imagination in the exclusive terms of the comic perspective. Only a holocaust, like that which Burke imagines, could strike so directly at the negative sense of the absurd, the grotesque and deformed, which thereby becomes the basis of moral judgment. It seems to me that to confront the holocaust with the "comic" criticism of man's impulses toward the holocaust is a half-morality, negative and restraining to a fine point. It has very little to say for "action" in the field which is left within the margins of the abyss. In that sense to draw limits on a space which contains nothing, or nothing that has a dramatized value to equal the dread of the holocaust, is to draw no meaningful limits at all. The tone of modern critical morality often has this quality of an evaporating content, articulate in warning but so empty of praise or devotion that the warning becomes pointless. The cult of tragedy may be able to make a claim for itself in contrast, on the premise that somewhere within the invited or uninvited ruin which is the theme of tragedy, there is a knowledge that does more than warn against action, but continues to affirm it.

III | THE CULT OF TRAGEDY

To confront modern fiction with the categories of the comic and the tragic is not at first view promising. And yet the discussion of these two intellectually attractive and frustrating concepts has great fertility as a means for approaching the problems we have been treating here. We have observed in stoic

naturalism a progressive tendency to produce the comic perspective, though it may actually conduct us to very dry and
neutral comedies. Again Bergson gives us relevant thinking.

> All that is serious in life comes from our freedom. The feelings
> we have matured, the passions we have brooded over, the ac-
> tions we have weighed, decided upon, and carried through, in
> short, all that comes from us and is our very own, these are
> the things that give life its ofttimes dramatic and generally
> grave aspect. What, then, is requisite to transform all this into
> a comedy? Merely to fancy that our seeming freedom conceals
> the strings of a dancing-jack, and that we are, as the poet says,
> ". . . d'humbles marionettes
> Dont le fil aux mains de la Nécessité." [11]

The question occurs, how much does modern fiction say for
our freedom and does it become thereby serious and tragic?
In my introduction I referred to Dostoevsky and Melville as
major figures to match Flaubert in the modern literary inheritance. I believe it would be plausible to call them neo-tragic
realists who contrast with a great neo-comic realist. One matter
cannot be disputed; the interest in tragic literature and in tragic
theory for this half-century has been exorbitant. It has reached
beyond writers and critics to philosophy, to religious theory and
to popular journalism. If we maintain our attention to the theme
of this essay, the problem of action and value, it is not difficult
to see why.

There is in the first place the general intellectual resemblance
between the situations offered to tragedy and to comedy. It was
clear, for instance, to one neo-tragic philosopher like Unamuno
that Don Quixote was easily carried across the line into tragedy.
In this resemblance tragedy again presents the broken synthesis,
the breach between human power and motives, or between
knowledge and action. Both comedy and tragedy are then out-
lets for the frustrated anthropocentric consciousness. They are,

11 Bergson, op. cit., p. 79.

it may be said, digressions from religious faith, compensations in the imagination for the uncertainty of the religious promise for life.

Karl Jaspers, another among the contemporary thinkers preoccupied with what he called "tragic knowledge," speaks to this point as follows:

> A yearning for deliverance has always gone hand in hand with the knowledge of the tragic. When man encounters the hard fact of tragedy, he faces an inexorable limit. At this limit, he finds no guarantee of general salvation. Rather, it is in acting out his own personality, in realizing his selfhood even unto death, that he finds redemption and deliverance.[12]

Jaspers emphasizes the premise that in tragedy we are dealing with broken or threatened metaphysical systems by asserting bluntly that " . . . Christian salvation opposes tragic knowledge . . . no genuinely Christian tragedy can exist." [13]

This is the issue, sharpened in expression, which brings us directly to the metaphysical theme of modern fiction. Within modern literature, I think, we find a highly developed genius and success with comedy, or irony, or serio-comic writing, and less success but a longing for expression in tragedy.* When we reason the distinctions between comedy and tragedy as, for instance, Bergson and Jaspers present them, we find the most relevant comments made for our own general discussion. Bergson stresses the contrast of perspectives, the outside as against the inside view of action. "Act in imagination with those who act," or participate in their personal sense of freedom, and you will be in a world that is grave and important. But step aside and

12 *Tragedy Is Not Enough,* Beacon Press, p. 42.
13 *Ibid.,* p. 39.
* Albert Camus, the modern writer who I believe had the consciousness best prepared for the writing of tragedy, promulgated the literary philosophy of the absurd. The "theatre of the absurd" is distinctively contemporary for its wedding of the philosophic substance of tragedy with the literary perspective of comedy.

look upon life as in disinterested speculation and you will have gained the perspective of comedy. "The humourist is a moralist disguised as a scientist."

An extreme objectivity in intellectual discipline would seem at the outset to forbid a tragic perspective, if we believe in the concept of identification, as Jaspers does in the following passage:

> The spectator partakes only through identification. What might befall him, too, he experiences as if it had already befallen him in fact. For he has merged his own identity with that larger self of man which unites him with everyone else. I am myself inside the human beings represented in the tragedy. To me the suffering addresses its message: "This is you." "Sympathy" makes man human—sympathy, not in the sense of vague regrets, but as felt personal involvement: hence the atmosphere of humaneness found in great tragedy.[14]

It is obvious that Jaspers does not mean identification in any naive sense, but he is not very explicit in describing how it is commanded. He suggests that the identity at stake is "that larger self of man which unites him with everyone," and this recalls Aristotle's insistence on the hero as a man who was neither perfectly good nor greatly bad, yet one who comes of high station and commands respect.

However, the protagonist's greatest demand for identification with him comes from his own action in the immediate crisis. Again Aristotle suggests more than his surface meaning when he describes the primacy of action in tragedy. It is the way in which action is made significant that defines heroes as heroes. Jaspers remarks that the hero faces an inexorable limit, but that he responds "in acting out his own personality, in realizing his selfhood even unto death." We have been brought to share in the dynamics of *action*, to the extreme degree, knowing the sense of choosing under great strain, the sense of the experience

14 *Ibid.*, p. 75.

which converges intensely on that choice, and knowing the meanings which pertain to that act and its great consequences. This, as Bergson suggested, is the sense of life which is serious.

The problem of tragedy is to relate action to meaning and to justify it, and though it confronts failure in the confrontation, to still insist in such a way that meaning *follows* action. Its distinction from the comedies of stoic naturalism rests on its insistence upon action, the dominance of value for what is done, so that the seriousness of the human cause is not released but maintains itself even within the ruins of meaning. The achievement of seriousness is the main point of a distinction. If what I have called the arc of action is not a bridge between great motives and great results, then we have a lessening of seriousness. If the focus of the action is not in himself strongly the *source* of critical action, then there will be a turn from seriousness. Perhaps most pertinent, if the field of vision is made distant from the field of action in such a way that the action in itself is diminished in the scale of events, then we will have a withdrawal from tragic seriousness, by which we mean ultimate seriousness, that which exists *within* crisis. There may be other forms of seriousness, a humanitarian seriousness, for instance, which penetrates so much social naturalism.

The ultimate goal of serious literature may be to activate the abstractions of faith or knowledge in the concrete and dramatic imagination. Tragedy, as we know it in the tradition, is at the peak of seriousness by its effect of accompanying action with the simultaneous break-up of established systems of judgment.* But this disintegration does not impugn the stature of the hero; rather, as almost any example would tell us, he is at the frontier of human powers. It is this combination of a great crisis and great faculties which press the action toward

---

* This approach to tragedy is largely indebted to both Kenneth Burke and Francis Fergusson for their theory of the tragic cycle, defined as dramatic stages in the growth of knowledge under the headings of "purpose, passion and perception."

finality, beyond the illustrating or predictive role of ideas. In this way, death is typically a final action, brought to the closest perspective, so close that it is bigger than consciousness and valuation—and the problem of tragedy is how to find a consciousness adequate to the action. The Aristotelian concept of the hero remains relevant. He must be large, he must fill the stage, he is the actor and he masters our sense of value by suggesting his power. He demands that the response of consciousness follow him. It does, overwhelmed and respectful, mastered by the action.

We have effects resembling this in Conrad's *Lord Jim*, as we follow him with Marlow the observer—effects which demand from our powers of valuation a means of justifying his life. In Conrad's novel, the action moves to the foreground and leaves behind predispositions of judgment. It even demonstrates the break-up of closed systems of value, as stressed in the subordinate but parallel story of Captain Brierly. Nevertheless *Lord Jim* seems to be a vivid case of a tragic theme struggling against strong limitations. Marlow is always with us to give the effect of the ubiquitous mind, doubting itself and screening the action subjectively. The break-up of values and judgment we have described is here influenced by the solipsistic effect, as if to say we are pressed by a skepticism which prohibits the possibility of judgment. We cannot be sure whether Jim is a romantic dreamer, a fool, or a hero, or whether he has any cause for action rooted in the actual world. The Quixotic pathos is with him throughout. With brilliant consistency Conrad draws the veil of ambiguity around the response of the world to his death, with Jewel, supposedly his greatest intimate in the world, being left at the end in her demoralized and embittered confusion. Finally Jim is encircled by a metaphysical sense of nature so powerful and so mystifying in its own implicit pattern, that he and all the others become diminished within it. This, too, is a response to influential naturalism and places Jim in the line of modern stoic heroes. The field in which he acts is too large and undefined to give the tragic sense of important motives leading to great results.

And yet of all the novels we have studied here, *Lord Jim* evokes the closest resemblance to tragic seriousness. I believe this is because of Jim's insistence on action, and our derived respect because of that. He begins to grow, to lengthen his shadow, because his enterprise has the will to extend itself over the world. It is a way of extension we can understand as necessary, as a response to actual reality from the largest need. It is important to make a distinction between Jim and Emma Bovary; the latter is the true dreamer who responds to her dream-like version of reality from a partial or highly selective need. Jim is in search of a character, that is, a *system* of values for action, whereas Emma is primarily in search of experiences, impelled by a more limited physiological subjectivity. The world that meets Emma is hard and defined and she is only a part of it, whereas the reality surrounding Jim more closely resembles the uncreated chaos. Upon this he imposes himself, as if in challenge; in Patusan he goes so far as to create a world which others can inhabit, a human design that achieves maximum actuality, like the world in which Oedipus and Lear once lived. Jim therefore conveys a tragic seriousness, because we perceive that he is easily the most interesting thing in the world which contains him. He dominates the patterns of fate, causation, forces in nature as well as the subordinate forces in himself, because his achieved character is more interesting than any of them, though of course his power is less. His *will*, which is the strongest thing he has in an unresponsive, confusing world, moves toward action, and his life, so to speak, is transcendent with indeterminate meaning, but a meaning nonetheless.

Faulkner's *Light in August* is even more deeply affected by a concept of naturalistic causation than Conrad's work. This diminishes the action possible from either Hightower or Christmas who share the central roles. If we took either of these characters out of the novel, what we would have left would be rather straightforward qualities of naturalistic writing. The auto-matistic, driven action of Joe Christmas is turned blindly by strong forces in his environment, his racial inheritance, and the given historical process. Hightower in turn would illustrate the pathos of the isolated consciousness, dreaming purposelessly, with ironic effect, within the drastic theatre of events. The special effect of Faulkner's novel comes from the fact that he has combined these two agents in the same work, and forced their attention upon each other. They face each other and achieve, not communication, but rather a passionate silent meet-ing that begs a communication. There is nothing in Christmas's mind at all when he runs to Hightower's house, and no one can imagine what they would say if there had been time to speak. This is a gesture, a frozen climax, but it raises both passive agents from their isolation. The synthesis of meaning and action is entertained at least as a possibility. The Christian emotion felt by Hightower, "the crucified shape of pity and love" he invokes, attempts to go further. It indicates the moral response which is the reduced basis of a relevant consciousness in High-tower, and a relevant meaning in Christmas' compulsive move-ment. For a moment at least we are in the mood of tragedy.

The effect of this in the novel, however, is like the crossing of a shadow, and that actually is what it is, the shadow of receptive judgment in the mind of Hightower. The actual strength of resolution in Faulkner's novel depends on something else, to which Hightower's Christian emotions are joined with greater conviction. The figure of Lena Grove takes precedence finally over Hightower's awakened moral commitment, though it supports it. Lena hardly needs the ministrations of Hightower at childbirth, and as for that agent of Hightower's moral sensi-bility, Bunch, it is clear that Lena leads Bunch to herself, rather than the reverse. A blessed compulsion, that erotic, life-giving maternity, stands dominant to give assurance to the struggling moral consciousness. The latter becomes secondary to it, comically following after, as Bunch follows Lena in the closing pages of the novel, an anecdote of the savage converting the missionary. The ultimate passivity of the equation is implicit; the cure for a disorder in nature, as Joe Christmas expressed it (and the strongest indication is that it is a disorder in human history that has done violence to nature), is found in the redemptive cycle of self-renewing nature itself.

Reviewing these considerations may help others to understand why I point toward tragic literature as a basis of contrast. I am fascinated by the possibilities of contrast because it seems to me that the body of tragic writing in the tradition throws a sharp light on naturalistically oriented literature. I think the sense of this supports the strong contemporary interest in tragedy, and led to such expositions as that of J. W. Krutch and more recently, George Steiner.[15] I believe they were right in thinking of the modern consciousness in literature by centering on the theme of the "death of tragedy." The instinct of judgment is sound, and the argument reaches to suggestive issues. Naturalistic thought, as such, and to the extent that it has locked the human figure in place in a monolithic structure of nature, stands in deepest opposition to the spirit of tragedy. However, this is not directly because the imagination has been deprived of the articles of a supernatural faith, or of the confidence that life possesses an absolute metaphysical support. It is not *primarily* because the anthropocentric drive of the imagination has been frustrated. We see rather that the tragic situation exists precisely where such a break-down occurs. It is here actually that the "modern temper" and what Jaspers calls tragic knowledge have their greatest affinities. The "crisis" aspect of naturalistic thought is then the point of resemblance, but the point of difference focuses on the extent that the crisis is passed over, and the issue is settled for the dominance of nature,

15 Joseph W. Krutch, *The Modern Temper.* George Steiner, *The Death of Tragedy.*

whether optimistically or negatively considered. It is here, cut off from independent action or definition, that the protagonist is furthest from the tragic role.

This is a theme that requires further exposition but I will put it here as an hypothesis: tragedy, as we have known it in Western literature, expresses a broken or threatened anthropocentric consciousness without conceding the essential human value—an intact and thriving will to action.

The agon or tragic dialogue becomes possible when the closed structural meaning of the universe has been challenged but no substitute order of values is formed to take its place. The conclusion of the tragic dialogue is never really positive in the sense that it reads a new meaning for life and the justice of God. It is rather more like an interrupted sentence, an active verb without its full predication. There is that kind of weight behind Hamlet's words to Horatio, or Othello's summation before the world. These messages confirm only the self-generating value of active man. He has acted in such a way that self-justification enters into action, in an area *beyond* creeds or beliefs. We observe this actor and are taught to believe. It is a scene where everything fails except the will to act and the moral faith required by it.

As a footnote to these remarks we should perhaps correct the implication that the tragic movement is toward action for its own sake. This would surely invite the useless tragedy of the holocaust which Kenneth Burke thought a threat, or the corrupted tragedy which Jaspers described in one cryptic sentence. "Tragic grandeur is the prop whereby the arrogant nihilist can elevate himself to the pathos of feeling himself a hero." [16] This may perhaps be the temptation of modern experiments with tragedy, or rather with generalized tragic emotions. However, the revelation contained in the great examples of tragedy is a mystery whereby the most deeply disturbed experience never

16 Jaspers, *op. cit.*, p. 101.

surrenders fusion with the sense of value. Its meaning is not a great suicide, but rather a generous inspiration which nourishes the energy for action at its *moral* starting point.

The contemplation of suicide is a dramatic center of crisis for what I have called stoic naturalism, as distinct from the naturalisms which are predeterminedly pantheistic or have the sanction of some other faith in nature's system. Camus' instinct in this respect was unerring for his choice of argument in *The Myth of Sisyphus*. The stoic pathos, which required the characteristic combinations of strict honesty and fortitude, has the quality of a greatly mannered death; it has the aura of suicide, though it may strike the greater poignance by refraining from it. This is the effect in stoic naturalism which most clearly brings to mind a resemblance to tragic literature. But the contrast I have in mind is a distinction between active and passive moods. In the tragic crisis, consciousness is indeed overwhelmed by a reality too strong to be controlled or understood; that is the issue of tragic suffering. Then what is the difference between tragic and stoic suffering? In the contrast, stoic suffering assumes the accommodations of defeat, a submission to what is left, as Camus' man resigns himself to his own lucidity, or as Joyce's craftsman intelligence resigns itself to the compensations of omniscience. There is a quality of self-consciousness in suffering, whether of sorrow or defiance, which results in gestures like that of Jake Barnes eating a hearty meal in a Madrid hotel, or Meursault invoking imprecations upon the people who will watch his execution. The hardness of these attitudes cannot finally conceal the note of self-pity. I think the essential element in such gestures is the solipsistic confinement of their effect. Every theory of tragedy, as well as every example, would suggest that the last act is a break-through for a profoundly shared experience. In simplest terms the message is to tell and retell Hamlet's story.

The narrowing of possible response is the characteristic "cornered" effect of the modern literature of passivity. That anti-climactic tone is struck in the first place by the sense of closed metaphysical possibilities as a premise of naturalistic thought. We feel that tragedy is written in the situation of the biblical Job, in the face of a comprehending God who has not made clear his justice, or that of Prometheus, in the face of a God who has abused or not yet learned his great function of a teleological justice. What is crucial in this view of the tragic situation is that possibilities are open, not closed. In the case of Prometheus, for instance, it was not necessary to postulate an omnipotent God, but rather a God who was capable of further creation and growth. That sense of a God who can be taught by human motives and suffering is present in the Orestes cycle and also in Sophocles' conclusion to the story of Oedipus. The great chance is really the chance of both man and God to achieve a reconciled order. This leaves the stress upon active motives and upon significant action. The difficulty in naturalism is in finding a focus for creative possibilities. There is no genuine contest between actions and the resistance they meet. Since the human agent is himself absorbed in the natural process, his role in questioning can be as grotesque as the metaphysical questioning of Leopold Bloom at the end of the long day which has swept him in its forces.

The touchstone
of tragedy

I am convinced that to bring some examples of tragic writing closely into view in the midst of intensive thinking about modern fiction, is to throw outlines into relief and obtain valuable insight. The process of definition or even generalized judgment is secondary; what we have in mind is an effect of critical awareness like that which Matthew Arnold conceived in his "touchstone" theory of criticism. One may agree with Arnold that this is one way of supporting judgments of value, but in the first instance the benefit pertains to the clarity of vision itself. We come away with more than a truism, that some modern novels resemble the model of tragedy and others do not, or resemble it in some ways and differ from it in others. The insights are specific, they deal with varying modes of conceiving human action and understanding human experience. The touchstone method in this sense is a device which goes beyond the need of classifying genre, or supporting appreciations. It is the means of pointing toward a common interest, a universal theme, in such a way that distinctions as well as the essence fall into place, for a moment at least. To compare *Madame Bovary* and *King Lear* directly would probably be pointless and a wasted project. To bring them next to each other as one considers the problem of knowledge and action in both, may heighten our awareness of each to a valuable intensity.

With this in mind, and not to dispose of tragedy with an inclusive definition, I proposed a concept of traditional tragedy which links it to the particular perspective of this book. As I stated it in the previous chapter, a major theme of tragedy, as we have known it in Western literature, expresses a broken or threatened anthropocentric consciousness without conceding the essential human value, an intact and thriving will to action. In the following pages I shall attempt to apply my meaning in a discussion of specifics in *King Lear*.

* * *

Robert B. Heilman says in a perceptive, close reading of *King Lear*, "The [tragic] flaws may be described, I think, as errors of understanding and *King Lear* may be read as a play about the ways of receiving truth." [1] He goes on to say that Lear's mistakes "are the terrible mistakes of a man of action, of a man whose action is a public action." The last emphasis is important, telling us again in the Aristotelian sense that the hero is a man whose knowledge has great responsibility.

When Lear divides the kingdom he is expressing the peak of his power and knowledge as well as the peak of his mistake. His power is signified in the act of giving up power, and his treatment of the world as known and knowable is implicit in the verbal demonstrations he expects from his daughters. These are the gestures of his securely defined world, and it is Cordelia who begins to shake that system. His reaction is a bigoted judgment against her, the more confirming the dogmatic as-

1 "The Unity of *King Lear*," *Critiques and Essays in Criticism*, R. W. Stallman, ed., Ronald Press, p. 155.

sumptions of his knowledge. He exclaims, "Thy truth then be thy dower."

By the rashness of his act he demonstrates his faith in the equivalence between reality and appearances. His absolute power as king would be conducive to that mistake. How is he to know of an ambiguity separating the will and the deed, the act and its meaning? Or to think of a separation between physical and moral power? Words and ceremonies are the sincere gestures of a world whose active principle is a moral order. As king he himself is a word in a human language, a definition of law and knowledge. As a king he has no need to defend himself against the world. His expectations and its design are a unity. As for the denials of Cordelia and Kent, his first reaction, done it must be said with a singular lack of self-questioning and grief, is to exclude their perpetrators by throwing them off. How shall we reconcile this act with the pain he suffers when his two eldest daughters deny him? Only in the sense that previously he has kept intact his world of intelligible reason and power and thrown out the rebellious agents. Now he has begun to lose the world itself, and the heartless irony is that all his power to hold fast to it depends on the number of his knights.

We notice then that as a king, Lear assumes the fusion of his knowledge, an active reality, and his power. His mission in the tragedy is to stand at that point of fusion, to suffer its disintegration and to endure experience until it or something quite different but also unifying is regained. This is a way of phrasing the tragic rhythm in the sequence of "purpose, passion and perception," the meaningful terms supplied by Kenneth Burke and Francis Fergusson, founded on the stages of ritual.

Appropriately in a passion, trying to quell the first threat of the deeper tragic passion, Lear says to Kent:

> . . . *Hear me!*
> *That thou hast sought to make us break our vow,*
> *Which we durst never yet, and with strain'd pride*

> To come betwixt our sentence and our power
> (Which nor our nature nor our place can bear): [2]

It is from this high state, where knowledge and action cohere, that the hero suffers his fall. The synthesis of knowledge and power in Lear is circumstantial in his role as king, and in that fusion his absolute power masks the quality of his judgment. He is a king, but the king is a man, the play tells us. Regan pronounces the theme: " 'Tis the infirmity of his age; Yet he hath ever but slenderly known himself." The king is a mere man, and when he falls from his estate it is apparently to a limitless depth, all the way to the "nothing [that] will come of nothing."

> Does anyone here know me? This is not Lear:
> . . . .
> Who is it that can tell me who I am?

In the passion of the play Lear is defined by his companions, the Fool, the naked poor Tom, and by his background, a storm in nature. It is where the beginning must be made, it seems, or the end forecast.

> L. Dost thou call me fool, boy?
> F. All thy other titles thou has given away.
>   That thou wast born with.

The king falls all the way to that point, and it is of the greatest importance in this play that the last step in the reduction to "nothing" goes beyond "foolishness" and beyond human madness, to a placeless, formless chaos in nature. Shakespeare, who does his thinking in images, gives us the deepest basis for thought in *King Lear* as we contemplate what are essentially two definitions of nature, the one classic and religious, the other modern and skeptical. The first is nature as the king himself

2 The Yale Shakespeare edition, Yale University Press.

might consider it at the start of the play; as Tillyard and others have described it, it is a developed medieval Christian principle of Moira whereby the human moral order and the order of nature have equivalence. This is a triumph of the anthropomorphic reason, and as an example it is the ideal point of fusion toward which the tested knowledge of the play strains. The word nature, most often used as an epithet, means a natural moral duty. Gloucester, in a stressed irony which plays on meaning, calls Edmund, "loyal and natural boy," and Lear, reasoning with Regan says,

> . . . Thou better know'st
> The offices of nature, bond of childhood,
> Effects of courtesy, dues of gratitude;

There is, however, the other nature in the play, nature set free, or nature unnatured, we might say. In the play's passion, all system breaks, and in that frustration of the reasoned will a new idea of nature appears, let us say a very modern one, a dark absolute of nature unreached by human purpose. This is the nemesis provoked by the "unnatural" actions of the daughters, a fierce disorder in nature, itself an ultimate power, as Edmund invokes her in his bravura speech, "Thou, Nature, art my goddess." This is a nature beyond the human, a sense of fact outside the sense of right, and the bastard, a mistake of the flesh, is its true sign. The tragic awareness strikes sharply here, that reality presents a violence of process and cause not to be contained in the human understanding, much less in the human power.

This is the nature he faces when Lear is stripped to nothing. All his metaphors of anarchy and betrayal proceed from it.

> Return to her? and fifty men dismiss'd:
> No, rather I adjure all roofs and choose
> To wage against the enmity of th' air:
> To be a comrade with the wolf and owl:

The storm on the heath is the sign of his passion but also we can say the cause of it, as though to show the broken world of man in an empty primeval violence. "Contending with the fretful elements," he sees life reduced to the same terms in the inexplicable treachery of its moral forms, and he understands that naked, mad Tom is the "thing itself," poor unaccommodated man.

Lear's passion, as we are considering it, is the suffering of reason and its natural extreme is madness, which together with the physical reduction, dominates the middle section of the play. However, Lear's madness is a reaction rather than a condition of the mind. There is no true madness in this play. (Poor Tom's madness is, of course, the mask of Edgar's persecuted reason.) Lear's mind is never lost, but is reasoning in its madness, suffering its great questions.

Madness, like the violent nihilism of the storm, is a tragic comparison, as "nothing" is invoked in the name of *something*, that great claim on life with which Lear began the play and to which as it ends it must give answers. Lear

> Strives in his little world of man t' out-scorn
> The to-and-fro-conflicting wind and rain.

This is the assertion of something in his nothing, and the play performs its brilliant paradoxes. His "little world of man" increases and extends its significance by his suffering until in the end it has dominance over nature. When he contrasts moral and physical suffering he asserts in his bearing the great primacy of the former.

> I tax not you, you elements, with unkindness;
> I never gave you kingdom, call'd you children,
> You owe me no subscription. . . .
> . . . Here I stand, your slave,
> A poor, infirm, weak, and despis'd old man.
> But yet I call you servile ministers,

Lear exhibits that he knows an essential human and moral reality superior to the physical, and that the threat of its extinction is the ultimate terror. This is the point of the great comparison on the heath. What Lear in his magnificent human presumption asks of nature, indifferent to its physical threat and challenging its moral indifference, is to discover "the wretch . . . unwhipped of justice."

> . . . Close pent up guilts,
> Rive your concealing continents, and cry
> These dreadful summoners grace. . . .

So long as nature's violence is a simulacrum of the Day of Judgment, we are in a world whose dramatic interest is the moral interest. This is the humanism of tragedy in essence—the world of things has taken its meaning from the world of men.

Nevertheless, having this claim to make, Lear must endure his punishing doubt, the epiphany of zero. Exposed to nature, he asks the great question, "Is man no more than this?" He is staring at the naked Edgar, "the poor, bare, forked animal," and he mocks his real consideration, saying, when they go into the hut, "Come, good Athenian." His real consideration is for the moral reason in the world. Again we stress that when Lear's world disintegrates and his despair makes him "mad," his mind by poetic license is clearer than ever. It is concentrated in a fury on the real problem which never leaves his lips. He asks for the good, he demands it, and the problem for Lear is not for a minute what the good is, but how it acts in the real world and whether it can exist there at all. It is true that Lear has come upon evil, but it isn't that he wasn't aware of evil before. What has broken him is learning the breach between things as they are and their intended values. Can one be so deceived is his outcry, and when he knows unaccommodated man, he questions the possibility of accommodation. How does value get into the world and who is true to it? What his daughters tell him is that all forms are flatteries and power is physical. So "Athenian" Lear debates the moral reason in the storm.

Perhaps if men fail, while still knowing the good, the good comes into the world from the gods, as ordainment and revelation. Men, naturally fallen, would then find themselves raised by supernatural example. Nothing seems more certain in my mind than that these terms, terms of a religious understanding, have no application to *King Lear*. The primacy of human good and evil, the sense of a lack of recourse above human action (Lear himself, the king, was the only source of such authority), would indicate that judgment. Lear seems at times to invoke the intervention of the gods, seeing their natural order broken, as when he says,

> Let the great gods,
> That keep this dreadful pudder o'er our heads,
> Find out their enemies now. . . .

But this is a rhetoric of expostulations. The real interest is not in the gods, their designs and interventions. They are in a sense only names for the force in events.*

Gloucester, when he is about to throw himself from the cliff, exclaims,

> O you mighty Gods!
> This world I do renounce, and in your sights
> Shake patiently my great affliction off.
> If I could bear it longer, and not fall
> To quarrel with your great opposeless wills,
> My snuff and loathed part of nature should
> Burn itself out.

This complains of indifference in the gods, whose inaccessibility, if not hostility, really encourages his suicide. This his

---

* Shakespeare is convenienced by the fact that he can use gods who are pagan and pre-Christian in the play. Accordingly this frees him to attribute to them an essentially passive, mechanistic function which would be impossible in a Christian world.

son Edgar would seem to refute when, picking his father up in
a new disguise, he says that a fiend led him over the cliff and,

> . . . Therefore, thou happy father,
> Think that the clearest gods, who make them honours
> Of men's impossibilities, have preserv'd thee.

But there was no fiend, no cliff, and I think we are entitled to
assume, there are no gods. It was Edgar himself, behind his
disguises, who produced all of these, and we must look then at
him as the forceful cause, that naked poor Tom, the unaccommodated thing, who is himself the effective, order-making man
in the drama.

We say that Shakespeare gives us humanistic tragedy but in
doing so he simply carries the principle of tragedy we have
stressed to its furthest point, where even modern humanists—
of absurdist reasoning, as Camus would say, strained by metaphysical disbelief—can read his imagination as if it were their
own. Lear's reduction is uncompromised, he falls all the way.
The world is a terror, but behind the sensible storm, it is
nothing; men are sharper than the storm, but behind their
treacherous forms they are naked and nothing. But are they?
Is man nothing? the play asks. To be stripped is to see him.
There is Lear, himself naked, but in his tragic sincerity, we
know a man making the heroic claim which is itself his substance to compel belief. It is perhaps that sort of "authority"
which Kent sees in his face, when Lear asks why he would serve
him.

Deeper than the harshness and great language of his challenges, a quiet but compelling note emerges, a relief which
may resolve everything perhaps. It is the paradox of human
companionship, of mutual regard, in that infinity of nothing.
To have an affinity is to count beyond the subjective one, which
is really a zero, and begin the rationalizations of order. The
storm is encompassing, that is its great point, as the little group
of men are joined about Lear on the heath. Kent urges him to

take shelter in a hovel, "Some friendship will it lend you 'gainst the tempest." And even as Lear's brain begins to turn, he thinks of that other reduced man, his friend, the Fool,

> . . . Come, your hovel.
> Poor fool and knave, I have one part in my heart
> That's sorry yet for thee.

Is despair then unselfish? If so it has already begun to answer itself. In the great reduction scenes on the heath, the company of the lost, the Fool, the madman, the King, discover in their nakedness a principle of sympathy which is itself the challenge to their state. So man accommodates himself. The "bare, forked animal," Edgar, is the man of the play, conducting his father back to a reconciliation in life, and the eventual champion who answers the trumpet to defend the human order.

In the powerful music of Shakespeare, these are rhythmic implications which grow even as their contrasts are dominant. The low point forecasts the high point, and the reduction in nature leads directly into a moral transcendence. Lear endures the limit but when his eyes are opened he sees Cordelia. What he sees is incarnate for the full world. It is not the world of ordained order and gesture it was for him in the first scene. Neither is it the natural anarchy he faces in the second and third acts. Her kiss awakes him and what he finds is simple in immediacy, a loving daughter, but he knows how to see her. Things fall into place and he has the tragic fullness of vision which can only have an immediate state of being for its focus. The audience moves with him and they can appreciate what he knows, but how can they know it?

The point is that the consciousness is full. What it is full of is reality, embraced with overflowing emotions and speech. Love itself has come into the play like a god and proclaims for itself the greatest offering of meaning, though the eyes are so concentrated on a simple object. The poetry of Shakespeare is the sign of the full consciousness, wholly fusing action with judgment. Cordelia speaks,

> Had you not been their father, these white flakes
> Had challeng'd pity of them. Was this a face
> To be expos'd against the warring winds?

Lear speaks in self-knowledge and every accent breathes an understanding the words cannot translate.

> Pray, do not mock me.
> I am a very foolish fond old man,
> Fourscore and upward, not an hour more nor less;
> And to deal plainly,
> I fear I am not in my perfect mind.

Actually that is where he is, or at the start of the perfect mind. Everything Lear has experienced has been brought to this moment of perception, symbolized by the new senses of the sleeper, awake to reality after his nightmare darkness. Lear says, "Am I in France?" and Kent answers, "In your own kingdom, sir." The moment of awakening has purity; it dramatizes a fusion between what is there and what is realized.

In a certain sense the moment of knowledge for Lear is so full because it is so much a moment of communication. The collapse of his world, his madness, and finally his sleep, had stressed that he was alone in the world, or alone in his own consciousness. Now in this time of recognition, the emotions of response are what are important. The consciousness celebrates what is, what certainly exists, "in my own kingdom," and that knowledge is tested by the response of others. There is a rush of confidence and trust.

> You must bear with me,
> Pray you now, forget and forgive, I am old and foolish.

In this way clear, indeed luminous reality, replaces tragic confusion, as when Gloucester thinks he falls over the Dover cliffs. The reality is that he is on solid ground, with Edgar at his side. Behind his disguise there is the true Kent. The fusion of appearance and reality is a flowering of knowledge. The suggestion after such a dark wandering and breach of the mind is that all that can be known is known. Life has given a meaning to Lear. If he accepts it, brimming with the passionate sympathy released by Cordelia, then we know that it is a great and positive meaning. He cannot perhaps tell us what it is, but its value comes to us. In that achievement of the full consciousness, spirit indwelling reality, the phenomenon of tragic knowledge explains itself.

The great rarity of this knowledge is its tangibility; we feel it, we know it in an action and its consequences in action. It is not mystical, though a mystery. It is not the knowledge which is a transcendent passion, as it might be in a romantic mode, with revelations expanding themselves into the inexpressible before death. Rather it is earthbound; it does not simply transcend limitations, it blesses them. All Shakespeare's tragedies end with a civic and political busyness on stage. The marshalling of the armies, the ringing of weapons, accompany Lear's meeting with Cordelia. That mysterious revelation accompanies daylight recognitions. Kent becomes known and says, testifying to the refreshing sobriety of all knowledge at this point,

> To be acknowledged, madam, is to be o'erpaid.
> All my reports go with the modest truth,
> No more nor clipp'd but so.

The world has a healthy, gladdening definition. The champion is summoned by a herald; he is Edgar in full armor (we might say naked Tom dressed in the uses and means of the moral life) to fight Edmund on the open field. The resolved paradox is that suffering, which has been and must remain personal, and in its depth incommunicable, has its tie to the overt life of the state and the moral order. The action of Edgar is endowed

with Lear's consciousness, which he has shared more than anyone in the grave passion of the play.

Even the carnage at the end has its part in the tragic exultation. One almost says there cannot be too much carnage, because every death has meaning. Judgment exists, that is the
important point, and all the action and the actors stand related
to it. The final universal eye which sees all and knows the value
of everything is a fatality itself endowed with the great the-
ophany of Lear's experience. Speaking with the limitations of
a secular, practical judgment which can be rewarded by the
knowledge gained in the play but cannot assume it, Albany
says,

> . . . *All friends shall taste*
> *The wages of their virtue, and all foes*
> *The cup of their deserving. . . .*

It is an irony attached to the secular world that Albany is
relatively distant from the major experience. The surviving man
with fullness of being is really Edgar, a fusion of achieved
wisdom and active power. We cannot forget that Edgar has
been mad Tom. He has become the tragedy's surrogate, Lear's
surrogate on the platform of life. The point about secular for-
tune and justice is that it comes as close to the tragic mystery
as it can, draws inspiration from it, and there it stops, for it
can go no further and still be what it is.

The tragic consciousness as I have said is really complete,
but it loses itself neither in mystical transcendence nor in
secular translation. It goes as far as the mystery itself, as far
as death, where it becomes tongueless and detached from further
considerations. The consciousness is complete because it is at
the limit of death and because it has achieved an essence, and
by that fact it goes further than practical and temporal results.
The issues of justice, obedience, the order of kingship, pass into
relative secondary position. Cordelia and Lear meet each other
as equals in suffering, not even as father and daughter, and he

plausibly would kneel to her. This humility and equality is the starting point, not concerned with the forms of entelechy but with the inspiration of entelechy itself, discovering the human love which is the source of idealized norms.

It is necessary that Lear and Cordelia lose, that is, that they lose the life of failure and success as it whirls around them. It is emphatic that the victory of right follows but does not save the tragic hero. In losing, however, Lear and Cordelia are given the chance to attest truth, communicated and made absolute. Knowledge can go no further than this. Their defeat is their chance to "sing," above the level of temporal success, transcending the ebb and flow of conditioned life.

> We two alone will sing like birds i' the cage:
> . . . So we'll live,
> . . . and hear poor rogues
> Talk of court news; and we'll talk with them too;
> Who loses and who wins, who's in, who's out;
> And take upon 's the mystery of things.
> As if we were God's spies; . . .

This is sincere hyperbole as well as the ironic exclamation of grief. It denotes the discovery by Lear of a great recompense in worldly failure.

> Upon such sacrifices, my Cordelia,
> The gods themselves throw incense. . . .

As I've said, however, it is a misemphasis to call this an apotheosis. Lear is no god and does not become one. Tragic realism has a great force; if pity and fear condition knowledge and make it the ultimate tragic knowledge, it is because the hero who suffers is a man. The obligation of the hero is to human knowledge, not to inspiration or ideal metaphysical faith. In his limitations he carries knowledge as far as it can go. And so in its great consistency, Lear's play ends with his incoherence and final darkness. Even while Albany is pronouncing for secular reason and justice, Lear staggers on stage with Cordelia dead in his arms, and shows how pathetically well-intentioned and limited such knowledge, the moral profit of the play, is in the face of death. All ends in grief and a great protest,

> And my poor fool is hang'd! No, no, no life!
> Why should a dog, a horse, a rat, have life
> And thou no breath at all? Thou'lt come no more.
> Never, never, never, never, never!
> Pray you, undo this button. Thank you, sir.
> Do you see this? Look on her! look! her lips!
> Look there, look there!

Knowledge carried to the limit demands that life bend to the incompletion or interruption of death, and all knowledge is false which does not include it. In classic tragedy death is the appropriate last act because it is the door into the last truth. The tragedy proposes that suffering has meaning. In the intellectual frame of the Greek play the gods understand and direct what men cannot either control or understand. Oedipus is the true scapegoat of knowledge because he is at the center where suffering (existence) and meaning come together. By his suffering and later by his death he *knows*. This of course needs the complement of *Oedipus at Colonus* to fulfill its meaning, and in that play Oedipus makes his ascension to the gods. This is the religious, the metaphysically self-confident understanding of death, but it is not really the "tragic" view of death. Oedipus, embraced and taken up by the gods, has transcended his own tragedy.

In *King Lear* I think we have a closer demonstration of tragic death as quite distinct from a redemptive apotheosis. The metaphysical resolution in Shakespeare's play is limited. In tragic realism Lear dies, and he names death not as a transcendence but as a final ambiguity. His language at the end of the play has the greatest immediacy of his personal grief, surpassing the question which throbs in such a line as this,

Why should a dog, a horse, a rat, have life,
And thou no breath at all?

He turns our attention again to the core of that knowledge which his passion obtained. He has discovered only the immediate not the metaphysical meaning of experience, so immediate it can hardly be called knowledge, his love for Cordelia, her answer to him. From that flows all that can accommodate man; without it, or with its negations, comes the naked chaos for which death would only be the final term of unmeaning.

The great antinomy in Lear's play is between undressed natural man and accommodated man. Lear learns where accommodation begins, in the moral response preceding all forms, and by himself leaving all contingencies, he produces his knowledge. By a final realism, stripped of all rationalization and idealization, the king finds his own moral essence. His energy which is passion becomes a moral energy. That vision of harmony and beauty which may be a god, which may be the moral right and the perfect state, has found its source—itself truly absolute because it has no fixed terms or intellectual definitions. We can understand that this absolute is the most concrete and intrinsic experience, an experience not a concept. It is a force which proves itself in the play through the action, before anyone knows that it is there or what to call it. Lear comes onto the stage at the end holding the dead Cordelia in his arms. He is in a passion, but from this passion, a greater reason, all structured human life has its source.

* * *

As we review the foregoing discussion we are brought to some broad conclusions. The conscious life of the hero is progressively forced into isolation, and the threat is that death will only complete the process of extinction. But to make the interior self and the full self known is the resisting force in the play. That counter movement anticipates a break-through out of solipsistic experience.

There lies the play's strongest reason for being, if we think of drama particularly as the intense expression of the anthropocentric impulse. It is molded by the strain for communication, not to express one thing, but everything. The dramatic art, speaking for other arts, and for religion and myth, suggests that the sensate state of being needs an outlet from itself or a fusion with externality. Every symbolic structure in the last effect argues for a seizure or possession of things by the human consciousness.

A communication, understood this way, is the struggle of subjective existence to obtain credence of itself by moving outward. It is a human necessity beyond survival, and if we could have our way every external object would become a piece of psychological furniture. The world would be furnished as the mind is furnished, by images which speak to each other, have histories, have futures, are active and not dead. They would live as a thought lives, with its active force gained from sensible life. This force we understand at its climax when we see it move toward religious communion with the personal God; here would be a fusion point of knowledge and actual being, power and the will to act.

That imagined apex of success is distant from the strategic retreats of modern thought. There are compensations, particularly for the priests of science and art, where detachment, or the self-transcendence of the human interest, wins its great rewards. One learns from such a limitation of teleological ambition how best to exploit fragmentary experience, both in the objective and subjective modes of applying focus. But then both truth and the man speaking it are fragmentary.

Nietzsche expressed this perfectly in describing the "objective man."

> He is an instrument, a piece of slave—the most sublime type of slave, to be sure, but in himself: *presque rien*. The objective man is an instrument, a precious, easily injured, easily clouded instrument for taking measurements. As a mirror he is a work

of art, to be handled carefully and honored. But he is not an aim, not a way out nor a way up, not a complementary human being through whom the rest of existence is justified, not a conclusion. And still less is he a beginning, an impregnation, or a first cause; he is nothing solid, nothing powerful, nothing self-reliant seeking to become master. . . . he is usually a man without substance or content, a "self-less" man.[3]

One is reminded generally of Stephen Dedalus; as a "mirror he is a work of art," or a worker of art, we should say, but then as Joyce stresses in Stephen's later phase, a particularly substanceless man, "nothing solid, nothing powerful." Nietzsche has provided an analytical note for application to the modern intellectual consciousness. Another is from Albert Camus; the "absurd man" and the "absurd creation" in his language are the response to the same great limitation.

All existence for a man turned away from the eternal is but a vast mime under the mask of the absurd. Creation is the great mime.

Further, returning to a passage I quoted in my introduction,

For the absurd man it is not a matter of explaining and solving, but of experiencing and describing. Everything begins with lucid indifference.

Describing—that is the last ambition of an absurd thought. Science likewise, having reached the end of its paradoxes, ceases to propound and stops to contemplate and sketch the ever virgin landscape of phenomena. The heart learns thus that the emotion delighting us when we see the world's aspects comes to us not from its depth but from their diversity. Explanation is useless, but the sensation remains, and, with it, the constant attractions of a universe inexhaustible in quantity. The place of the work of art can be understood at this point.[4]

3 *Beyond Good and Evil*, Henry Regnery, Chicago, 1955, pp. 125–126.
4 *The Myth of Sisyphus*, Vintage, p. 70.

An intelligent indifference has its own road to power, and we can guess that its "emotions delighting us" come from more than satisfied curiosity. That pleasure must linger in the connotations of the word "absurd," in irony, in self-awareness, in the lucidity of the comic spirit. All this the reading of modern fiction can tell us, but the contrast with the deepest note of tragic drama becomes visible. In the latter the mind *suffers* under such restriction and makes an issue of such interrupted knowledge. Explanations are *not* useless, if the alternative to them is unreasoned existence, a zero like that which threatens Lear.

Knowing that this is the mind struggling on the stage, we are prepared to understand something about tragic relief, and are reminded of that classically difficult concept, the Aristotelian catharsis. What most attempted definitions have in common is, put simply, that the catharsis means a kind of victory over the suffering in the play. We feel an exultation in the death of Hamlet, various critics have told us, and despite differing explanations we are led to general assent. Yeats was certain of it: "We know that Hamlet and Lear are gay. . . . Gaiety transfiguring all that dread." The question renews itself, what is the dread and what is the gaiety?

At the first the dread must come from the fall of the hero from his place. That is the sound Aristotelian principle. The power of the king, the hero, is large. One questions, is it as large as circumstance? His will would assume coincidence with reality, or at least among men he has the best chance of doing so. When he falls he dramatizes the breach between power and circumstance. As a reduced man he is beleaguered by an oppressive reality which ignores his pretensions.

The approach of death only emphasizes the more explicit threat to his full existence. The play postulates that the circuit of reason or intelligibility which should flow from the world to the hero's will has been broken. He is crushed by ignorance, weakness, doubt. Isolated as he is in his subjective corner, teeming with consciousness, perhaps this is where catharsis begins. The more he is forced into his isolation, the more we, in the audience, understand him. The less communication he has with a meaningful fate, the more he has with us. But this is probably a modern sympathy. If this were all it would hardly be called "exultation." That mode of understanding the misunderstood might keenly evoke the characteristic notes of irony and pathos, fixed in the modern temperament of writing, but that road turns off from the tragic effect; it is the empathy aroused by weakness, and its effect requires that the protagonist surrender himself, both to the world and his audience.

This is a communication in a small voice; the effect largely depends on the surrounding silence. Communication in the tragic catharsis would by contrast seem full, it would fill up the world, if "gaiety transfigures all that dread." The original challenge was great and relief, if it is to be a relief, must match it. The challenge or the issue, as we have said, confronted ultimate powers and questioned human strength against them. That strength fails, in the metaphysical sense; as we have said, the god does not need to appear in the play, and the "exultation" does not depend on him. What has happened is a conversion of the appeal from gods to humans.

We can say that the tragic anxiety is metaphysical but the action which relieves it is not. In a conversion of terms the anthropomorphic judgment purges itself of the possibility of error but accepts its own inner impulse. The metaphysical need sheds like a thin covering before a rising and dominant illumination which is moral. But it is a morality which pierces being and occupies it. It gives the basis for a faith in life, but this is a seizure of real being by men rather than a reassuring message from the universe itself. We find we can borrow our words from Camus again, when he says that Oedipus "gives the recipe for the absurd victory." He goes on to define the "absurd victory" in the ringing tones of a hero himself, forced to rise from his own "lucid indifference."

I conclude that all is well! says Oedipus, and that remark is sacred. It echoes in the wild and limited universe of man. It teaches that all is not, has not been, exhausted. It drives out of this world a god who had come into it with dissatisfaction and a preference for futile suffering. It makes of fate a human matter, which must be settled among men.[5]

The tragic hero follows knowledge as far as he can, and remains human. If he could go further he would go beyond tragedy and in fact leave this world. To the modern mind certainly, *deus* is always *ex machina*. The play affirms that whatever else exists, malevolent or benign powers, indifferent or insane intelligence, the essential regime of action is human and the inspiration for action is human. The hero creates an identity at the very center of his destruction. This is independent of metaphysical support. He unites mind and being in a paradoxical triumph over the difficulties of the play, and does so apparently by making his awareness so great, his power to judge so passionate, that mind, the human mind, convinces us that it is large enough to contain reality.

The explanation of this respect for man which tragedy releases is in the power of the hero, not a god, to take a meaning from action and to make action out of meaning, and in doing this, demonstrate his active will within the shadow of great suffering and death. Oedipus and Lear offer a moral paradigm for all experience, taking out of themselves a principle of good and evil and subjecting *themselves* to it. This is in danger of being crudely understood because the behavior injunction is slight in tragedy. It has no activist doctrine to preach. In essence the hero makes fate intelligible by supplying motives for action which transcend either the empirical or metaphysical meaning

5 *Ibid*, p. 91. This surely expresses a great deal more than the delight of "experiencing and describing" the world. In writing *The Myth of Sisyphus* Camus was actually forcing his way out of such a cold and abstract justification. His estheticism was a stringent irony, defending the human search for knowledge, but he knew that Oedipus was involved in more than looking at the stars.

of events. He does this by taking full responsibility for the events of his own life, as Oedipus does, even illogically and when he could claim his ignorance, or by applying full judgment within the ruins of his life when it is too late, as Lear does. The effect in these plays is that all action or presented reality has been made to turn, as upon a fulcrum, at the center of a man's conscious experience. When he takes this responsibility, without being able to explain it, he finds a center for meaning. This purveys a moral intelligibility which absorbs metaphysical intelligibility and thereby asserts dominance for the human principle. The hero reverses the "suffering" of the play and from an atom of consciousness thrown about in punishing circumstances, he has become a microcosm of the world whose experience explains the world. In Nietzsche's words he becomes a human being "through whom the rest of existence is justified."

The communication with reality which has put the human spirit back into it has been supported by a communication among men. In the last resort the metaphysical loneliness has been answered by the human companionship. That communicable world then is a real world. If he were not to die the hero would seem redisposed for action, for he has restored within himself the adequate motives for action. It would be more accurate to say, of course, that he has restored it for others. In that sense he is an offered sacrifice, for the finality of his suffering makes him available for full entrance into the consciousness of others.

The supremely affirmative effect is to rebuild the bridge between motives and a real world. Tragedy concentrates on the reality of human judgments, so magnified that they give credence to a coherent universe. When Lear gives his tenderness to his daughter, all of life seems to begin again, and the illusion of the world finds its rock. We can live in any dream so long as we are convinced of the reality of the dreamer. The teleological crisis of belief in tragedy has counter-valence in only one way, the assent of the audience to the existence of a man.

Index